AFTER THE NATURAL LAW

John Lawrence Hill

After the Natural Law

*How the Classical Worldview
Supports Our Modern Moral
and Political Values*

IGNATIUS PRESS   SAN FRANCISCO

Cover images from us.fotolia.com

Cover design by Carl E. Olson

© 2016 by Ignatius Press, San Francisco
All rights reserved
ISBN 978-1-62164-017-2
Library of Congress Control Number 2015930773
Printed in the United States of America ∞

To my children, Ananda, Gwyneth, John, and Devin

The Sea of Faith,
Was once, too, at the full, and round earth's shore
Lay like the folds of a bright girdle furl'd.
But now I only hear
Its melancholy, long, withdrawing roar,
Retreating, to the breath
Of the night-wind, down the vast edges drear,
And naked shingles of the world.

—Matthew Arnold

CONTENTS

INTRODUCTION

In 1948 the *Atlantic Monthly* published a remarkable essay by the philosopher W. T. Stace, a man of little religious sentiment. His essay, "Man against Darkness", opened with a startling pronouncement: "The Catholic bishops of America have recently issued a statement in which they said that the chaotic and bewildered state of the modern world is due to man's loss of faith, his abandonment of God and religion. For my part I believe in no religion at all. Yet I entirely agree with the bishops." Stace went on to claim that our loss of the sense of a purposeful plan for the world is nothing short of an unmitigated catastrophe for humanity. A world destitute of all spiritual foundations is a world devoid of meaning, purpose, and ultimately morality.[1]

Only half a century earlier, another philosopher, Friedrich Nietzsche, pronounced God dead with Promethean glee:

> The greatest recent event that God is dead, that the belief in the Christian God is no longer believable is already beginning to cast its first shadows over Europe.... [A] long plentitude and sequence of breakdown, destruction, ruin and cataclysm ... is now impending.... Indeed, we philosophers and free spirits feel, when we hear the news that the old god is dead, as if a new dawn shone on us; our heart overflows with gratitude, amazement, premonition, expectation. At long last the horizon appears free to us again.[2]

Sadly for Nietzsche, his horizon was far from as open as he thought. He wrote these words in 1882, six years before he lost his sanity at the age of forty-four, and spent the last decade of his life in a syphilitic haze. Yet his words were eerily and horribly prophetic. The half century or so that separates Nietzsche from Stace was quite plausibly the

[1] W. T. Stace, "Man against Darkness", *Atlantic Monthly* 182 (September 1948): 54.
[2] Friedrich Nietzsche, *The Gay Science* (New York: Vintage Books, 1974), 279–80.

worst period of breakdown, destruction, ruin, and cataclysm in world history: two world wars, worldwide economic depression, the rise of global communism and National Socialism, the carpet bombing of industrial centers in London, Dresden, and other cities on a mass scale and the use of the atom bomb on noncombatants in Japan. Easily one hundred million lost their lives in the trenches, the gulags, and the concentration camps in a period of only three decades.[3]

The new dawn that Nietzsche celebrated and Stace lamented was both more and less than the loss of God. It was the twilight of a worldview—the classical worldview that had slowly assumed its form over the course of some twenty-five hundred years, beginning with Plato and Aristotle and culminating with Thomas Aquinas' grand synthesis of Christian theology and Aristotelian philosophy. The classical worldview first took root in the soil of a philosophical system known as teleology. The teleological idea holds that the world is an ordered, purposeful, and ultimately intelligible place. As Plato put it almost four hundred years before the birth of Christ, "the world is the product of a Mind which sets everything in order and produces each individual thing in the way that is best for it."[4]

Plato's vision of reality presaged the Christian worldview in striking ways. His student Aristotle also prepared the way by implanting Plato's transcendent Forms in the real world of material things. The transcendent was mingled with the terrestrial, and the eternal with the evanescent. Aristotle's philosophy came to represent the middle way between Plato's idealism and philosophical materialism, which was already being defended in Plato's time. From the soil of Aristotle's philosophy and the life-giving water of Christianity flowered the natural law tradition. This tradition achieved its most luminous synthesis in the thirteenth century, in the Christian teleology of Thomas Aquinas. Aquinas' theory of the natural law was the theological, philosophical, and moral completion of the classical worldview—a

[3] More eerily still, Nietzsche predicted in another work the immanent consequences for Europe of the loss of faith: "As the will to truth thus gains self-consciousness—there can be no doubt of that—morality will gradually *perish* now: this is the great spectacle in a hundred acts reserved for the next two centuries in Europe—the most terrible, most questionable and perhaps also the most hopeful of all spectacles." Friedrich Nietzsche, *On the Genealogy of Morals* (New York: Vintage Books, 1989), 161.

[4] Plato, *Phaedo* 99d.

worldview that retains a powerful hold on our own contemporary moral, philosophical, and political ideals.

Nevertheless, all Creation groans in futility: even great theories are destined to decay. Within half a century of Aquinas' death, William of Ockham and those who followed him labored—sometimes from purer motives, sometimes for political reasons—to jettison from Christian thought what they regarded as the contaminating influences of pagan philosophy. Ockham is the true originator of modern thought. Underlying the Platonic vision was the striking intuition that reality falls along an ontological continuum, that different kinds of things such as material objects, ideas, numbers, shadows, thoughts, and God must possess varying *degrees of Being*. For Plato and those who followed him, some things are literally *more real* than others. Ockham denied this. He insisted that only individual things exist and that anything that exists is as real as any other thing—a position known as nominalism. Ockham's denial of the Forms was a fateful philosophical move that began a cascading series of intellectual consequences that unfolded over the course of the succeeding four or five centuries. The ultimate result was a disaster, not only for theology but for philosophy.

In Ockham's wake early modern thinkers, including Descartes, Locke, and Hume, slowly distilled form from matter, the soul from the body, the moral law from the physical law, and God from the world. What Aquinas recognized as an integrated whole was slowly sundered into halves, one eternal and one material. Descartes' dualism in the seventeenth century was the high-water mark of the early modern attempt to preserve both halves of the earlier whole, but Cartesian dualism was ultimately philosophically unsustainable. By the eighteenth century, what had been cleaved from matter was abandoned altogether as the terrestrial half of the older dualism became the new whole. The soul became the mind, and the mind became matter in motion. Christianity withered into deism, and deism into atheism. Natural law disintegrated into utilitarianism and Kantianism, each of which isolated and then distorted parts of Aquinas' older ethical theory until these, too, decomposed into sundry forms of moral relativism.

In the course of a few centuries, the dualism of the early modern period simply collapsed into materialism, the view that any explanation for the world must be sought within, rather than beyond, the natural, material world. The world is an accident and has arisen from visionless causes. There is no divine plan or Planner, no objective purpose, and no meaning other than that which men create by fiat. All morality is a human construction. *We* decide what is good and bad, right and wrong. We are not bound by moral standards existing independently of us. If ethics has any ground, it must be the quest for pleasure or happiness in this world, not in the next. As one of its most recent defenders put it, materialism is the view that "earthly things are all that we have or are ever going to have."[5]

In a very strange way, we have come full circle. Contemporary debates about the meaning of morality and the purpose of human life—particularly disagreements between moral relativists and moral realists—echo eerily and revealingly the philosophical exchanges of Plato's time. Intellectually, history has proven to be not a progression but a pendulum that swings between the poles of materialism and theism. This book explores the arc of this pendulum.

To explain and defend sympathetically the classical worldview of Plato and Aristotle, Augustine and Aquinas, as this book does, is not to suggest that we must take every facet of these theories literally today. It is certainly not to argue that we should ignore the findings of modern science. None of these thinkers—in particular, Aristotle (who was perhaps the most accomplished scientist of his age) and Aquinas (who always insisted that there is one truth, that science and theology complement each other)—would have countenanced such a thing. To defend the classical worldview is rather to suggest that it is a far closer approximation of our own self-understanding than is the materialistic outlook with which the modern scientific quest is often conflated. What classical thinkers have provided is not so much an empirical hypothesis about the nature of reality as it is, as John Finnis put it, "an analogue model" for the speculative interpretation of the facts of our world.[6] This tradition, which culminated with Aquinas, also provides a far more plausible foundation for our modern moral and political ideals—for liberty, equality, dignity, and the sanctity of human life—than do the successors of Hobbes and Locke, Descartes and Kant.

[5] Christopher Hitchens, *God Is Not Great: How Religion Poisons Everything* (New York: Twelve, 2007), 5.

[6] John Finnis, *Natural Law and Natural Rights* (Oxford: Oxford University Press, 1980), 393.

Part I of this book traces the development of the classical world-view. Chapter 1 examines materialistic atheism in antiquity. Chapter 2 focuses on the pre-Christian tradition of Plato, Aristotle, and the Stoics. Chapters 3 and 4 trace the intellectual influence of Christian philosophy: chapter 3 focuses on the natural law tradition, and chapter 4 on the classical conception of the person, the relationship between the soul and the body, free will, and the ethical integration of human character.

Part II traces the decline of the natural law tradition and its consequences for our modern moral and political ideals. Chapter 5 examines four foundational thinkers of modern thought—William of Ockham, René Descartes, John Locke, and Thomas Hobbes. Chapter 6 explores the disintegration of the concept of the soul and the self in modern philosophy and psychology. Chapter 7 surveys the modern attempt to reconcile traditional ideas of freedom and responsibility (which depend on some version of the traditional concept of the self) with contemporary materialism, which denies the reality of freedom of the will. Chapter 8 follows the moral consequences of the modern rejection of natural law. It shows how natural law theory disintegrated into utilitarian and Kantian ideas of morality and why these theories, in turn, have collapsed, leaving various forms of moral relativism. Chapter 9, finally, draws together the lines of argument from the previous chapters and examines the three core moral and political ideals of modernity: freedom, responsibility, and human dignity. This chapter argues that these concepts become meaningless outside a framework grounded on the idea of the natural law.

Part I

The Classical Worldview

I

The First Materialists

All that exists are atoms and the void.

—Democritus

The Origins of Western Philosophy

Western philosophy arose not in Athens, where it ultimately flourished, but in the Ionian city of Miletus on the coast of Asia Minor and later in Elea on the sunny southeast coast of Italy. It was there in the sixth century B.C. that a group of thinkers sought to provide a purely scientific understanding of the world. They began from two apparently unquestionable assumptions: something exists, and it changes. Of all that exists, they asked, what does reality consist of most basically? Is there some primordial substance out of which all things are made? We can call this the question of *substance*. The second question concerns the nature of change and movement in the world. What causes things to change—to be born, to grow, and to disintegrate? This is the question of *process*.

Pre-Socratic thinkers attempted to answer the substance question in terms of one or another basic physical element. Thales (fl. 585 B.C.), usually regarded as the first genuine philosopher in the Western tradition, was the bumbler-savant who is said to have predicted an eclipse in 585 B.C. Aristotle reported that Thales grew wealthy by cornering the market on olive oil presses after accurately predicting a

It is not clear whether it was Democritus or his teacher Leucippus who first said this. Some have doubted that Leucippus was even a real person—e.g., W.K.C. Guthrie, *The Greek Philosophers from Thales to Aristotle* (New York: Harper and Row, 1950), 56–58—but ancient sources recount his life. See Diogenes, *Lives of Eminent Philosophers*, trans. R.D. Hicks (Cambridge, Mass.: Harvard University Press, 1972), 2:438 (Leucippus) and 442 (Democritus).

21

bumper crop in olives. Yet Aristophanes lampooned Thales for falling into a well while looking up at the stars. Thales' main contribution to philosophy was to argue that everything in the world is made
of water—a conjecture that seems to have been based on the fact that
the world is made mostly of water and that moisture is essential to the
reproductive process.[1]

What came next were variations on the same theme. A younger
associate of Thales, Anaximenes (ca. 585–528 B.C.), propounded the
view that there was indeed one basic element but argued that it must
be air. Slightly later, Heraclitus (ca. 535–475 B.C.), a nobleman from
Ephesus, thought that fire best mirrored the nature of reality since,
like all things in the world, fire is forever seeking, never satisfied,
always consuming everything it touches on pain of its own extinction. Empedocles (490–430 B.C.) adopted the still more democratic
idea that there were four elements—water, air, fire, and earth. Finally,
Anaximander (ca. 610–546 B.C.) reached the striking conclusion, later
to influence Aristotle, that matter in its most essential form could not
be described as one or another element at all, that "it was something
more basic, mutable and primitive", a prime matter that took many
forms but could not be finally reduced to any particular element. He
called this prime matter *apeiron*, meaning a formless, indefinite, and
limitless substance from which all things spring.

If answering this first question of substance was divisive, the question of change split philosophy along a second dimension. In fact, the
earliest thinkers began to suspect that there existed a tension between
the two questions. They recognized that things combined and dissolved, evaporated and condensed, grew and decayed, but they
found it difficult to understand change without compromising their
understanding of the eternal substance: if what is basic and eternal is
characterized by its changelessness, as they assumed, then it seemed
that the most basic and eternal element could not change at all. But
how, then, were they to make sense of the constant change that takes
place in the world?

Parmenides of Elea (fl. 500–450 B.C.) posed the dilemma in this
way: things that are real, he reasoned, cannot arise from things that are
not real, since Being can never come from non-Being. For anything
to change, something existing must cause this change since every

---

[1] Guthrie, *The Greek Philosophers from Thales to Aristotle*, 23–27.

effect has a cause. But this cause must already exist before the effect in order to bring about the effect. And if *this* cause has itself arisen from something else, then this still more basic cause must underlie *its* effect. Underlying all change there must be something unchanging since, otherwise, there would be an infinite regress. At every moment, there must be some basic ground of Being that is unchanging and eternal. All change is an illusion of the senses, and all we can say of reality, Parmenides concluded, is that "it is"—complete, indivisible, unchangeable, and eternal.[2]

Heraclitus took the opposite position. Change and the diversity of things in the world were too obvious to deny. The senses do not lie. Yet because Heraclitus accepted the premise that Being can never come from non-Being, he concluded that *there simply is no most basic thing*. Ours is a world of process, not substance. Change is simply inexorable, the very fabric of reality itself. Heraclitus declared that "we never step into the same river twice." Ours is a world of constant Becoming, but never Being. Individual things come into being and pass away, but there is nothing "deeper"—nothing that *is*—but the *Logos*. The Logos was a divine ordering principle through which the substanceless and impermanent world finds its "hidden attunement". It is little wonder that the term *Logos* was later adopted by the Stoics, who associated it with the mind of God, and that it found its way into the Gospel of John.[3]

---

[2] Diogenes, *Lives of Eminent Philosophers*, 2:428–32; W. K. C. Guthrie, *A History of Greek Philosophy* (Cambridge: Cambridge University Press, 1965), 2:26–50; Frederick C. Copleston, *A History of Philosophy* (New York: Image Books, 1993), 2:47–53.

[3] Change, Heraclitus argued, is relentless, the product of a mysterious and all-pervasive force he called "Strife", which constantly turns the wheel of experience, churning and propelling reality onward in its kaleidoscopic and ever-metamorphosing manifestations. Strife is the mother of all tension and conflict in the world, but it is a tension that is nonetheless necessary for order. Heraclitus insisted that "we must know that war is common to all and that Strife is justice, and that all things come into being and then pass away through Strife." Underlying the interminable conflict was a deeper order that he described as "the hidden attunement of the universe", a principle he called the "Logos". Guthrie, *History of Greek Philosophy*, 1:419–35.

The idea of the Logos is the mother of all natural law ideas. Heraclitus went so far as to associate the Logos with an impersonal, pantheistic godhead, "the one wise thing", which is willing and unwilling to be called Zeus. The Stoics were later influenced by Heraclitus' pantheistic conception of God and made the Logos the basis for the natural law. The Logos even finds its way into Christian theology in the Gospel of John, where it is associated with the Word, the disincarnate Christ in John 1:1. For a discussion of the Logos, see Heinrich Rommen, *The Natural Law: A Study in Legal and Social History and Philosophy* (Indianapolis: Liberty Fund, 1998), 6.

It is worth observing that the same two extreme positions of Parmenides and Heraclitus recur in Eastern philosophy: Hinduism, in its philosophical form, shares the Parmenidean belief that all change is *maya*, illusion, and that true reality is a changeless, eternal One. Buddhism, in contrast, is Heraclitean to the core: everything is impermanent; there is no enduring substance or truth in the world. These two opposed philosophies—radical monism and radical nihilism—are the equal but contrary results of failing to see that between Being and non-Being lies a third possibility, an idea that Aristotle discovered 150 years after Heraclitus.

Materialism

Plato tells us that his teacher, Socrates, became disillusioned as a young man with the speculations of these natural philosophers, the "scientists" of his era. Then one day he heard someone reading from a book by the philosopher Anaxagoras.[4] Anaxagoras was the first thinker in Western philosophy to draw a clear distinction between *hylo* and *nous*—or, as we would call them today, "matter" and "mind". The distinction almost immediately galvanized armies of thinkers on what would become the two sides of philosophy's great Maginot Line: either mind precedes matter, or it is simply the product of material processes.

Anaxagoras declared for mind. He wrote that nous was limitless and existed completely independently of matter. It is "the finest and purest of all things" and has "set everything in order".[5] Anaxagoras' nous was the first genuinely philosophical intuition of God in Western thought. So distinct was his discovery that Aristotle later said Anaxagoras stood out like a single sober man among the pre-Socratic philosophers.

On the other side of the debate (then, as now) were those who insisted that the world is the accidental result of visionless natural causes that have, against all odds, spun dust into DNA and distilled

---

[4] Plato, *Phaedo* 97c.

[5] W. K. C. Guthrie, *A History of Greek Philosophy* (Cambridge: Cambridge University Press, 1965), 2:273.

sunlight into human consciousness. This is the worldview known as materialism. Materialism is not the product of modern scientific thought, as some believe. It is as ancient as philosophical theism.

Materialism arose from the attempt to reconcile the world of change with the idea that Being, the basic stuff of reality, is eternal. The first materialists were Leucippus (fl. 430 B.C.) and Democritus (460–370 B.C.). We know very little about the shadowy Leucippus (Epicurus, who lived a little more than a century later, doubted that there ever was such a person). About Democritus, we know much more. Born in Abdera in northern Greece, he was known as the Laughing Philosopher for his easy disposition. He traveled throughout the known ancient world—to Egypt, Persia, and Ethiopia—accumulating knowledge in every recognized intellectual field, including physics, astronomy, botany, anatomy, chemistry, philosophy, and ethics. No one but Aristotle equaled his scientific learning. Stories about his Sherlock Holmes–like powers of observation—some of them, undoubtedly, apocryphal—abound.[6] He said many edifying things—such as that the essence of happiness is tranquillity and that "speech is the shadow of action." We are also told that Plato, who lived at the same time as Democritus and hated his materialism, wanted to engage in that most time-honored form of censorship—to burn all of Democritus' books. Plato did not get his way but never mentions Democritus anywhere in his *Dialogues*, even to refute him.[7]

Leucippus and Democritus harmonized Parmenides' enigmatic logic with the obvious fact of change by shrinking Parmenides' One into the atom. It was an ingenious solution. Atoms are the most basic unit of reality, they reasoned—imperceptibly small, solid, impenetrable, and, crucially, indivisible (*atom* literally means "undividable"). Democritus pointed out that, if matter were indefinitely divisible, the very concept would dissolve in an infinite regress as each "level" would have to be explained by another deeper level, ad infinitum. As Epicurus later put it, dividing the atom "into even smaller parts to infinity ... consume[s] existing things by reducing

---

[6] Diogenes tells us that one morning Democritus greeted a friend's maidservant, saying, "Good morning, maiden." A day later he greeted her again, "Good morning, woman." Later it was revealed that she had been seduced the previous night. Diogenes, *Lives of Eminent Philosophers* 2:453.

[7] Ibid., 2.449–51.

things to nonexistence".[8] Like the universe itself for all Greeks, the atom was eternal: it could be neither created nor destroyed. It thus satisfied the Greek conditions for a thing to qualify as the most basic stuff of reality.

Democritus taught that atoms and empty space were the only two things that exist. (Space, by definition, was made up of nothing.) Atoms were infinite in number and of endless variety and shape. The things of the ordinary world come into and pass out of existence as a result of the combination of atoms as they become "hooked" onto each other. The void—space—had to be empty since a universe packed with contiguous atoms would make movement and change impossible.[9] Democritus argued that atoms move through space, colliding and rebounding in innumerable ways, producing the aggregations of atoms that comprise all things, from plants to planets and from minerals to man. All material things in the world are in this way formed, persist for a while, and then deteriorate into their composite, still indestructible atomic components.

Unlike their modern successors, the ancient materialists did not deny the existence of mind or the soul. Democritus thought the soul the object of all ethical inquiry. Still, it was made of atoms— though the finest and smallest of atoms, which, alas, disperse at death, leaving no trace of the substance of the person. Democritus also

[8] Epicurus, "Letter to Herodotus", in *The Essential Epicurus: Letters, Principal Doctrines, Vatican Sayings, and Fragments*, trans. Eugene O'Connor (Amherst, N.Y.: Prometheus Books, 1993), 28. The ancient materialists were scandalized by the idea that material things might be infinitely divisible. Lucretius wrote that if the atom were not indivisible, impenetrable, and eternal, the smallest things would equally consist of an infinite number of parts, a proposition that true reason cries out against. Lucretius, *On the Nature of the Universe*, trans. R. E. Latham (New York: Penguin Books, 1977), 45.

[9] As Lucretius, a materialist who lived around the time of Julius Caesar, wrote:

> Thus, there is void, intactile empty space:
> If there were not, then there would be no way
> For things to move.

Worse still, without movement there could be no change since:

> if there were not void,
> they'd not so much be lacking speed and movement
> as never, in reason, have come to be at all
> in a world of matter, tight-packed and motionless.

Lucretius, *On the Nature of Things* 1.334–36, 342–45.

taught, as later materialists would, that everything happens by necessity. His determinism left no room for free will, but Epicurus, a later materialist, went to great lengths to salvage free will, as we will see.

Materialism proved barren ground for the broadly liberal and humanitarian instincts of most of its adherents. It took less than a generation for the cold, pristine materialism of Leucippus and Democritus to dissolve into the glossy, cosmopolitan skepticism of the Sophists—thinkers such as Protagoras and Gorgias. The Sophists were the secular humanists of their day. The parallels, in fact, are striking. For one thing, they had no place for God in their worldview. Protagoras, who had been a student of Democritus, famously began one book advocating agnosticism: "As to the gods, I have no reason of knowing either that they exist or that they do not exist. For many are the obstacles that impede knowledge, both the obscurity of the question and the shortness of human life."[10] The Athenians thanked him for his skepticism by exiling him and burning his books. It was also Protagoras who said, "Man is the measure of all things"— virtually the defining maxim of modern humanism. Anticipating the moral relativism of our age, Protagoras claimed here that all moral standards come from us: there is nothing beyond our own values by which we can measure our actions.

The Sophists elevated sensation above reason. They taught that whatever impression the senses receive must be regarded as true insofar as these sensations *appear true* to us. In fact, Protagoras declared that "no one thinks falsely." Moral judgments, in particular, are in the eye of the beholder.

Unfortunately, this ecumenical acceptance of the validity of all impressions turns quickly into its opposite—skepticism. If what you see or believe does not conform to what I see or believe, then each of us has the right to reject the other's judgment as binding on us. Knowledge itself becomes relative to the observer. Thus, the still more radical Sophist Gorgias—a postmodernist among the premoderns— famously declared his three skeptical truths: that nothing exists; that if anything did exist, it could not be known; and that if anything could be known, it could not be communicated. (That he was attempting to communicate this truth seems not to have bothered him.) The

---

[10] Diogenes, *Lives of Eminent Philosophers* 2:465.

Sophists were thus the first to inflate and then totally devalue the currency of knowledge.[11]

The Moral and Political Consequences of Early Materialism

The most important materialist of antiquity was Epicurus (341–270 B.C.) (for whom we still use the eponymous *epicurean*). Epicurus did more than any other materialist thinker to draw out—and to try to mitigate—the moral and political consequences of materialism.

He was of Athenian descent, born on the island of Samos off the coast of Asia Minor as Athens was being absorbed into the Macedonian Empire of Philip II and his son, Alexander the Great. He was about nineteen when Aristotle died. Rather than following the latter's doctrines, Epicurus took the materialist side in the great war of philosophy. He espoused political withdrawal and a gentle hedonism, counseling that pleasure was the highest good. His social philosophy was relativistic and egalitarian; he admitted men and women, and freemen and slaves alike to his Garden. He exhorted his students to live a life of natural simplicity and independence. His pithiest advice to his followers was "Live unseen!"—a principle Descartes later claimed to follow.

Thus, in some ways, Epicurus' philosophy seems a precursor to the shibboleth of the 1960s—"Tune in, turn on, drop out." Yet this comparison can be misleading. Though his association with hedonism has condemned him in the minds of many—Dante placed him in the sixth level of hell for having denied the immortality of the soul, and some of his contemporaries maliciously gossiped that his Garden was the secret venue of riotous orgies—Epicurus would have been horrified by the permissive ethos of modern culture. Enough of his writings have survived to paint a clear picture of his nuanced thought, including three philosophical letters, the brief *Principal Doctrines*, several fragments quoted in other philosophers' works, and the *Vatican Sayings*, a collection of aphorisms discovered in a Vatican manuscript in 1888.[12]

---

[11] Copleston, *A History of Philosophy*, 2:87–95.

[12] I have drawn from several sources on Epicurus' life. The classical source was originally book 10 of Diogenes' *Lives of Eminent Philosophers* 2:528–675. See also Friedrich Albert Lange, *The History of Materialism and Criticism of Its Present Importance* (London: Routledge and Kegan Paul, 1925), 93–125. More contemporary sources include Eugene O'Connor,

Epicurus' theory of knowledge followed closely on that of the Sophists. He taught that the only way to judge the goodness or badness of an action is by the sensation of pleasure or pain it produces. As an ethical hedonist, he thought that the Good is equivalent to happiness, which, in turn, is simply pleasure. Like the Sophists before him and empiricists such as David Hume much later, Epicurus subordinated reason to the senses as a faculty of knowledge. He insisted that reason cannot second-guess our sensations of pleasure and pain since reason draws its knowledge from the senses. "If you do battle with all your sensations," he wrote, "you will be unable to form a standard for judging even which of them you judge to be false."[13]

These assumptions lent themselves to a broadly relativistic view of morality and knowledge, as for the Sophists before. Yet what Epicurus took in principle he more than gave back in its application, tempering the hedonistic principle at every turn. He argued that pleasure is nothing but the reduction of pain, counseled that the best way to maximize pleasure is to reduce our desires and needs, and taught that it was far better to do the right thing and suffer ill fortune than to do the wrong thing and succeed through luck. He said that it was nobler to do a kindness than to receive one and that the suffering of the soul is far worse than the suffering of the body.[14] In each of these ways, it is fair to say, Epicurus' practical judgment far surpassed the apparent implications of his philosophy.

Epicurus' moral and political views were the forerunners of a characteristic set of positions later taken by Enlightenment political thinkers. He was an ethical relativist, a utilitarian of sorts, and he subscribed to a social-contract view of social relations. Morality is

---

introduction to *The Essential Epicurus*, 9–17; Whitney J. Oates, general introduction to *The Stoic and Epicurean Philosophers* (New York: Random House, 1940), xiii–xv; Copleston, *A History of Philosophy*, 1:401–11.

[13] Epicurus, *Principal Doctrines*, no. 23, in *The Essential Epicurus*, 72. Compare with Lucretius, *On the Nature of Things* 4.469–521.

[14] Epicurus, *Principal Doctrines*, no. 3, in *The Essential Epicurus*, 69; "Letter to Menoeceus", in *The Essential Epicurus*, 68. As Epicurus put it: "When we say that pleasure is the goal, we are not talking about the pleasure of profligates or that which lies in sensuality.... [I]t is freedom from bodily pain and mental anguish. For it is not continuous drinking and revels, nor the enjoyment of women and young boys ... but sober reasoning which examines the motives for every choice and avoidance, and which drives away those opinions resulting in the greatest disturbance to the soul." Ibid., 66. For a discussion of Epicurean ethics, see Copleston, *A History of Philosophy*, 1:408–11.

simply the name we give to the body of rules we fashion together to
make life livable. Moral conventions serve a utilitarian function and
are grounded on a hypothetical social contract. Almost two thousand years before Hobbes argued that the fear of death is the tap-
root of the social contract, Epicurus wrote that "natural justice is a
pledge ... to prevent one from harming others, and to keep oneself
from being harmed."[15] When David Hume wrote in the eighteenth
century that "public utility is the sole origin of justice", he was
following the same train of thought as Epicurus, who declared that
"[t]here is no such thing as justice in itself; it is always rather a certain
compact made during men's dealings with one another in different places, not to do harm or to be harmed."[16] Hume and Jeremy
Bentham would also have found equally congenial Epicurus' idea
that "that which is proven to be beneficial in the business of men's
dealings with one another is the guarantor of justice."[17] Even that
most sanctified of all ancient relationships, friendship, for Epicurus
"begins in need". Then as now, utility, convention, and self-interest
were the three corners of the materialist's ethic.

Materialism leads political thought in the opposite direction of
natural law theory in several respects. Aristotle taught that our society is the natural expression of our human telos. It is natural not
only in the sense that it arises from our natural needs but in the
greater sense that it perfects the individual—that society gives us
our "second nature". When Aristotle declared that "the State is by
nature prior to the individual",[18] he was pointing out that the State
is *formally* prior to the individual in the same way (as we shall see)
that the form of a thing is prior to its matter. Aristotle saw plainly

---

[15] Epicurus, *Principal Doctrines*, no. 31, in *The Essential Epicurus*, 74.

[16] David Hume, *An Enquiry Concerning the Principles of Morals*, in David Hume, *Essays Moral, Political, and Literary*, ed. T. H. Green and T. H. Grose (London: Longmans, Green, 1907), sec. 3, pt. 1; cf. Epicurus, *Principal Doctrines*, no. 33, in *The Essential Epicurus*, 74. Hume was less sympathetic than Epicurus to the social contract idea but thought, with Epicurus, that justice was utility, and utility was derived from men's needs, not supernatural standards.

[17] Epicurus, *Principal Doctrines*, no. 37, in *The Essential Epicurus*, 75. He elaborated: "If someone makes a law which does not result in advantage for men's dealings with each other, it no longer has the nature of justice. Moreover, when circumstances change such that a prac-tice once thought to be just is no longer advantageous, then the practice was once just but no longer is." *Principal Doctrines*, nos. 37, 38.

[18] Aristotle, *Politics* 1.2.

what no one but a brilliant misanthrope like Rousseau could deny—that the individual owes his humanity, even his individuality, to our social institutions.

Epicurus denied much of this. Anticipating thinkers such as Hobbes and Rousseau, he maintained that the State was an artificial convention: there is nothing natural about it. Where Aristotle exalted civic participation in the polis, Epicurus advocated political withdrawal. Epicurus' later Roman follower Lucretius (ca. 99–55 B.C.) wrote that the State, at best, secures and perfects the natural freedom that we have in the state of nature and that, in entering society, we trade our precarious natural freedom for security and submission. Hobbes would argue the exact same thing two thousand years later. At its worst, moreover, government is a ruse perpetrated by the wealthier but less numerous on the landless and clueless. One cannot read Lucretius' account of the state of nature and the origins of civilization without suspecting Rousseau of plagiarism.[19]

The deepest problem of all for Epicurus, Lucretius, and their contemporary ethical followers is explaining the *oughtness* of morality. If morality is merely a social convention, how can it ever be used to provide a normative critique of our social institutions? If "good" and "bad" are simply social constructs, then the reformers of the world—the Socrateses and the Ghandis and the Martin Luther Kings—will always be "wrong", *by definition*, since they oppose prevailing conventions. Moreover, if following moral rules is simply a matter of social convention (or even self-interest), why should anyone who can perpetrate an unjust act to his own advantage without suffering social sanction refrain from doing so?

---

[19] Lucretius imagined that society arose through three stages: the benign state of nature, in which men are simple, strong, and well disposed toward their fellows; the idyllic life of the happy villagers who first settled down to agriculture; and modern civilization—venal, debased, besot, and weakened with material overindulgence. Everywhere Lucretius sounds the themes that kindled Rousseau's fame eighteen hundred years later: the state of nature is benign, civilized society is artificial and unnatural; natural man is simple but self-sufficient, whereas modern man is corrupt; the State is the tool of the wealthy and powerful; etc. "Through ignorance they often served themselves poison; grown wiser, they serve it now to others." Lucretius, *On the Nature of Things* 5.1009–10; cf. Jean-Jacques Rousseau, *The Discourse on the Origins of Inequality* (1754). Yet whereas Rousseau and his modern-day followers insist that all these problems can be solved if only the State can be democratized, Epicurus and Lucretius were content to counsel self-sufficiency and a turning away from politics.

In Plato's *Republic*, the character Glaucon mentions the tale of the ring of Gyges. The ring permits its wearer to turn invisible so that he can perpetrate any evil or fraudulent act without detection. Gyges uses the ring to infiltrate the Lydian royal household, seduces the queen, and murders the king to assume control of the kingdom. What mortal, Plato asks, is virtuous enough to forsake this power, given the opportunity to use it?[20] Epicurus knew the story well, and yet the only reason he could give to explain why people should not be unjust was that the unjust man will spend the rest of his life fearing apprehension.[21] For the materialist, the source of all moral obligations is none other than the unvarnished threat of punishment.

The Fate of Materialism

Epicurus died around 270 B.C. His most illustrious follower was Lucretius, who developed materialism into a comprehensive world-view in his book-length poem *On the Nature of Things*. By this point in history, Stoicism had become the dominant philosophy in the Greco-Roman world, and materialism began to wane. With the coming of the Christian era, materialism largely vanished from the scene, reemerging only in the seventeenth century in the philosophy of Thomas Hobbes, among others. In our age, however, materialism is again ascendant. It disguises itself under different labels—secularism, humanism, post-agnosticism, et cetera—but these doctrines all share the same basic elements of the materialist's worldview, though frequently cast in the quasi-religious idiom of a "religion of humanity".[22]

The basic tenets of Democritus' atomism remained largely unchanged until the end of the nineteenth century. Yet in the

---

[20] Plato, *Republic* 2.359d.

[21] "For right up to the day of his death, it remains unclear whether he will escape detection." Epicurus, *Principal Doctrines*, no. 35, in *The Essential Epicurus*, 74.

[22] For example, the *Humanist Manifesto*, published in 1933, defends a broadly materialistic, agnostic, and socialistic worldview, though it casts this in quasi-religious terms, i.e., as a new religion to replace the older, God-centered religions. The *Humanist Manifesto II*, published in 1973, dropped the religious overtones altogether, declaring that belief in God "is unproved and outmoded". A third manifesto followed in 2003. The central tenet of these manifestos closely tracks materialism—that there is no God or immortal soul and that morality is purely a human construction.

twentieth century, relativity theory and quantum physics have left hardly a trace of the concept of matter as Democritus would have understood it. Whereas atomistic theories assumed that mass was an intrinsic property of matter reflecting the absolute quantity of "stuff"—i.e., the more matter, the greater its mass—we now know that mass varies relative to the position of the observer. This makes matter a very queer kind of thing indeed. Nor does anyone now hold Democritus' "particle" theory of matter. The atom has now been dissolved into the subatomic substrata of electrons, neutrons, and protons and then the subtler quarks and wave-particle functions and the like. The Schrödinger-Heisenberg theory understands the atom as a field of energy rather than as a concrete material particle. Modern string theory, which attempts to reconcile quantum mechanics and Einstein's general relativity, postulates that subatomic particles are vibrating one-dimensional strings (they have length but not width or height) and requires that we postulate the existence of several unobservable dimensions of reality. Even the looser concept of mass energy is a philosophical anomaly today.[23] The universe is clearly a much weirder place than the materialists of antiquity ever dreamed.

On the other side of philosophy's Maginot Line, the opponents of materialism—men such as Socrates, Plato, and Aristotle—began to reason their way to a very different resolution of the apparent conflict between Substance and Process. Their ideas became the most important philosophical tributary to an understanding of the world that would flower into the Christian natural law tradition.

---

[23] Joseph Levine, *Purple Haze: The Puzzle of Consciousness* (New York: Oxford University Press, 2001), 17–21. What remains is largely the idea of energy. As Bertrand Russell, who remained a physicalist, put it, "There is no longer any reason to believe that there is such a thing as matter consisting of atoms that persist and move. There is a collection of events ordered in the four-dimensional manifold of space-time. There is something called energy." Bertrand Russell, *On God and Religion* (Buffalo: Prometheus Books, 1986), 155.

2

The Classical Worldview before Christianity

But we must not follow those who advise us, being men, to think of human things, and, being mortal, of mortal things, but must, so far as we can, make ourselves immortal, and strain every nerve to live in accordance with the best thing in us.

—Aristotle

An old Chinese proverb declares, "When the finger points at the moon, the idiot looks at the finger."[1] Modern man is an idiot savant. We know more than we ever thought possible about the *hows* of physical reality even as its *whys* have faded almost entirely from view. We understand the mechanisms of the finger of the world but have lost sight of where it is pointing. Classical thinkers, including Plato, Aristotle, and St. Thomas Aquinas, thought that we cannot even claim to know a thing without knowing its purpose, its end—its *why*. To understand the world, and ourselves, we must understand the direction in which we are pointed.

Philosophers use the term *teleology* (from the Greek *telos*, meaning "end", "goal", "purpose", or "fulfillment") for the idea that men, among other things in the world, have a particular end, or form of fulfillment. Our end points us in a certain direction and tells us how to live. Plato was the father of the teleological worldview. He taught that each thing in the world has a particular form of perfection—an

Aristotle, *Nicomachean Ethics* 10.7.1177b31–78a2.

[1] Edward Feser, *The Last Superstition: A Refutation of the New Atheism* (South Bend, Ind.: St. Augustine's Press, 2008), 267.

end—toward which it inherently strives.[2] Aristotle later used the word *essence* to describe the inherent nature of a thing that embodies its form and strives toward its telos.

To know a thing's end is to know its specific form of perfection, which, in turn, is to understand what that thing really *is*. Thus, for Plato, Aristotle, and later classical thinkers, there is no radical separation between the world of facts and the world of value. The Good of each thing is the unfolding of its essence, and this essence is a fact. To understand a thing's purpose in the world is to understand what that thing is. To put it a bit poetically, teleology means that the *what* of each thing cannot be separated from its *why*. To discover what any particular thing is, one must discover "how it was best for that thing to be, or to act".[3] And to discover this is to discover a thing's nature or *form*.

Plato and the Teleological Worldview

Plato was born into an aristocratic family in 427 B.C., near the zenith of Athenian cultural and military dominance. For the previous half century, from its defeat of Persia in 479 until Pericles' time, Athens was the intellectual and commercial center of the Mediterranean. But all of this began to unravel with the outbreak of conflict with Sparta a few years before Plato was born. Plato's youth was marked by the hardship of a war that lasted, with some intervals, for over twenty-five years. The war ended in 404, when Plato was about twenty-three, but by then Athens had been severely weakened, economically and militarily. It never fully recovered. With

---

[2] The telos, or concept of an end, has two aspects: positively, it embodies the particular form of fulfillment toward which a thing strives to actualize its manner of perfection, and, negatively, it reflects a thing's limit beyond which it is not meant to go. We use the word *end* to reflect both this positive goal of its fully actualized state and the ontological terminus. Plato was deeply influenced, in the second respect, by Pythagoras, who extolled the virtues of limit and proportion among the parts of things. In fact, Pythagoras contrasted light, unity, and limit, which were all good things, with darkness, plurality, and the unlimited, which were bad. These ideas influenced Plato's conception of justice as the appropriate proportion among the parts of a greater order. W. K. C. Guthrie, *The Greek Philosophers from Thales to Aristotle* (New York: Harper and Row, 1950), 36.

[3] Plato, *Phaedo* 97c7–d1.

the Athenian defeat, the aristocratic class with which Plato's family was associated was displaced by a more democratic party. Prevented by these events from pursuing a life in politics, Plato turned to philosophy. When his beloved teacher Socrates was executed by the democrats a few years later, in 399, Plato resolved to carry on Socrates' mission and used Socrates' name to represent his own philosophy in his dialogues.

Plato founded his Academy to teach philosophy to the aristocratic young men of Athens, but it was not until he was well into his forties that he began writing his dialogues. He thought that philosophy should not even be studied until the student approached middle age. While in his sixties he made an attempt to convert to his philosophy the elder and younger Dionysius, the father and son rulers of the city of Syracuse, and he traveled there two or three times before falling out with the younger Dionysius. Plato apparently never married and lived to the age of eighty-one.

Plato's deepest interests were always on the interior side of the human condition. He was more interested in the soul than in the body, the nature of the Good rather than the laws of the physical world, the idea of justice rather than the mechanisms of government. He wrote poetically of time as "the moving image of eternity" and said that all true philosophy was a preparation for dying. Whereas today we believe that there is no middle way between existence and nonexistence, Plato taught that there are degrees of Being—that some things possess more reality than others. Material things fall low on the scale. In his allegory of the cave, Plato compared material things to shadows and insisted that the ordinary world was one of Becoming but not Being.[4]

---

[4] Plato gave us two memorable descriptions of the degrees of reality in his *Republic*. In his description of the divided line, he imagines a line cut in two, representing, respectively, sensible and intelligible things. Each of these segments is further divided between what is more and less real in each realm. Thus, the line has four segments, AB, BC, CD, and DE. The sensible realm is represented by CD and DE. DE, the least real thing, represents shadows and reflections of ordinary objects. CD represents the objects themselves. BC comprises the realm of thought, and AB, the most real of all, comprises the realm of the Forms. The realm of thought (BC) is a reflection cast by the Forms (AB), just as shadows (DE) are reflections cast by the objects they reflect. Plato, *Republic* 509d7–e3.

In his allegory of the cave, Plato analogizes ordinary men to prisoners chained in a cave. The prisoners spend their lives watching shadows cast from a high wall behind them, which they cannot see. The shadows they see represent the lowest grade of reality; the objects casting these shadows are like the ordinary material objects in the sensible world. If one of the

As for harmonizing an enduring world of Being with the obvious fact that our world changes, Plato rejected atomism altogether. Instead he divided reality between the changeless Parmenidean world of the Forms and the ever-changing Heraclitean real world of ordinary objects. The things of the real world are imperfect replicas of their Forms. Whereas materialism holds that all changes in the world are driven from behind by the causes and conditions that necessitate them—that prior causes lead to later effects in a deterministic fashion—Plato thought that change occurs when the things of the world are drawn forward toward their greater perfection by a process of attraction to their own Forms. Behind this process of attraction lies something still greater, as we will see shortly.

Plato was the first to ask what makes all things in the same class of objects—all trees or triangles or instances of redness—*resemble* one another. To the modern mind, this is a strange question and seems to put the problem backward. Today we are inveterate nominalists: we live in a world of particular *things*, not forms. We think that it is the *name* we give to things that unites them in a commonality (ergo, *nominalism*). We think that we simply use the word *tree*, for example, to relate a bunch of things that bear a superficial resemblance to each other. But Plato wondered why we apply the same concept to these, and only these, objects. He answered that there must be something beyond the many individual instances of trees that makes them all alike, instances of the *Form* of the tree.[5] Our language captures this reality but does not create it.

---

prisoners were to be unchained and dragged outside, he would see not only the real world of objects but also the sun, which illuminates all. If this same prisoner were to return to the cave to free the others, he would be laughed at, if not killed. So, too, the masses prefer the life of the senses to real knowledge, which only the philosopher sees fit to pursue. Plato, *Republic* 514–17d.

[5] Nominalists have a response, but it fails. They argue that we look at this white thing and that white thing, blocking out all other aspects of the two things, comparing them by the quality that remains—their whiteness. But this does not explain why they seem similar, nor does it explain how we know both things share the same quality, whiteness, before beginning the comparison. The nominalist may say that the two things just resemble one another, but this just pushes the problem back one level. Not only does this not explain what it means for one thing to resemble another without appealing to a universal, but *resemblance itself* is a universal that specifies a type of relation between two or more things. Two white things resemble each other in one way, and two intelligent things resemble each other in another way, but there is a resemblance between the two resemblances, a metaresemblance. Thus, the nominalist has just pushed the problem back another step without ridding himself of universals. For a comparison of Platonic realism with nominalism and conceptualism, see Feser, *The Last Superstition*, 39–49.

The Forms (or universals, as they were later called) also explain the enigmatic nature of thought and communication. Thoughts themselves—my thought of redness and your thought of redness— are obviously distinct things, yet there is this ineluctable something that we are able to share, something that "connects" our thoughts, that permits you and me to have *the same idea* in our heads notwithstanding our having *two distinct thoughts*. Our minds meet, so to speak, in contemplating one and the same eternal Form, or universal.

Plato's eternal Forms are the fundamental things of reality and the true objects of our knowledge. They draw together diverse physical things in resemblance and similarly unite separate minds in the process of communication. No sentence can be uttered that does not include a universal.[6] Nor do we seem to be able to explain relations (e.g., being greater than or being the son of) without some conception of a form, since relations do not exist in the physical world as such, or as ideas in someone's head. (A star is bigger than a rock whether or not anyone has ever thought about it. One event occurred before another even if everyone has forgotten the events.) Indeed, it is impossible to explain what the laws of science are without reference to Forms, or universals. So impoverished does our world become when we deny the reality of universals that even several modern materialists have concluded that they are indispensable to philosophy and science.[7]

At the pinnacle of Plato's hierarchy of Being is the Form of the Good. He taught that the Good was the single most *real* thing in the world and the highest object of contemplation. Plato tells us that "the greatest thing to learn is the idea of the Good and that even if ... we should know all other things ... it would avail us nothing without knowing the Good."[8] The Form of the Good is the single most attractive thing in the world, drawing all things to it according

---

[6] Though Plato limited the realm of Forms to nouns (trees, triangles) and adjectives (red), we can also think of all actions in the language of universals. Running, eating, existing—these also seem to fit the definition of universals. Bertrand Russell, *The Problems of Philosophy* (New York: Barnes and Noble, 2004), 65.

[7] Atheist Bertrand Russell championed Plato's theory of Forms, with some modifications of his own, as one of the most important and successful contributions to philosophy. Ibid., 63. Other naturalists or materialists who have accepted universals include D. M. Armstrong and W. V. O. Quine. Feser, *The Last Superstition*, 274n14.

[8] Plato, *Republic* 6.505a.

to their own nature. Men, too, naturally seek the Good, though we see through a glass darkly in our quest for the Good. Because we are easily led off course by our appetites and our lack of understanding, we continually miss the mark, chasing things that we believe to be good but that lead us astray as often as not. All things are moved by their perception of the Good, "which every soul pursues and for its sake does all that it does, with an intuition of its reality, but yet baffled and unable to apprehend its nature".[9]

Plato's Form of the Good is, in sum, an adumbration of the Christian idea of God. As the most real thing, the highest object of contemplation, and the thing that is most worthy of love, Plato's idea presages St. Thomas Aquinas' idea of God as the absolute ground of Being, Truth, and Goodness.[10]

Naturalizing Teleology: Aristotle

It fell to Aristotle (387–322 B.C.) to call Plato's Forms down from the heavens and implant them in the things of this world. If Plato was the poet, Aristotle was the scientist. For Aristotle, science was an extension of philosophy and metaphysics a foundation for science. Aristotle was an encyclopedic natural scientist who wrote on biology, zoology, botany, anatomy, physics, astronomy, and meteorology. He studied and dissected the new specimens of plant and animal life that his student Alexander the Great sent home from military expeditions. He was, without a doubt, not simply the greatest philosopher but the most learned scientist of his age.

[9] Ibid., 505e.

[10] Plato was himself notoriously uncertain about the status of the Form of the Good. In the *Republic* he seems to acquaint it with *nous*, the divine agent in the universal order, but in his *Timaeus* he makes the Demiurge the creative and mindlike entity that brings order from chaos. Most scholars have concluded that Plato did not intend to equate the Form of the Good with God and that the functions of God are divided between the Form of the Good and the Demiurge. See, e.g., J.C.B. Gosling, *Plato* (Boston: Routledge and Kegan Paul, 1973), 118; R.M. Hare, *Plato* (New York: Oxford University Press, 1982), 44–45; John P. Rowan, "Platonic and Christian Theism", in *God in Contemporary Thought: A Philosophical Perspective*, ed. Sebastian Matczak (New York: Learned Publications, 1977), 402–3. Against this current, David Conway has recently argued that Plato used these different terms to refer to one and the same entity, which he equated with God. David Conway, *The Rediscovery of Wisdom* (New York: St. Martin's Press, 2000), 34–52.

Aristotle was born in the Thracian city of Stagira. His father was court physician to the Macedonian king, and Aristotle is supposed to have married a Thracian princess. As a youth, he went to study philosophy in Athens, where he sat at the feet of Plato for some twenty years until Plato died in 347. By the 330s, Macedonian power was expanding under Philip II, the father of Alexander the Great. Athens was absorbed into the Macedonian Empire in 338, and Aristotle became the tutor of the young Alexander. While still in his twenties, Alexander conquered much of the known world to the east, but he died suddenly at the age of thirty-three in 323 B.C., leaving a power vacuum. The Athenians rebelled against Macedonian suzerainty, and Aristotle was accused of impiety, one of the two charges brought against Socrates. Aristotle fled Athens, lest, as he put it, the Athenians sin against philosophy a second time. He died in exile of natural causes a year later.

Aristotle's most important overall contribution to philosophy was to naturalize teleology—to recast Plato's teleological idealism in more natural, scientific terms. Central to this project was Aristotle's discovery of the concept of substantial form. Aristotle was no idealist, let alone a mystic. He was a commonsense philosopher. Against Plato, he insisted that natural things are not mere shadows, imperfect replicas of immaterial Forms. Nor are they simply the random composites of atoms that have somehow flown together to form objects, as the materialists taught. The truth, characteristically for Aristotle, falls between Democritus' materialism and Plato's idealism. Aristotle found in the ordinary world an order and a beauty that Plato thought could be found only in the immaterial realm.

Consider a flowering plant. It has a holistic, organic structure of its own. This particular organization and characteristic form of flourishing is inherent in the plant's structure (it makes the plant what it is) and in its dynamic development (it unfolds and develops in accord with its built-in blueprint). The plant does not grow and change because of the lower-level changes at the atomic level, as the atomists taught. Rather, the structure of the plant as a whole operates in a top-down manner, regulating its internal, component processes. Like all other natural things, Aristotle argued, the plant is a *substance*, a concrete unit of reality distinguishable from other substances by the fact that each particular thing is similarly self-contained. Substances are the true units of reality, he thought, and each material thing is its own substance.

But what are substances, exactly, and how is Aristotle's approach distinguishable from materialism? Aristotle taught that all things are made of matter, as our senses plainly tell us, but that there is a second basic constituent of all real things as well. It is here that we find Plato's most important contribution to Aristotle's philosophy. *Substances are composites of form and matter.* Plato was right to insist that we must understand each thing in terms of its Form, but he was wrong to think that form existed independently of matter. Form and matter are inseparable. It is the form of a thing—its having the form of a hyacinth, for example—that "organizes" the matter in the plant. The form of a thing is its core *essence*, which gives each thing its intrinsic nature and ensures that it unfolds at it should to realize its nature. And since knowing a thing's nature is to understand what it should be at its best, each thing's form is key to understanding its telos, the end, or form of excellence, at which it aims.

Aristotle next distinguished the substance of a thing from its properties. A particular apple is round, red, sweet, et cetera—these are among its properties—but there is a core "thingness" to the apple, which Aristotle called its substance. Properties do not exist separately from things. Redness, tallness, and intelligence are qualities that exist *in* things. Properties inhere in substances. Some properties are expressions of the essence of a thing (e.g., rationality is an essential property of humanness), and other properties are accidental (e.g., a person's height or weight or hair color).

A substance is the ontological center of gravity for each thing. The concept of substance explains the tendency of ordinary things to persist through time even as they change. The leaves of the tree sprout in the spring, turn verdant in summer, and then become sere and brown before falling off the tree in late autumn. Each leaf changes and yet somehow persists through the process of change until it finally disintegrates. A person, too, grows and matures and continually develops, yet in some sense he is still the same person throughout his life. Aristotle argued that it is precisely the substance of the leaf or the tree or the person that is the enduring subject of change. The tree or the person is real because each is a form-matter composite, a genuine locus of reality with a nature and a telos of its own. Aristotle argued that it is the form of the thing that unites it with others of its kind, while its matter differentiates it as a particular physical thing distinct from all other things. This concept of substance will be crucial, as we will see in chapter 4, to explain how the person or self can persist over time even as every molecule in his body is constantly replaced by new ones.

Aristotle's most striking departure from materialism was his claim that form is so intrinsic to each thing that it is *metaphysically prior to matter*. Not only is there a nonmaterial aspect embedded within all things, but it is this nonmaterial aspect that is the more important constituent of each thing. In saying that form precedes matter, Aristotle was asserting that *function determines structure*, rather than the other way around, as materialists believe. The modern Darwinian insists, for example, that mankind has developed its intelligence in part because our ancestors evolved hands and an opposable thumb, which permitted them to manipulate things and, through a process of natural selection, proved essential to their survival and success as an evolving species. Aristotle would insist that this has it backward. Because form is prior to matter, the physical structure of man unfolds as a consequence of the form of humanness, which Aristotle took to be rational animality. Nature has fitted mankind with hands because we were born to have the intelligence to use them; we did not develop intelligence because we first, as a random fluke, developed hands.

It is important to understand that Aristotle's point here is metaphysical, not physical. A modern Aristotelian need not deny the Darwinian evolutionary chronology, but he will insist that there is a purposive element inherent in the evolutionary process, which is evidenced in a powerfully circumstantial way by the upward spiral of evolution. We have evolved through a physical process in time, but this historical, natural process has slowly unfolded the form of humanness, which was implicate in the order of the world from the beginning.[11] It should be clear from this that the form-over-matter

---

[11] In light of Darwin's discoveries, Aristotle would insist that our evolutionary development must be understood in teleological terms as a process of purposive development (i.e., that God has fitted us for our purpose through the course of our evolutionary development). (For an excellent discussion of the implications of a teleological account of evolution, see Étienne Gilson, *From Aristotle to Darwin and Back Again* [San Francisco: Ignatius Press, 2009].) Of course, the modern skeptic may ask: What is the point of evolution? Why did God need

principle will ultimately lead us back to an understanding of God, since the Forms originate in God's mind.

The most important corollary of the form–over–matter principle is Aristotle's observation that we cannot explain causation as materialists do, purely in terms of material and efficient causes. Aristotle taught that there are four kinds of causes for any phenomenon—the material, efficient, formal, and final causes.[12] The material and efficient causes are, respectively, the internal and external aspects of the physical nature of a thing, and the formal and final causes are, respectively, the internal and external aspects of its formal element. For example, the matter of which a mustard seed consists (the material cause) is watered and fed by the soil and the sun, which are the efficient causes of its growth (i.e., they are the external, physical causes). But the mustard plant develops in a certain way in accordance with its intrinsic formal structure (its formal cause). The plant maintains this form as it works toward its final end, its telos: its fully realized structure as a mustard plant. This is the work of the final cause. The final cause is the most important of the four causes. Since each thing exists for a purpose, with an end in view, the final cause unites the other causes by explaining why a thing exists and what it is in its finest form. For this reason, Aquinas later called the final cause the "cause of causes".[13]

---

to invent dinosaurs and a myriad of other lower physical organisms on the way to evolving us? Evolution, it might be said, is an incredibly inefficient process involving a great deal of destruction on the way to achieving its ultimate triumph: us. St. Thomas might have answered that this is itself a profoundly self-centered perspective. He pointed out that we are not the sole point of Creation: "Since the divine goodness could not be represented by one creature alone, God produced many and diverse creatures.... Thus, the whole universe together participates in the divine goodness more perfectly and represents it better than any single creature whatever." Thomas Aquinas, *Summa Theologiae* Ia, 47, 1, cited in Robert Barron, *Thomas Aquinas: Spiritual Master* (New York: Crossroad, 2008), 144.

[12] Aristotle, *Metaphysics* 1.3, 10; *Physics* 2.7. Since all things are made of matter and form, each thing has both formal and material causes. The formal and final causes are aspects of the formal nature of things, and the material and efficient are material causes. Causes can be divided along a second dimension as well: there are intrinsic causes that are inherent in a thing and extrinsic causes that operate from outside the thing to bring about some change. The material and formal causes are internal; the efficient and final are external. See D. Q. McInerny, *Metaphysics* (Elmhurst, Pa.: Priestly Fraternity of St. Peter, 2004), chapters 13 and 14, for a description of causation in terms of these two dimensions. But we must remember that the four causes are not entirely distinct in nature but are different ways of thinking about the process of change. Jonathan Lear, *Aristotle: The Desire to Understand* (New York: Cambridge University Press, 1988), 28–42.

[13] McInerny, *Metaphysics*, 266.

For Aristotle, it is the form, and not the matter, that represents the *active* principle in all things. Form is responsible for the characteristic way a thing unfolds and develops, and it is also what produces all changes in things. Matter, on the other hand, functions purely passively to limit the range of changes that can be brought about by a form.[14] As we will see in part 2, the modern assault on teleology was based in part on modern thinkers' rejection of formal and final causes.

Aristotle's conception of form, matter, and substance answered the first question of metaphysics, the question of what ultimately exists. But his second great insight solved the problem of change that had bedeviled philosophy from Parmenides' time. Everyone accepted Parmenides' postulate that Being cannot come from non-Being. But how is change possible, then, since every state of affairs seems to bring something new into existence?

One of Aristotle's most original flashes of insight was to argue that there is a third category intermediate of Being and non-Being, actuality and nonactuality—a category he called potency or potentiality. All things in the ordinary world (water, seeds, men), he argued, have potentialities, latent capacities waiting to be actualized, given the right external causes. A potency is an unrealized property or capacity hidden within a thing. Water can be frozen to create ice. Seeds can be planted to grow. Men can become either morally virtuous or debauched. Each thing has a myriad of distinct and often conflicting potentialities. A potentiality can never realize itself; it is something within that requires something from without to realize it, since Aristotle accepted that, with the exception of God, "all other things move by being moved".[15]

---

[14] Aristotle concluded that forms can be transmitted in at least three ways: biologically, through the process of reproduction; manually, through artistic creation (e.g., as when a sculptor sculpts a block of granite); and linguistically, through the process of teaching. In each case, a form is transmitted (the form of humanness in the case of human reproduction, the form of the sculpted bust in the case of artistic creation, and the form inherent in the knowledge transmitted in the course of teaching). Yet in each case the matter that receives the form places limits on the form a thing can take. A sculptor cannot carve a bronze bust from a granite block, nor can an animal be taught to do algebra. Moreover, the giver achieves a greater degree of perfection by transmitting a form. Lear, *Aristotle*, 33. The artist becomes a better artist by doing art, a teacher actually learns the subject matter better in the process of teaching, and a man becomes a better man by being a parent.

[15] Aristotle, *Metaphysics* 11.7.1072b3.

All change, then, requires three things: the substantial thing, which is the subject of change (the seed), the external cause or causes of change (the soil, water, and sunlight), and the potentiality embedded within the thing's nature (its potency to grow into a tree). In fact, actuality and potentiality *require* each other. They are intelligible only in relation to each other. The two always go hand in hand with one exception, God. All other things have potencies, possibilities for transformation. No material thing can ever completely achieve its potentiality; there are always aspects of a thing that must go unfulfilled, unrealized. Indeed, this is necessarily true for finite material things since the realization of one potentiality may forever frustrate the realization of another. Potentiality is what permits a thing to change, whereas actuality is what changes a thing; it is the active force in change. Since form is active and matter is potentiality, it follows that matter and form are specific instances of potency and actuality. Just as matter cannot exist without form, so potency cannot exist independently of an actual thing.

This way of thinking about the world of ordinary things later led the Scholastics to observe that existence itself must be first and primarily an *act*, rather than a thing. Before we *are* anything in the predicative sense—a tree or a man—we simply *are* in the existential sense, in the sense that each thing first exists. Aristotle's philosophy is, as Étienne Gilson suggested, the true existentialist philosophy.[16]

Aristotle's Ethical Philosophy: Teleology and Virtue Ethics

Teleology implies that human beings have a distinct form of flourishing, which entails the unfolding of our essence. The ethical good is measured by this natural human end, i.e., the realization of our distinctly human telos. To achieve our telos, we must, Aristotle observed, "like archers ... have a mark to aim at". Thus, teleological ethics is a form of moral objectivism. The goodness of an act is real, a feature of objective reality. Yet Aristotle saw clearly, in a way that some modern moral thinkers do not, that ethics is not an exact science. In the opening paragraphs of his *Nicomachean Ethics*, he

---

[16] Étienne Gilson, *God and Philosophy*, 2nd ed. (New Haven, Conn.: Yale University Press, 2002), 67.

says that we cannot achieve the same degree of precision in ethics as in the natural sciences.[17] He distinguished between theoretical wisdom, or *sophia*, which is knowledge of fixed truths, and practical wisdom, *phronesis*, which involves judgments about more contingent matters. Ethics belongs to the sphere of *phronesis*. The goal of ethics is action, not knowledge, and the sphere of action always involves changeable reality, not the fixed sphere of essences. Ethics, in sum, is a practical pursuit that involves experience, judgment, and, as we will see, a cultivated character.

This emphasis on the practical and active nature of ethical inquiry has a vitally important consequence in Aristotle's (and, as we will see in the next chapter, Thomas Aquinas') thought. From Socrates on, some thinkers have held the overly optimistic belief that "virtue is knowledge", i.e., that the acquisition of virtue is a purely intellectual affair. Some think that a person can be persuaded to do good by an argument or by being educated and, conversely, that vice is always the product of ignorance. Aristotle reveals a deeper psychological savvy in his skepticism toward such sunny Socratic rationalism. The bad man simply will not see the point of being good because the impoverished state of his character prevents it. "The best good", Aristotle observed, "is apparent only to the good person, for vice perverts us and produces false views about the principles of actions."[18] Decisions—ethical and otherwise—are always made through the prism of one's character, not simply through the lens of acquired intellectual knowledge. This explains why Aristotle thought the ordinary man of good character was a more reliable judge of goodness and far more likely to pursue goodness than the philosopher who understands the subtleties of ethical theory without having integrated this knowledge into his character.

So how does one acquire good character if not by studying ethics? Aristotle taught that good character can be achieved only through action. One can judge the Good only by being good, and one can become good only by habitually acting in a virtuous way. We literally integrate goodness into our very souls by doing good deeds. Good *doing* precedes good judgment, though good judgment subsequently

---

[17] Aristotle, *Nicomachean Ethics* 1.2.1094a24, 1094b14–15.
[18] Ibid., 4.1144a35–b1.

guides our actions. (See chapter 4 for a discussion of the moral integration of the personality.) Aristotle's insight takes on an even deeper spiritual significance when it is read through the prism of Christian spirituality. To attain the deepest spiritual understanding of the world, one must reorient one's soul to the steady performance of good actions. As Athanasius put it, "Anyone who wishes to understand the mind of the sacred writers must first cleanse his own life, and approach the saints by copying their deeds."[19]

Though teleology obviously embodies a strongly perfectionist element, it is ultimately a happiness-based ethic. Teleology begins from the twin assumptions that all actions are directed toward some end and that the most general end, which is desired for itself, is happiness.[20] It is both natural and good for men to be happy. But what is happiness exactly?

Aristotle's idea of happiness steers a middle way between the extremes of hedonism and asceticism. Aristotle would have found both the Epicurean pursuit of pleasure for its own sake and the Stoic's ataraxia, a state of total disinterest in our material condition, to be equally distorted goals. In contrast to the Stoics, he taught that we are bodily creatures with material needs. Though money cannot buy happiness, external goods are still necessary in moderate proportion to ensure the good life.[21] But material things, and pleasure in particular, should not be the object of our actions either, contrary to Epicurean philosophy. Happiness is a side effect of achieving our good. The unvarnished pursuit of pleasure predisposes the soul to a debilitating, subhuman passivity. It diminishes us, makes us recipients rather than givers, consumers rather than full actors in human affairs. The object of our actions should not be a state of passive feeling but a way of living—an active, virtuous condition of life that seeks for the highest form of human fulfillment.

Aristotle called this particular form of human fulfillment *eudaimonia* (good spiritedness). Eudaimonia is not merely a subjective state of mind—happiness in the narrow sense of enjoying some momentary pleasure. It is rather a *state of being* of the virtuous. It is not a

---

[19] Athanasius, *On the Incarnation*, chap. 9.
[20] Aristotle, *Nicomachean Ethics* 1094.
[21] Ibid., 1174a7–8.

momentary state, for true happiness is a condition of life as a whole, subjectively experienced as a wise, stable, and contemplative state of being.[22] Virtue, moreover, is not simply a means to eudaimonia; it is itself constitutive of eudaimonia.[23] In other words, acting virtuously brings us closer to our fulfillment, but our fulfillment then naturally emanates in virtue.[24] As we come closer to the goal, we naturally act more in accordance with our end and find enjoyment in doing so. Happiness is a natural emanation of the life well lived. To this Aquinas would add a distinction between imperfect (earthly) happiness, which will always be incomplete, and beatitude, the only condition capable of completely fulfilling human longing.[25]

If the virtuous life is the way to eudaimonia, what is virtue exactly? We must not understand the word in its Victorian sense as the priggish observance of what is "socially acceptable". There is still something in Aristotle of the older Homeric idea of virtue as a power or capacity to find our telos. Virtue is a power that consistently seeks the appropriate mean, relative to us, in our actions. Plato, Aristotle, Cicero, and other pre-Christian thinkers consistently held that there are four cardinal virtues (*cardinal* means "hinge", for the cardinal virtues are hinges on which the good life hangs[26]). These are prudence, fortitude, temperance, and justice. Prudence is the capacity to judge rightly the appropriateness of an action under the circumstances; fortitude, or courage, is the ability to maintain one's commitments in difficult circumstances; temperance is self-control and moderation in acting; and justice is giving each person his due. To these, the Christian tradition has added the three theological virtues—faith, hope, and love.[27] In chapter 4 we will explore how the virtues help us to integrate our character and to bring out our true self.

---

[22] Ibid., 1100a4.

[23] Lear, *Aristotle*, 158.

[24] Ibid.

[25] "Final and complete happiness can consist in none other than a vision of the divine essence." Thomas Aquinas, *Summa Theologiae* I-II, 3, 8c. This end, moreover, is achievable only in the next life, though we can achieve a kind of analogical understanding of God in this life.

[26] For two excellent treatments of the virtues, see Romanus Cessario, *The Moral Virtues and Theological Ethics*, 2nd ed. (Notre Dame, Ind.: Notre Dame Press, 2008); Peter Geach, *The Virtues* (Washington, D.C.: Catholic University Press, 1977).

[27] See 1 Corinthians 13:13.

The Stoics: The Origins of the Natural Law

Aristotle died in 322 B.C., and his Academy soon splintered into competing factions. The next century was a period of intellectual ferment, giving rise to classical antiquity's last important philosophical tradition: Stoicism.

The term *Stoicism* comes from the Greek word *stoa*, "porch", as the first Stoic thinker, Zeno of Citium (334–262 B.C.), lectured from a porch open to the public. Zeno had been a wealthy merchant who, according to one story, turned to philosophy after losing a fortune in a shipwreck. On returning to Athens he wandered into a bookshop, where he discovered a work by Crates the Cynic, whose philosophy provided him with some solace for a time. Eventually he founded his own school and became so beloved by the Athenians that they erected a gold statue in his name and deposited the keys to the city with him.[28] Stories about Zeno's life abound. He is reported to have tripped in his old age and fallen to the ground. Pounding the dirt with his fist, he cried out, "I come of my own accord; why then do you call me?" He died a few days later.

Zeno's philosophy blended elements of materialism with the philosophies of Heraclitus, the Sophists, the Cynics, and Socrates. He taught that the universe was animate, good, and wise, that all things were ordered by Providence, and that the end of life was to live in accordance with this order, which was one and the same with Nature and reason. A later follower, Chrysippus (281–208 B.C.), systematized Zeno's doctrines into a coherent philosophy. The movement continued to attract followers in the Roman world through the first two centuries after Christ. The Roman orator and statesman Cicero (106–43 B.C.) was deeply influenced by Stoicism, as were three of Rome's greatest thinkers—Seneca (4 B.C.–A.D. 65), Epictetus (A.D. 55–135), and Marcus Aurelius (121–180). These were men who had the benefit of witnessing firsthand the vicissitudes of Roman virtue and depravity. Seneca was courtier to the emperors Caligula and Claudius. His student Nero demanded that Seneca open his veins in response to an assassination plot in which Seneca was probably not

---

[28] Diogenes, *Lives of Eminent Philosophers*, trans. R. D. Hicks (Cambridge, Mass.: Harvard University Press, 1972), 2.113–17.

involved. Epictetus had been an educated slave in a wealthy Roman household before gaining his freedom. And Aurelius was a Roman emperor who wrote the *Meditations*, a book of epigrammatic exhortations arranged by subject.

The Stoics were neither true materialists nor theists. Rather, they were pantheists, holding that God is one and the same with the physical cosmos. All things in the natural world are part of God, emanate from God, and in due course are reabsorbed into God in an endless cycle of cosmic creation and destruction. Every event, every human action, is destined to recur again and again eternally, unfolding exactly as it must in accord with the unvarying laws of Nature—sort of a cosmic *Groundhog Day* without the happy ending. (Nietzsche borrowed this idea for his own theory of the eternal recurrence two thousand years later.)

The Stoics were materialists of sorts because they thought that everything in the world, God included, was physical in nature. Yet their philosophy was nothing if not deeply religious. They conceived of God as the active principle of the physical world: He is to the physical universe what the soul is to the human body. They adapted Heraclitus' Logos, equating it with the rational principle that pervades and orders the universe. The Logos is providence, God's will, as it is expressed in the physical laws of Nature and in a universal and unchanging moral law. The Stoics called this overarching set of laws—both the physical laws of science and the moral law that guides men—the natural law. Thus, while Plato and Aristotle had clearly grasped the distinction between conventional morality and true justice, and between human law and ideal law, it was the Stoics who arrived at a coherent doctrine of natural law.[29]

Cicero summed up the idea of the natural law in this way:

> Law is right reason in harmony with nature. It is spread through the whole community unchanging and eternal, calling people to their duty by its commands, and deterring them from wrong-doing by its prohibitions.... The law cannot be countermanded, nor can it be amended, nor can it be totally rescinded.... There will not be one

[29] Plato used the term *natural law* or *natural justice* only once or twice in his dialogues. In neither case does it have the meaning with which we now associate the term. See Plato, *Gorgias* 484 (where *natural justice* means the "right" of the stronger to impose his will); *Timaeus* 83e (where the term refers to the physical laws of the universe).

such law in Rome and another in Athens, one now and another in the future, but all peoples at all times will be embraced by a single and eternal and unchangeable law.[30]

We participate in the Logos in virtue of our reason and consciousness. Thus, while all things are part of God, there is a genuinely divine element in human nature, for we partake of the very principle of order that governs the universe. Reason and order are part of us, as we our part of God.

Just as the moral law is unalterable, so, too, the physical laws of the natural world are governed by Fate. All things unfold exactly as they must by necessity. Nothing can be other than it is. Here we find the Stoics reverting to the determinism of earlier materialists.[31] Thus, where Plato and Aristotle defended (what would later be called) free will, the Stoics denied that man has any real freedom. All there is of freedom is the recognition of our being bound by Nature. The task of the wise man is to reconcile himself to this order, which, after all, is nothing more or less than the expression of God's will. As Epictetus put it in the first century A.D.:

> Conduct me, O Zeus and O Destiny,
> Wherever your decrees have fixed my station.
> I follow cheerfully; and, did I not,
> Wicked and wretched, I must follow still.
> Whoever yields properly to Fate, is deemed
> Wise among men, and knows the laws of heaven.[32]

There was a subtle inconsistency in this, of course, since, in a deterministic world, even our attitudes and dispositions would happen with necessity.[33] But the Stoics thought there was at least

---

[30] Marcus Tullius Cicero, *Republic* 3.33.

[31] This, however, did not change the Stoic attitude toward punishment. Zeno is reported to have caught a slave stealing. When the slave responded that, according to Zeno's own philosophy, he was destined to steal, Zeno responded, "Yes, and to be beaten, too." Diogenes, *Lives of Eminent Philosophers*, 2:135.

[32] Epictetus, *Enchiridion*, trans. T. W. Higginson (Indianapolis: Bobbs-Merrill, 1955), 39.

[33] Epictetus opened the same work declaring, "Some things are in our control and others not. Things in our control are opinion, pursuit, desire, aversion, and, in a word, whatever are our own actions. Things not in our control are body, property, reputation, command, and, in one word, whatever are not our own actions." Ibid., 17.

enough freedom in the interstices of the human soul to fix one's attitude toward the nature of the world. Disillusionment, anger, and despair are irrational and fruitless in any event, since things all work by necessity. The world simply is the way it is, and we have nothing to say about it; rather, we must adjust our attitude. True virtue, they taught, consists in living a life free of all emotional reactions, which are nothing but "false opinions" and which only increase the pain produced by bad circumstances.[34] The Stoic goal was to reach a state of *apatheia*, a condition not of apathy (as the modern connotation would suggest) but of an undisturbed equanimity of soul, in which one lives in complete harmony with Nature and reason.

The crux of the Stoic worldview was to try to combine the best of materialism and theism and to reduce to one what other philosophers took to be two essential ingredients of reality (spirit and body, form and matter, God and world). The Stoics labored mightily—and unsuccessfully—to overcome all these dualisms. The later Stoics tried to split the difference on questions that appear to admit of no middle way. They said there is a soul but claimed that it is not immortal (although some suggested that the soul of the Stoic sage lives on from death until the next conflagration). They waffled on the question of freedom, as we have seen, arguing that necessity does not penetrate to the inner sanctum of the human will. But it was concerning the nature of God that they had the most trouble.

Officially the Stoics were pantheists: for them God and the physical world were one and the same. But is God or the Logos a *conscious* entity or merely a purely impersonal ordering force in Nature? If the Logos is impersonal, why equate it with the mind of God? On the other hand, if God is indeed a conscious, personal entity who governs the world, He must have a degree of autonomy and separation from the world. God's consciousness and intentions, after all, govern the world. The charge of inconsistency is only heightened by the quasi-religious nature of Stoic philosophy. The Stoics claimed to be materialists, but they universally condemned atheism: Seneca taught that God will help the man committed to a life of virtue, and later Stoics seem to have decided that God must be fully personal: "Every

---

[34] Seneca said, "Pain is slight if opinion has added nothing to it.... It is according to opinion that we suffer." Seneca, *Moral Letters to Lucilius* 78.13–15.

one of [our] acts", the great Epictetus declared, "is seen by God."[35] In this, as we will see, he may have been influenced by Christianity.

The greatest Stoic legacy to modern thought, along with the idea of the natural law, is the Stoics' ethical doctrines. In many ways Stoic doctrines supplemented Plato's and Aristotle's ethics, and in other ways they represent a definite moral advance over them. In Stoic thought there is, for the first time, a real emphasis on the inward dimension of our moral life, on the significance of the will, and on the battle between sin and the spirit that St. Paul so deftly described.[36] The Stoics taught that it is the inner intention with which an act is performed, not its consequences, that is most significant in measuring the goodness (or evil) of an act: "The essence of good and evil", Epictetus wrote, "lies in an attitude of the will."[37]

Finally, their emphasis on the lawlike nature of the moral order led the Stoics to an entirely new idea in ethics—the notion of moral *duty*.[38] To follow the laws embodied in the Logos, as expressed in Nature and known by human reason, is to act according to one's duty. The law is more than a mere prudential guide to our happiness and self-fulfillment; it is binding upon us, rationally and morally. The consequences of our acts are beyond our control, but the intention with which we perform an act falls squarely within the province of the will. The Stoic emphasis on the will, on duty, and on the priority of intention over the consequences of an act not only influenced Aquinas' theory of natural law but in many ways presaged Kant's deontological ethics two thousand years later.

It is also in Stoic thought that we find the origin of so many of the noblest values shared by Christianity and secular humanitarianism. The Stoics gave us the idea of the brotherhood of man and the

[35] *The Discourses of Epictetus* in *The Stoic and Epicurean Philosophers*, ed. Whitney J. Oates (New York: Random House, 1940), 229, 250.

[36] "I can will what is right, but I cannot do it. For I do not do the good I want, but the evil I do not want is what I do" (Rom 7:18–19).

[37] Epictetus, *Discourses* 1.29.

[38] Aristotle's ethics are essentially eudaimonistic—the wise man will act rightly because doing so is conducive to happiness and self-fulfillment. There was still something of this in Stoic doctrine, for the virtuous were, after all, happy according to Stoic doctrine. But, for the Stoics, this happiness was inseparable from doing one's duty. Diogenes reported that Zeno was the first to use the word *duty* and to write an entire treatise on the concept of duty. Diogenes, *Lives of Eminent Philosophers*, 2:137.

values of human dignity and moral equality. As against Aristotle's unfortunate contention that some men are natural slaves, the Stoics condemned slavery. Epictetus, who had once been a slave himself, denounced slavery as "the law of the dead". The Stoics were the true cosmopolitan thinkers of antiquity, teaching that the commonality of men transcends all national boundaries, that all men are morally the same by means of their reason and virtue. No less an authority than the Roman emperor Marcus Aurelius wrote, "My city and country, insofar as I am Antonimus, is Rome, but insofar as I am a man, it is the world."[39] Nor was this a purely abstract cosmopolitanism, for the Stoics were true humanitarians who taught that it is our highest calling to love and respect others. Seneca wrote, "Wherever there is a human being there is room for benevolence", and Aurelius echoed Jesus' injunction to love God with all our heart and to love our neighbor as ourselves with his pithy, if bald, exhortation: "Love mankind, follow God."[40]

At the source of the Stoic devotion to human dignity and equality was the understanding that every person participates in the Logos and thus has a share in providence. The Christian concept of the *imago Dei*, that our nature is itself a mark of the divine imprint on human nature, has its precursor in Stoic thought.[41] That providence works to the good of the man who conforms his will to God's,[42] that the care of the soul is infinitely more important than external goods,[43] and that we should love all men as ourselves[44] are equally Stoic and Christian themes. Perhaps we should not be surprised that Seneca was rumored to have carried on a friendly correspondence with St. Paul and that Epictetus is said to have honored Christ as a true moral prophet.

[39] Marcus Aurelius, *Meditations* 4.44.

[40] Ibid., 5.17.

[41] Two centuries before Christ, Zeno's student Cleanthes wrote:

> O' God, most glorious, called by many a name ...
> We are thy children, we alone of all
> On earth's broad ways that wander to and fro,
> Bearing thy image wherever we go.

Frederick C. Copleston, *A History of Philosophy* (New York: Image Books, 1993), 1:393.

[42] "We know that in everything God works for good with those who love him" (Rom 8:28).

[43] "For what does it profit a man, to gain the whole world and forfeit his life?" (Mk 8:36; see also Mt 16:26).

[44] "You shall love your neighbor as yourself" (Mt 19:19).

3

Thomas Aquinas and the Natural Law

The natural law is nothing other than the light of understanding placed in us by God.

—Thomas Aquinas

The Limits of (Greek) Philosophy

G. K. Chesterton said that philosophy tries to explain the world by giving us a pattern, whereas Christianity gives us a Person. In a number of striking ways, Greek thought anticipated many of the central truths of Christianity. Yet the Greek vision was doomed to incompletion, even incoherence, because it saw the world only in terms of patterns—forms—rather than in terms of a personal Logos through whom these patterns are manifest. When Aristotle declared that "Nature has an end", he meant that the things of this world work toward a specific form of completion, yet he specifically denied that the world as a whole had a divine purpose. Perhaps, more sympathetically, we could say that, thinking from the ground up, the Greeks discovered the essential structure of the world without achieving the only overarching vision that could give it coherence. That yearning for truth that turned the young Socrates from science to philosophy remained, at the end of the era, fundamentally unfulfilled.

The Greeks anticipated the God of Christianity in various inchoate ways. Anaxagoras' nous was the divine, intelligent ordering principle of the world, but even Aristotle recognized that it was a "god of the gaps", a deistic device he appealed to when no physical explanation for some phenomenon could be found. Plato's Form of the

Thomas Aquinas, *Collationes in Decem Praeceptis* 1.

Good was a cosmic final cause toward which all things are drawn, but it was no personal God, and his Demiurge ordered but did not create the cosmos. Aristotle's Unmoved Mover—the eternal, simple, immaterial, immutable Thought Thinking Itself, which somehow sustains the world—came closer. But Aristotle's God neither created nor intervened in the world since he thought that any contact with changeable reality would have tainted God's perfection.[1] And where Aristotle excessively separated God from the world, the Stoics committed the opposite error of treating God and the world as one.[2] It is thus poignant to read in Acts that when St. Paul visited Athens around A.D. 60, he was especially moved to find an altar dedicated to "an unknown god".[3]

Pre-Christian ethics offered some promising starts as well. Plato insisted that the care of the soul was the most important task in life, anticipated the golden rule, and taught that the soul of the wrongdoer suffers far more harm than the one he has wronged. Aristotle showed how happiness and virtue were reconciled in the fully integrated character. The Stoics salvaged Heraclitus' idea of the Logos as the ordering principle of the universe, gave us the natural law, and discovered the doctrine of the brotherhood of man. But Plato could never have exhorted his followers to love their neighbor with all their heart, and Aristotle's human ideal, his great-souled man, would have been scandalized by the self-emptying of the Cross. Even the Stoic sage Epictetus seems to have been moved far more by duty than by love. In sum, the Greeks gave us *arête*, but it was Christianity that gave us *agape*.

---

[1] Aristotle's most famous sentence about God was that God is "thought [that] thinks itself as object in virtue of its participation in what is thought". Aristotle, *Metaphysics* 1072b19. Aristotle's God cannot know the changeable world since Aristotle thought that the nature of thought depends on the nature of its objects. God cannot think about changeable, material things without Himself being changeable, which God is not. So God can think only eternal truths, including the essences of things.

[2] For the Stoics, God was to the world as the human soul is to the body. As Alexander Pope later put it:

> All are but parts of one stupendous whole
> Whose body Nature is and God the soul.

Frederick C. Copleston, *A History of Philosophy* (New York: Image Books, 1993), 1:388.

[3] Acts 17:23.

It is little wonder that some subsequent Christian thinkers came to see philosophy as a preparation for Christianity, while others eyed philosophy warily, suspecting it of introducing heretical, pagan elements into the pure body of Christian theology. Characteristically, Thomas Aquinas held a third, intermediate view. Philosophy is neither a foundation for nor a threat to Christianity. It is a pedagogical tool, a heuristic stepping stone—a lamp to light the way for the darkened mind.[4] In the very first question of his masterwork, the *Summa Theologiae*, Aquinas declared that theology "can accept something from philosophical disciplines, not that it requires them out of necessity, but that it might make more manifest those things that are treated".[5] Philosophy rescues the blinkered soul from Plato's cave, drawing the unenlightened mind into the noontime sunlight of Truth. To adapt Ludwig Wittgenstein's famous metaphor, philosophy is a ladder. Those who reach the roof can push the ladder away as they look out upon the world as it is. The rest of us must keep climbing—never looking down, hopeful that we, too, may one day reach the top.

Thomas Aquinas: Christianity Meets Aristotle

Thomas Aquinas (1225–1274) was among the first generation of Westerners in a thousand years to read Aristotle's philosophy, preserved by Muslim philosophers and rediscovered in the wake of the Crusades. Aristotle's work had been lost and found several times during the centuries after his death but disappeared from the West entirely by around the third century A.D. Thus, it was Plato who influenced Christianity philosophically during its first millennium. If St. Augustine Christianized Plato, Aquinas baptized Aristotle.

---

[4] As the apostle Paul put it, "But thanks be to God, that you who were once slaves of sin have become obedient from the heart to the standard of teaching to which you were committed.... I am speaking in human terms, because of your natural limitations" (Rom 6:17, 19). "For now we see in a mirror dimly.... Now I know in part; then I shall understand fully" (1 Cor 13:12).

[5] Thomas Aquinas, *Summa Theologiae* I, 1, 5, as quoted in Robert Barron, *The Priority of Christ: Toward a Postliberal Catholicism* (Grand Rapids, Mich.: Brazos Press, 2007), 148 (discussing philosophy's role in understanding God).

St. Thomas was born in Roccasecca, Italy, the seventh of seven sons in a powerful and well-connected aristocratic family. When his father, a count and cousin to the Pope, learned that Thomas wanted to give his life to God, he tried to set him up with their well-placed relatives with the expectation that he might someday become a cardinal or even Pope. Aquinas wanted no part of this. He joined the humble Dominicans, becoming a begging friar. His family responded by sending two brothers to snatch him from the road while en route to Paris. He was kidnapped, bundled off to a fortress, and locked in a room with a seductive courtesan, whose task it was to bring the young man to heel. Thomas, as the story is often told, grabbed a burning brand from the fireplace and drove the astonished woman away. Eventually his relatives relented.

The other story comes from the end of his life, though it was not published until fifty years after his death. In December 1273, while saying Mass, he had an experience—a vision—that abruptly ended the service. For days he would not even say what had happened until, upon being repeatedly pressed by his secretary, he simply reported the God had given him a glimpse of the ultimate truth, which made all he had written seem like "bushels of straw". Having been vouchsafed a glimpse of a reality greater than anything he had conceived intellectually, he said he could no longer write and was prepared to die. And so he did, about three months later, in March 1274.

Though Aquinas is remembered as the synthesizer of Christian theology and Aristotelian philosophy, he had a genuine worldview of his own, which drew upon other elements but which also freely departed from these when they were inconsistent with Christian doctrine. Characteristically for an Aristotelian, he often found himself in the middle on several important questions of his day. His insistence that there can be only one truth—that science, theology, and philosophy do not teach different lessons, ultimately—meant that he was often embroiled in a war on two fronts: with conservatives who distrusted the influences of pagan philosophy and with more unorthodox theologians, including the Latin Averroists, who were more inclined to follow philosophy than Church doctrine. The spirit of compromise is evident in Aquinas' conception of faith as a position midway between opinion and knowledge: faith is more than opinion because it involves an act of commitment, the assent of the will, but less than knowledge because knowledge requires no act of assent (since what is known is evident on its face). Aquinas accepted much of Aristotle's system of metaphysics. He accepted Aristotle's notions of substantial form, his formal and final causes, and his moderate realism, in other words, the view that universals exist as the essence of particular things. He followed Aristotle in calling the soul "the substantial form of the body", an idea that departed in striking ways from the Platonic Idea, as we will see in the following chapter. Yet in each of these ways he read Aristotle through the lens of the Christian virtues and the Christian conception of God.

What we will have to say in the next few paragraphs may seem very abstract, but I hope the reader will bear with us, for the central idea is vitally important to understanding Aquinas' conception of God and reality. A central principle of Aquinas' metaphysics is that the various things of the world possess gradations of Being corresponding to their goodness. Some things are literally *more real* than others, and they are more real in virtue of their capacity to attract, as goodness does. To the modern mind, of course, the alternatives are starker: either something exists or it does not. If it does exist, it is as "real" as any other existing thing. The problem for us moderns is to decide what *does* exist. Does a shadow exist? Is it as real as the object that casts it? What about the number three: are numbers real or abstractions? Do past events—such as the battle at Thermopylae—still exist in some sense? Is my love for my children really an existing thing, independent of the chemicals in my brain when I feel this love? And what about ideas—does the idea of Santa Claus exist, even if Santa Claus does not?

Because we have a binary conception of existence, we have to make draconian decisions about each of these, deciding whether to put the entity in the column of "existing things" or "nonexisting things". But recall that Plato taught that the various things of the world have degrees of Being—that some things are more real than other things. He also argued that all things aim at the Good. In fact, he thought that all things have Being insofar as they participate, through their own Forms, in Goodness. The Form of the Good was for Plato the highest thing in reality, the single most real thing, since it moves all other things. All other things share in this reality—*have Being*—to the extent that they move other things through their

attractive capacity. The shadow literally has less *Being* than the object
that casts the shadow, and the object has less reality than its particular
Form because this Form is the moving principle in matter.

Aquinas concluded that Plato was largely correct in looking at the
world this way. Some things are more real than others. But what is it
about the various things of the world that makes some more real than
others? Aquinas answered as Aristotle did: it is a thing's *active* nature,
its capacity to transmit forms and to move other things, that makes
it real. Crucially, there is a connection between the reality of a thing
and its goodness. Being and Goodness are convertible concepts for
Aquinas: Being and Goodness are one in *reference* and distinct only
in *sense*.[6] A "thing is perfect", he declared, "to the extent that it is in
actuality."[7] For a thing to be actualized is for it to be closer to achieving its fully realized form, its essence, its telos.[8] The convertibility of
Being and Goodness is what provides the necessary link, so central to
classical natural law theory, between the world of facts and the world
of moral "oughts".

Because Goodness is Being, its opposite—evil—is non-Being, a
privation. Evil literally has no essence. The greatest evil would be
nothing at all.[9] At the other end of the ontological scale is the Greatest Good, which is also the most real thing in the world. Medieval
theologians obviously did not believe that God was possessed of a
physical body, but some seemed to conceive of Him as an immaterial
spirit. St. Augustine, who was deeply influenced by Plato's idea of
Being, recognized that God was not a spirit existing independently
of the world. Rather, God must in some sense be "in" all things.[10]
Augustine wrote that God is "intimior intimo meo" ("closer to me
than I am to myself").[11]

[6] Thomas Aquinas, *Summa Theologiae* I, 5, ad. 1.

[7] Thomas Aquinas, *Summa Contra Gentiles* I, 39, cited in Eleonore Stump, *Aquinas* (New
York: Routledge, 2003), 63.

[8] According to Eleonore Stump, "When Being is considered in this second way, it is
correct to say that, in a certain respect, there is an increase in Being for that thing." Eleonore
Stump, *Aquinas* (New York: Routledge, 2003), 67.

[9] Ibid., 68.

[10] Thomas Aquinas, *Summa Theologiae* Ia, 8, 1, as quoted in Robert Barron, *Thomas Aquinas: Spiritual Master* (New York: Crossroad, 2008), 90. As Barron explained, God is modally,
not spatially, distinct from the world.

[11] Augustine, *Confessions* 3.6.11, as quoted in ibid., 89.

Following the same line of thought, Aquinas concluded that God is not another *thing* in the world at all—not even the greatest thing in the world. God is not a Being among beings but is, rather, the Ground of all Being. Aquinas adapted Aristotle's insight that God is the one thing whose existence is not divided between actuality and potentiality: God alone is pure actuality, drawing all things to Himself by drawing them first to their own greater perfection. God is the only entity whose existence is not contingent. God's very essence *is existence.*[12] His Being and Goodness are perfect and are one with each other.

This conception of God permitted Aquinas to draw a powerful theological connection to the biblical understanding of God. Because God is not in space and time, He cannot be apprehended by the senses or conceived by the intellect.[13] We cannot lay hold of Him, or particularize Him; we should not try to make of Him a thing. Yet, of course, it is human nature to *want* to particularize Him. But this, Aquinas pointed out, is the subtlest form of the sin of idolatry. Even to conceive of God as the Supreme Being is to make of Him a thing that we can categorize and conceptualize and hold on to. Aquinas drew here a remarkable parallel to the scene from Exodus in which the Jews want to be able to give God a name. Moses asks God for His name, and God answers, "I AM WHO I AM." He tells Moses to tell

[12] The etymological similarity in modern English between *act* and *actuality* reflects a deeper philosophical connection between the two ideas, but it also obscures an important difference. *To act* is a verb, and *actuality* is a noun denoting "that which exists". There is a connection here: on an Aristotelian-Thomistic view, to be actual—to exist—is itself the primary act. Metaphysically and logically, before a thing can have a form, it must exist. Existence is the primary act of all things. In describing the Thomistic implications, Robert Barron wrote, "A limited thing is that whose act of existence is poured into a particular mold or structure that is essence." God's essence and existence, on the other hand, are not distinct. This is what theologians mean by God's simplicity. God is formless. There is no distinction between existence and essence. Barron, *Thomas Aquinas*, 78–79.

Modern English loses this distinction by using one verb, whereas Latin distinguishes *esse*, "to be", from the noun *ens*, which denotes what is actual. *Ens* designates substance, whereas *esse* is the act of existing that underlies the concept of substance. *Esse* is metaphysically and logically prior to *ens*. As Étienne Gilson concluded, "[E]sse is much harder to grasp because it lies more deeply hidden in the metaphysical structure of reality.... To understand this is also to reach, beyond the level of essence, the deeper level of existence." See Étienne Gilson, *God and Philosophy* (New Haven, Conn.: Yale University Press, 2002), 63–64.

[13] Indeed, Aquinas thought that we can know God's nature only negatively, by comparison with what it is not—that God is not corporeal, or made of form, or in time, etc.

the Israelites that "I AM" has sent Moses to them and that this "is my name for ever". In sum, God cannot even be named: He simply *is*. His essence is *to be* and *to act* without being acted upon.[14]

Beyond this God of the philosophers, however, is a personal God, Whose image we share. Our tendency may be to believe that we ascribe to Him our attributes, but the truth is just the reverse: He is the exemplar of what it means to be a person, and each man is but a replication of the divine personhood.[15] Man's final end is to love and glorify God. But God's glory is not something wholly separate from our natural, human good. In this sense, the *natural* is indelibly infused with our supernatural end. Man attains his true end by reflecting and manifesting God's goodness. Thus, we come closer to God by perfecting ourselves, and, in doing so, we realize this good subjectively. When Jesus sums up the essence of God's commandments by exhorting us to love God with all our heart, mind, and soul, and to love our neighbor as ourselves,[16] He invites us to seek God's goodness for our own well-being and to reflect it outwardly to others. Thus, the idea of the *imago Dei*, the notion that we have been made in God's image, has a double implication. God has created us in His image, but we can truly attain our end only by becoming "the clear pools in which God's reality can be mirrored".[17] We achieve our own highest good by seeking to become as much like God, as far short as we will inevitably fall, as it is possible for us to be.

Aquinas, finally, read Aristotle's theory of knowledge through a christological lens. Plato, Aristotle, and other classical thinkers held that all knowledge is knowledge of form, not matter. The mind knows each thing by knowing a thing's form, but form is communicated materially, through sensation. Aristotle held that matter can be perceived but not understood, whereas form can be understood

---

[14] About Ex 3:14–15 Aquinas observed, "Now every name is intended to signify the nature or essence of something.... It remains that the divine act-of-being itself is the essence or nature of God." Thomas Aquinas, *Summa Contra Gentiles* I, 22. Indeed, as Barron pointed out, Aquinas argued that God is not even a Form; He is beyond form. Barron, *Thomas Aquinas*, 79–80.

[15] As Alvin Plantinga put it, "God is the premier person, the first and chief exemplar of personhood ... and the properties most important for an understanding of our personhood." Quoted in J.P. Moreland and Scott B. Rae, *Body and Soul: Human Nature and the Crisis in Ethics* (Downers Grove, Ill.: InterVarsity Press, 2000), 24.

[16] See Mt 22:37.

[17] Barron, *Thomas Aquinas*, 162.

but not directly perceived.[18] We perceive the tree by sensing (seeing, feeling) the matter of which it is made, but we *know* the tree as a tree by intuiting its form. Aristotle used the term *essence* to refer to the form as it is known to the intellect. The essence, we might say today, is the subjectively grasped side of form. Perhaps the most remarkable consequence of Aristotle's and Aquinas' theory of knowledge is that, in knowing something, the mind in a sense *becomes one with the object*. As Aristotle put it, "Actual knowledge is identical with its object."[19]

But how is this possible? Why should Aristotle's eternal universe be preordered so that the activity of the mind mirrors the ontological structure of reality? Nothing short of a supernatural explanation can provide the answer.

Aquinas recognized that the clues for this understanding were scattered throughout Scripture. The Gospel of John refers to Jesus as the Logos, the primordial intelligibility of the order of things, the principle through which all things were created.[20] To be intelligible is to have form, and to have form is to participate in the Logos,

---

[18] Aristotle, *Physics* 3.6.207a24–32. We grasp universals through sensible particulars. As Aristotle put it, though one perceives the particular, perception is of the universal. Aristotle, *Posterior Analytics* 2.19.100a17–b1. Aristotle adopted Plato's distinction between sensible and intelligible things, but rather than associating the intelligible with the realm of the Forms and the sensible with ordinary particulars, as Plato did, Aristotle concluded that ordinary things have both a sensible and an intelligible aspect.

[19] Aristotle, *De Anima* 3.5. As Aquinas later put it, the mind is *quodammodo omnia* ("in a certain sense, all things") since it takes the form of anything it knows.

Aristotle developed his philosophy always with one eye on its implications for science. Since matter in the abstract is completely unintelligible, science should concern itself with the study of structure, organization, form. Aristotle, *Physics* 2.2. Aristotle was clearly in sympathy with the empiricist outlook of the scientist, but he insisted that in studying objects as they exist in nature, what we learn about are the relationships among the parts of a thing, the functions of each, and the way they work together to produce the overall structure of the thing. The examination of form leads us in two directions at once: as we study the total form of a thing we are led downward to study its material parts, from the heart to the vessels to its capillaries, for example, and again upward from the study of a thing's parts to the structure as a whole. The form of a natural thing is always the form of the entire organism or structure, not the parts. Aristotle's philosophy is thus holistic. We can know the essence of a thing only by knowing its overall structure and purpose, not its component parts. Aristotle tells us that the true object of architecture is not wood or timber but the house; and so the principle object of natural philosophy (science) is not the material elements, but their composition, and the totality of the substance, independently of which they have no existence. Aristotle, *Parts of Animals* 1.5.645a, cited in Jonathan Lear, *Aristotle: The Desire to Understand* (New York: Cambridge University Press, 1988), 48.

[20] Jn 1:1–5.

which emanates from the mind of God Himself. To say that form is prior to matter, and that essence precedes existence, is to say that God knew us before we existed in material form.[21] Knowledge can be identical with its object only if the activity of the mind mirrors the very structure of reality. To participate (by degrees) in the intelligibility of the Logos is, as Paul declared, to have "this mind ... which was in Christ Jesus".[22]

In sum, reason—the Logos—is the light that falls simultaneously upon mind and object, preparing the ground for the mutual participation of both in an order that transcends yet connects them. Plato and Aristotle's idea of Form was none other than the highest human way of understanding how the knower and the known *coinhere* in the same rational order.[23] Without the Logos, through whom men participate in the rational order of the world, there would be nothing to connect the world of mind with the world of things.

Aquinas' Ethical Theory

Moral theories are usually divided between those that hold that morality is in some way real or *objective* and those that deny this. Moral-realist theories hold that moral principles such as "Murder is wrong" are in some sense real facts that are true and that exist independently of what we may happen to desire or to believe. Because they are true independently of what we happen to believe, a person or a culture can hold incorrect moral beliefs just as we can hold incorrect

---

[21] "Before I formed you in the womb I knew you" (Jer 1:5).
[22] Phil 2:5.
[23] Robert Barron puts this beautifully:

First, the light of divine Logos must fall upon the object of vision and, second, the one who sees must share to some degree in that same light; there must be a correspondence based upon mutual participation.... Since all has been made through, and will be ordered by, a divine rationality, there must be form in all finite being as a whole, and in each particular thing that exists; what comes to be through Logos is, necessarily, logical. This implies, of course, that there is an unavoidable correspondence between the activity of the mind and the structure of Being; intelligence will find its fulfillment in this universal and inescapable intelligibility.

Barron, *The Priority of Christ*, 148, 154.

scientific beliefs. Moreover, because these facts exist independently of us, moral realists hold that we discover rather than invent moral truths. Because they are truths of the world, they are binding upon us, individually and collectively. It is no more possible, at least over the long haul, to ignore a moral truth than to ignore a physical truth.

Plato, Aristotle, and Christian thinkers such as Augustine and Aquinas have obviously defended versions of moral realism. Yet moral realism is itself a rather large tent. Moral philosophers generally distinguish between three varieties of moral realism: virtue ethics, consequentialism, and deontology. Virtue-ethics theories, such as Aristotle's, emphasize the moral character and virtues of the actor as the most important ingredient of morality. If the actor is acting from a well-formed character—if he acts virtuously—he will live a good and happy life and will bear good fruit in the world of activity. Consequentialist theories, by contrast, de-emphasize the character of the actor, making the consequences of the action the primary focus of morality. Consequentialist theories of ethics (including utilitarianism) measure morality by the act rather than by the character of the actor. If the consequences of an act are beneficial, however the theory may define this, then the act is "good".[24] If the consequences are harmful, the act is "bad". Deontological theories, such as those of Immanuel Kant, focus neither on the overall character of the actor nor on the consequences of the act. Rather, acts are right if they are well intended or properly motivated (if they have the right object or purpose), and they are wrong if they do not.

Aquinas' theory of ethics is complex and possesses aspects of each of these three approaches to moral theory. It is primarily a virtue-based ethic, following Aristotle in this respect. What counts most at the end of the day is the goodness of the soul, the virtue of the whole man. Aquinas devoted 170 questions in his *Summa* to the virtues, which include the moral virtues (prudence, fortitude, justice, and temperance), the theological virtues (faith, hope, and charity), and the intellectual virtues (wisdom, knowledge, and understanding). Because the virtues are central to Aquinas' theory of the integration

---

[24] There are forms of "rule utilitarianism" according to which we are to follow rules that generally maximize the best consequences. But even here the "best" rule is the one that maximizes the best consequences overall, as measured by the specific acts required by a rule.

of human character, we will consider this aspect of his theory at greater length in the following chapter.

Underlying Aquinas' virtue ethics, however, is a background theory of the nature of goodness. What makes an actor virtuous, after all, is that he habitually acts for the Good. So what is the Good? Aquinas defines the Good, following Aristotle, in broadly teleological terms, as that which promotes the realization of the human telos.[25] In this respect, Aquinas' ethical theory is consequentialist: acts are good to the extent that they result in the fulfillment of the human good.

But there is also a powerful deontological component in his thought reminiscent of Stoicism and appropriate to an ethic based on Christianity.[26] Aquinas gave a great deal of attention to the rightness or wrongness of the actor's *intentions*. Though the goodness and badness of various acts in general (acts of theft, for example, versus acts of charity) are measured by their tendency to promote or frustrate the human good (the consequentialist aspect), Aquinas also placed a great emphasis on the moral quality of the *purposes* and *motives* of the actor (the deontological aspect). The tendency to act rightly over a longer period is, finally, indicative of the state of a person's character (the virtue-ethics aspect). As if to give effect to the biblical admonition that "you will know them by their fruits",[27] Aquinas taught that we can judge the state of a person's soul by looking to his actions and the motivations for these actions.

One aspect of this deontological focus is the greater attention Aquinas gave to the voluntariness of free human acts. He distinguished

---

[25] "All substances seek their own perfection." Thomas Aquinas, *Summa Theologiae* I, 6, 1. The realization of this human telos is simply the achievement of our full perfection.

[26] Teleological systems of ethics connect the Good with some conception of human flourishing grounded on the idea that we have a distinct human essence and telos. Good actions are those that conduce to human flourishing, and bad actions frustrate human flourishing. By contrast, deontological ethics, most commonly associated with Kant, connect the rightness of an act with the moral intention of the actor, rather than with the consequences of the act. Thus, an act may be morally required even if it does not produce some specific set of consequences—happiness (as with utilitarian consequentialism) or human flourishing (as with teleological ethics). Deontology is a duty-based ethic (*deon* means "duty") that views certain actions as morally obligatory or morally objectionable, independently of the consequences they produce. Thus, it is sometimes said that teleological and consequentialist systems make what is "right" derivative of what is good, while deontological systems make what is good derivative of the more fundamental rightness of an action.

[27] Mt 7:16.

mere "behavior" (*actiones hominis*), which includes even involuntary acts, from human actions in the strict sense (*actiones humanae*), which are acts that issue from a deliberate act of reason and will. Only the latter fall within the sphere of morality, strictly speaking. Involuntary acts may produce harm, but only deliberate acts can be *morally* wrong or sinful. In acting deliberately, moreover, it is primarily the *object* of our will, the species of act that we seek to perform, that defines its goodness or badness. Acts of murder, theft, or rape are wrong generally insofar as they frustrate the human good. This is, again, the teleological component of his thought. But the real focus of morality is on the actor, not the act. The person who chooses to do bad acts is wrong because the object of his intention is bad. This is the deontological component of Aquinas' ethical thought. What makes an act right or wrong is our acting with a good or bad intention.

Aquinas does recognize, of course, that the circumstance of an act can worsen or mitigate the moral quality of the act. Thus, while theft is generally wrong, filching a loaf of bread to feed a starving family is less wrong than theft motivated by selfish reasons. Conversely, good acts—such as almsgiving—are less good if the actor is motivated by a desire to show off. No deliberate human action, finally, is morally indifferent. Every act is either good or bad to the extent that it is conducive to, or obstructive of, achieving our human end.[28]

This multifaceted nature of Aquinas' ethical thought means that ethical decisions are often very difficult to make. There will be disagreements—not because general moral standards are not objective but because there are so many points at which even reflective, morally advanced actors may differ. Aquinas was thus in total agreement with Aristotle that, as we descend to particulars, there will inevitably be less certitude in our ethical conclusions. Throughout his writings we find the admonition against thinking that we can reason in a purely syllogistic fashion, from general principles to specific conclusions, in moral matters.[29] The reason for this is that theoretical reason and practical reason have two entirely distinct ends: "A theoretical or speculative inquiry ... is directed toward discovering truth

[28] Thomas Aquinas, *Summa Theologiae* I-II, 18, 9.

[29] This observation recurs in Aquinas' conception of the way in which natural law principles must be adapted to particular circumstances and conditions. Thomas Aquinas, *Summa Theologiae* I-II, 91, 3, ad 3; I-II, 94, 4; *Commentary on the Nicomachean Ethics* I, lec. 3, no. 34.

considered in itself. [Practical wisdom], on the contrary, is directed toward the doing of something. The purpose of speculative inquiry is truth while the purpose of practical inquiry is action."[30] Thus, moral truths do not cease to be real because we sometimes disagree about the right thing to do in particular situations.

The Natural Law

Though the natural law tradition had been developed by Christian thinkers for a thousand years before Aquinas, no other thinker did more to distill, synthesize, and refine the idea of the natural law. Aquinas defined *law* as an ordinance of reason for the common good that is made by the one who has care for the community and is promulgated.[31] But following the Stoics, he used the word *law* as we still use it, to refer both to the physical laws of the universe (i.e., the laws of science) and the moral law. All laws bind, as the etymology of the term itself (from the Latin *ligare*, "to bind") indicates, but the moral law binds in a manner different from that of physical laws.[32] The laws of science bind by physical necessity, and the moral law binds through the force of reason and conscience.

Aquinas distinguished four kinds of law: eternal law, divine law, natural law, and human law.[33] The eternal law is law in the broadest

[30] Thomas Aquinas, *Commentary on the Trinitate of Boethius*, 16.5.1, cited in Anthony J. Lisska, *Aquinas's Theory of Natural Law: An Analytic Reconstruction* (New York: Clarendon Press, 1993), 214. This is not to say that Aristotle did not believe that one should act in accord with what is right. He explicitly defended the goodness of sacrificing oneself for a friend, for example. *Nicomachean Ethics* 9.8.1169a18–26. But he did not have a clear idea of moral *duty*, of being morally (rather than merely prudentially) bound to do something.

[31] Thomas Aquinas, *Summa Theologiae* I-II, 90–94. Thus, there are essentially four requirements of law: that it conform to reason, that it be directed to the common good (rather than a matter of individual self-interest, for example), that it issue from the political or moral leader of the community, and that it be publicly disseminated.

[32] Ibid., 91, 1. John Finnis argues that it is law in the moral sense that is the more basic of the two senses. True law binds not through compulsion but by an appeal to reason and to virtue. As Finnis put it, "Aquinas strongly insists that law is something addressed by one mind and will to others—by one freely choosing person to other freely choosing persons.... The central case of law is an appeal to the mind, the choice, the moral strength (*virtus*) and the love of those subject to the law." John Finnis, *Aquinas: Moral, Political and Legal Theory* (New York: Oxford University Press, 1998), 307.

[33] Thomas Aquinas, *Summa Theologiae* I-II, 91.

sense, law as the Stoics used the term to refer to God's multilevel physical and moral order for the world. The eternal law binds each level in the hierarchy of Creation in its own way. As we ascend this hierarchy, things move and respond not only in a more complex way, but in a way that makes their participation in God's order increasingly its (our) own.[34] Inorganic things—such as the planets and the interactions of chemicals—are moved from outside by physical necessity, as materialists believe all things are moved. These, too, are governed by final ends, but these ends are in God's mind. The organic world of plants and lower animals, on the other hand, operates in part from principles within those creatures, from their own internal "entelechies", as Aristotle called them. Plants grow toward the sunlight; animals pursue prey in response to hunger, et cetera. At the apex of the natural hierarchy, men participate in a more direct way in God's order by acting purposively for their own ends. When we align our ends with God's ends, as we discover them through reason and our understanding of nature, we follow the natural law.

The second species of law—the natural law—is simply our participation in the eternal law. It is the way in which we share in God's divine providence. We participate in God's providence in two ways—rationally and by natural inclination (by our appetites and desires). In a sense, we know what is right "through the light of reason" and by our natural inclinations. We reason our way to the Good, but there is something deeper—a capacity God has laid at the foundation of the human soul. We are hardwired to develop the capacity to distinguish good acts from evil acts: it is literally written on our hearts, as St. Paul put it.[35]

This is not some crude ethical innatism. Aquinas did not think that we are born with full knowledge of ethical truth, but neither did he think we were "tabulae rasae" (blank slates), as Locke and the empiricists later claimed. Rather, we possess an inborn propensity to grasp basic ethical principles, a propensity Aquinas called "synderesis". Through education, reflection, and habituation to right behavior, we

[34] Heinrich Rommen, *The Natural Law: A Study in Legal and Social History and Philosophy* (Indianapolis: Liberty Fund, 1998), 40–41.

[35] See Rom 2:15; 2 Cor 3:2–3. For a lively discussion of the natural law in contemporary ethics, see J. Budziszewski, *What We Can't Not Know: A Guide* (San Francisco: Ignatius Press, 2007).

actualize synderesis, in other words, we develop a fully formed conscience.[36] This process of moral development can be frustrated by unchecked vicious dispositions, bad habits, or a corrupt culture, leaving our conscience deformed and our ethical understanding blunted or distorted.

But natural law is "in us" in another way as well: it is built into our natural inclinations. "The order of the precepts of natural law", Aquinas wrote, "accords with the order of natural inclinations."[37] By this he meant that morality is not opposed to our properly ordered inclinations, as some later thinkers, including Kant, thought. To the contrary, our natural inclinations are directed to our human good—to our telos—so that, by following our inclinations rationally, we are led to our good.[38] This is another way in which we find a patterned correspondence between what lies outside us and what lies within. The eternal law is built into the fabric of human nature. Thus, the natural law is in us not only in the sense that God has given us the capacity to recognize what is good, but in the way in which He has given us a natural inclination to pursue it.[39]

The third type of law, divine law, was Aquinas' term for revelation. Whereas all men, as rational creatures, participate in the natural law through reason and conscience, divine law has been promulgated

[36] Aquinas considered synderesis a dispositional capacity to know the good and the bad. He compared synderesis to our dispositional capacity for speculative understanding—e.g., that the whole is greater than the part. In each case, we are born with a disposition to understand, but only experience and training can actualize the disposition so that we may fully understand the ethical or speculative principle. Thomas Aquinas, *Commentary on the Sentences of Peter Lombard* 24.2.3c.

[37] Thomas Aquinas, *Summa Theologiae* I-II, 94, 2c.

[38] Aquinas obviously did not believe that every inclination leads to our good. Inclinations can lead us to eat gluttonously, to use alcohol immoderately, to engage in promiscuous sex, or to be greedy. Here, as always, the crucial qualifier is that the inclinations must be educated and ordered rationally. In fact, Aquinas thought that human life was influenced by a "law of sin", which leads us to act in ways contrary to our highest ends. Ibid., I-II, 91, 6. The law of sin leads us to mistake the momentary pursuit of pleasure for true human fulfillment.

[39] Robert Pasnau and Christopher Shields, *The Philosophy of Aquinas* (Boulder: Westview Press, 2004), 222. Our natural inclinations are dispositions that lead us to our natural and supernatural ends. To put this in Aristotelian language, our dispositions are the formal causes that lead to our final cause. Or as Anthony Lisska put it, "The natural law, in the mind of Aquinas, is nothing more than the determination of the natural ends—read final cause—of the dispositional properties of the essence—read formal cause—of the human person." Lisska, *Aquinas's Theory of Natural Law*, 124.

to aid our faltering human judgment and to bind us internally in ways that cannot be judged from an external point of view.[40]

Human laws, finally, participate in the eternal law insofar as they partake of reason and have as their object the common good.[41] Human law is truly law only if it conforms to the moral order, which is also the order of Nature. Human statutes that contravene or violate the moral order are not law in the fullest sense of the word. As St. Augustine said, "An unjust law is no law at all."

Now, in what sense is the natural law *natural*? Since the eighteenth century, modern thought has placed Nature and law in opposition to each other. We think of laws as being socially constructed, artificial, man-made. Similarly, whereas Aquinas and the Scholastics equated reason with Nature, later thinkers—most notoriously, Kant—gave them diametrically opposed meanings. For us moderns, law is associated with the *overcoming* of Nature, whereas, for Aristotle and Aquinas, law (even in the human sense) is Nature's ultimate expression. As the meanings of nature and law have drifted increasingly apart in the last two centuries, *natural law* has an oxymoronic ring to us today. Nature is what we instinctively do: the natural—as in "doing what comes naturally"—is for us opposed to social duties and imposed obligations. It is anything but legal.

But for Aquinas the "natural" was what we *should* do as well as what we are normally led to do by uncorrupted natural impulses. The division between reason and Nature, and between our duties and our ultimate happiness, was far less stark for him than it is for modern thinkers. Because God has ordered the world, we should not expect every choice to be a zero-sum game. To act naturally is to pursue our telos, our true end. Nature is in this sense eminently reasonable. And it is lawlike in binding us through the power of conscience.

One last point is in order, but it is vitally important, since an emphasis on law can begin to give our view of Nature and morality a rigid, draconian character. In Aquinas' philosophy, Creation is bound externally by law, but it is bound internally by love. Love attracts us, moving us to our fullest human expression, our telos. This love is motivated by desire. The highest expression of this love is the desire

---

[40] Thomas Aquinas, *Summa Theologiae* I-II, 91, 4 and 5.
[41] Ibid., 93, 3.

to know the Good, and the desire for union with God. Thus, God is both the ultimate source of all love and its ultimate telos. Through this love, which is, again, the internal side of law, all Creation is moved to its final end.

Natural Law and the Dilemma of Moral Obligation

One last issue remains to be discussed. Teleological theories of ethics, such as Aristotle's, are sometimes criticized for lacking a theory of moral obligation. Even where we may agree on what the Good is in a particular situation, why should we perform the Good? What motivates the good man to sacrifice his self-fulfillment for the benefit of another? Why be good when doing so runs contrary to our self-interest? Moreover, what motivates the bad man, or even the marginally good man, to become better? Bad men notoriously doubt that virtue is its own reward, and even marginally good men may have a difficult time motivating themselves to take the necessary steps to move to the next stage of moral development. For all his exhortations to excellence, one can only imagine Aristotle's shock at the biblical injunction to pluck out the eye that makes one stumble.[42] Aristotle's theory tells us that the virtuous life will make us happy, but it does not seem to make the pursuit of the Good morally *obligatory*.

This issue of moral obligation, of why we should pursue the good, is the human side of this question, but there turns out to be a closely related set of issues that can be raised from God's side. The question can be put this way: What is it about certain acts that makes them good or evil? What is the source of the rightness or wrongness of an act? Are certain acts good or bad because God has willed them to be, or does God will them to be because they are good or bad in and of themselves? Aquinas' approach to the natural law helps us to resolve this dilemma and supplements Aristotle's deficient theory of moral obligation.

Plato first raised this problem in his dialogue *Euthyphro*. For example, is murder wrong because God has forbidden it, or has God forbidden it because it is intrinsically wrong? From God's side, the

---

[42] See Mt 18:9.

problem is about the source of our moral values (whether God's decrees *determine*, or simply *ratify*, good and evil). From the human side, the problem is about the source of our obligations. Are we obligated to pursue the Good and avoid evil because God has commanded it or for some independent reason?

Philosophers use the term *moral voluntarism* to describe the position that holds that certain acts are good or bad because God has willed them so. From God's side, voluntarism holds that moral value is conferred by an act of God's will, in other words, by God's choosing it. From the human side, voluntarism holds that we are obligated to follow God's commands because God has willed them and because we will suffer some punishment if we do not conform to God's will. In both respects, moral voluntarism puts the emphasis on will rather than on reason. God's will creates moral value, and men are compelled to obey, not because it is reasonable, but because God has commanded it. As we will see in chapter 5, William of Ockham, John Calvin, and John Locke, among others, were moral voluntarists.

Moral voluntarism is an unattractive view for many reasons. It implies, first, that moral standards are not fixed (that God could change them by changing His mind—making adultery a "good" thing and charity "bad", for example). The moral quality of the same act could be "good" at one moment and "bad" at another, depending on God's orientation to the act at any particular time.

Second, voluntarism seems to entail that we cannot reason about morality without knowing God's will since, again, it is only God's will that measures the rightness or wrongness of an act. Voluntarism thus drives in the direction of a biblical fundamentalism since things "just are" right or wrong in virtue of God's decrees and since it suggests that human reason is inadequate to the task of moral inquiry. Third, voluntarism just seems inaccurate. We *know* murder is wrong, and we *know* it independently of knowing God's will. Even those who do not believe in God have recognized the wrongfulness of murder and the goodness of values such as charity and self-sacrifice. For these reasons, many thinkers—Plato among them—have rejected voluntarism.

Why, then, have so many been drawn to voluntarism? For essentially two reasons: from God's side, voluntarists believe that it is the only way to preserve God's sovereignty and freedom. If moral standards are not created by God—if they are in some way prior to, or independent of, God—then they must limit God just as much as they bind us. Voluntarists want morality to be within God's control, not God within morality's. God must be able to will whatever He wants—even to change His mind if He wishes. To say that God's judgment and will are bound by moral principles outside Him is to say that God is not omnipotent and not truly free.

The second reason voluntarism has attracted some followers is that it provides an easy answer to the question: Why be good if it is not in one's self-interest? The answer is: *Because God says so*. God has decreed that we behave in a certain way, performing certain kinds of acts and avoiding others, and backs this up by the threat of divine punishment. What voluntarism lacks in subtlety it makes up for in simplicity. Again, from man's side and from God's, moral voluntarism gives primacy to the will, not to reason: we are obligated not because we have reasoned our way to the truth but because we have been commanded to act in a certain way.

The alternative to voluntarism is moral rationalism. Moral rationalism holds that good and evil are qualities intrinsic to actions, in other words, that murder is wrong, that it will always be wrong, and that it would be wrong even if God did not exist. For all the reasons we have discussed, Plato took the side of the moral rationalists in the *Euthyphro*. Good and bad acts are such by their very nature; they are fixed for all time, and we can reason about them even without knowing God's will on every subject. God commands us to do good deeds not because He declares them good, but because they *are* good. God's commands are ratifications of good and evil; they do not themselves *determine* the rightness or wrongness of the act.

For all its apparent advantages, however, moral rationalism has its own defects. From God's side, there is the problem we have just discussed, in other words, that this seems to limit His sovereignty. There is a second problem as well, however. Where do moral standards come from, if not from God? If the standards of right and wrong emanate from some source other than God, what is it? Is God somehow subject to these standards in roughly the same way that we are? The problem gets even worse for a natural law ethic. If the Good is measured by human nature and exists independently of God's will, then God is ultimately limited by the standards implicit in human nature—which God Himself has created. This seems to make God dependent on His Creation rather than His Creation dependent on Him. And from the human side, how can a pure appeal to reason motivate disinterested goodness? Why should the bad man (or the marginally good man) behave himself if he is not subject to some threat of punishment? The rationalist cannot explain either the source of morality or the springs of moral obligation.

Aquinas' theory of the natural law resolves—or perhaps more accurately, dissolves—this dilemma.[43] His conception of God's nature and that of morality implies that the *Euthyphro* problem is a false dilemma: from God's side, moral standards are not independent of God (as the rationalist claims) and are not based simply on His will (as voluntarists claim). Rather, moral standards are a finite reflection of God's essence. God has created Nature and human nature as a reflection of His own nature. He wills the Good for us as a reflection of His nature because He loves Himself and because He cannot act inconsistently with His nature. Morality is a reflection of the divine essence, which is itself immutable. Thus, God cannot arbitrarily change His (and our) moral standards, as rationalists insist, but neither is He limited by standards that exist independently of Him, as voluntarists fear. Morality is literally a central part of God's very nature. It emanates from God, so that moral standards are not prior to or independent of God, as voluntarists fear, but they do not issue forth as acts of divine fiat, as rationalists fear.

This is Aquinas' answer to the *Euthyphro* question from God's side. But what obligates us to follow these dictates from the human side? Aquinas answered that it is our participation in the Logos—in God's reason. Since God is, above all, reasonable and since we participate in this reason via the natural law, we can know morality through reason. And it is reason that obligates us. When we discover these principles through reason, we discover them by participating in the eternal law, which, having the force of law, binds us as rational creatures.

In this way, natural law theory goes well beyond the prudential ethic of Aristotle and, at the same time, answers the vexing question of the source of moral values first raised by Plato in the *Euthyphro*.

---

[43] Aquinas nowhere addresses the *Euthyphro* problem by name, but his overall theory provides the response to the dilemma. Thomas Aquinas, *Summa Theologiae* I, 63, 1.

Three Objections to Natural Law Considered

Among the various objections raised against natural law theory, three are standard and repeated so frequently in different forms that any account of natural law must address them. We will call these the anthropological objection, the metaphysical objection, and the liberal objection, respectively.

The anthropological objection: If the natural law existed, there would be a much higher level of uniformity among the moral practices of different cultures over time. Individuals, too, would more readily agree about what is right and what is wrong. Instead, when we look at different cultures and at different historical epochs, we find a dizzying moral diversity. Infanticide, and its religious form of infant sacrifice, was a common practice throughout the pagan ancient world. Infanticide is still practiced in Asia and is now gaining ground in the modern West as Christianity is abandoned. Prostitution is considered immoral in many places and, in any event, is considered antithetical to the practice of religion. Yet in the past, cult prostitution was practiced in certain religious devotions in India, parts of the Near East, and other places. Social dispositions toward a myriad of other practices and attitudes—interracial marriage, abortion, euthanasia, homosexuality, even wife burning—have varied so widely at different times and places that we can hardly assume that there is a uniform standard of judgment that all men share.

Even when there is agreement in principle, there are a myriad of individual and cultural responses about how to apply the principle. For example, we may agree that killing is generally wrong, yet people who share this principle will disagree about when self-defense is justified, or whether capital punishment should be permitted, or when it is legitimate to kill during war. This diversity of judgment is powerful evidence, the objection holds, against the existence of a natural moral order in which all men participate.

Aquinas and other natural law thinkers were certainly aware of this historical and cultural diversity of moral judgments. Aquinas himself often referred to the Germanic tribes who exalted the virtues of theft (at least when committed against other tribes), and he was certainly aware of more permissive pre-Christian attitudes toward prostitution, homosexuality, and infant exposure, among others. But he had three responses to this obvious diversity, for "although there is necessity in the general principles [of practical reason], the more we descend to matters of detail, the more we encounter defects."[44]

First, as we have already seen, the flexible character of natural law is a function of the practical, rather than the theoretical, object of ethical truth: ethical judgments are about *doing*, not knowing. Consequently, ethical arguments do not always lead to one determinate right answer. Practical wisdom, *phronesis*, is an art, not a science. Thus, "while speculative reason is busied chiefly with necessary things, which cannot be otherwise than they are ... practical reason is busied with contingent matters."[45] Two persons with equal judgment and rectitude may reach different conclusions in the same situation.[46]

A related reason for this contingency of moral reasoning is that Aquinas followed Aristotle in believing in the role of equity in ameliorating the sometimes draconian consequences of hard-and-fast rules. For example, the right of private property may be relaxed in cases of true hardship. None of this implies moral relativism. Among a range of possible responses to a moral problem, some options are affirmatively wrong. Yet there may be more than one appropriate response within the range of permissible responses. In any event, in some cases equity requires that rules be relaxed as a practical matter.

A second reason for the diversity of ethical practices is that the natural law must always be adapted to differing social or cultural circumstances. A nomadic culture will evolve different concrete practices concerning property, for example, than an agrarian culture. A society that must constantly defend itself from attacks from outside will develop a more timocratic social structure than a society without

[44] Ibid., I-II, 94, 4.

[45] Ibid.

[46] John Finnis has made a particularly compelling case for the "naturalness" of this diversity of judgments, given the complexities of practical reason. In his work developing the "new natural law" theory, he argues that there are seven basic goods—life, knowledge, play, aesthetic experience, friendship, practical reasonableness (or prudence), and religion—and eight methodological prerequisites of ethical decision making (including avoiding arbitrary preferences among the basic values, among persons, the limited significance of consequences, and following one's conscience). John Finnis, *Natural Law and Natural Rights* (Oxford: Oxford University Press, 1980), chaps. 4 and 5. As Finnis concluded, given the number of values and the complexity of these requirements, "we can see how 'natural' is that diversity of moral opinion which the skeptic makes such play of." Ibid., 127.

these threats. A wealthy culture will appropriately evolve different secondary rules of distributive justice than a poor culture. Thus, "truth or practical rectitude is not the same for all, as to matters of detail, but only as to the general principles."[47] This flexibility is also a virtue of natural law theory, not a vice.

A third reason for the diversity of practices and judgments follows from the fallibility and corruptibility of human judgments. Aquinas concluded that both aspects of the natural law within us—our reason and our natural inclinations—can be corrupted by the ways of a vicious culture, by bad arguments, or by a perverted character: "Both ways ... are imperfect, and to a certain extent destroyed, in the wicked, because in them the natural inclination to virtue is corrupted by vicious habits, and, moreover, the natural knowledge of good is darkened by passions and habits of sin."[48] While synderesis is the ineradicable source of moral judgment that lies within us, conscience—our everyday awareness of right and wrong—can be distorted by custom, habit, or argument. This explains why it was so important for a society's social and legal structures to support the development of good character in its citizens. Good laws support the flowering of synderesis into a well-formed conscience.

In sum, we should expect a diversity of moral practices because of the variable character of moral judgments, the diversity of social circumstances, and the corruptibility of human character. As Leo Strauss put it, the diversity of moral opinions is not an obstacle to natural law; it is the very precondition for the emergence of natural law theory.[49]

The metaphysical objection: A more theoretical objection to natural law is that natural law depends on teleology, the existence of formal and final causes, the notions of essence and the concept of the human telos. But if the world does not operate on teleological principles, natural law theory loses its foundation: if there are no essences and final ends, there is no distinct human telos, and if there is no distinct human telos, there is no one particular form of human flourishing. Nor can the concepts of virtue and happiness be easily harmonized if Nature does not operate purposively in human behavior.

---

[47] Ibid.

[48] Thomas Aquinas, *Summa Theologiae* I-II, 93, 6.

[49] Leo Strauss, *Natural Right and History* (Chicago: University of Chicago Press, 1953), 10, cited in Finnis, *Natural Law and Natural Right*, 29.

The problem goes much deeper, in fact. As modern thought began to tear away at the fabric of the teleological worldview (see chapter 5), it inevitably led to a sundering of the realm of facts from the realm of values. Only if teleology is true—only if the human moral good is grounded in facts about human nature—can human nature serve as a ground for moral judgments. To put it in the most general terms, only if Nature is ordered to human happiness does it make sense to draw moral conclusions from our natural condition. If Nature is random and accidental, as the materialists claim, perhaps we can ignore Nature, or even change it. Thus, David Hume's famous objection that one cannot logically infer an "ought" from an "is"—that facts about nature ("is" statements) in no way entail moral conclusions ("ought" statements)—follows from the modern skepticism about teleology.[50]

This is indeed a blockbuster objection. Defenders of the natural law tradition have responded in two ways. One response is to agree that natural law does depend on teleology and then to defend the teleological worldview. There have been several recent defenses of teleology and natural law along these lines.[51] The purpose of this book, too, is to provide a kind of reductio ad absurdum argument for teleology—to show that if we reject teleology, several powerfully unpalatable and counterintuitive conclusions about human nature

---

[50] As Hume put it:

In every system of morality, which I have hitherto met with, I have always remarked, that the author proceeds for some time in the ordinary ways of reasoning, and establishes the being of a God, or makes observations concerning human affairs; when all of a sudden I am surprised to find, that instead of the usual copulations of propositions, is, and is not, I meet with no proposition that is not connected with an ought, or an ought not. This change is imperceptible; but is however, of the last consequence. For as this ought, or ought not, expresses some new relation or affirmation, 'tis necessary that it should be observed and explained; and at the same time that a reason should be given; for what seems altogether inconceivable, how this new relation can be a deduction from others, which are entirely different from it. But as authors do not commonly use this precaution, I shall presume to recommend it to the readers; and am persuaded, that this small attention would subvert all the vulgar systems of morality, and let us see, that the distinction of vice and virtue is not founded merely on the relations of objects, nor is perceived by reason.

David Hume, *A Treatise of Human Nature* 3, 1, 1.

[51] See, e.g., Lisska, *Aquinas's Theory of Natural Law*; David Oderberg, *Real Essentialism* (New York: Routledge, 2007); Russell Hittinger, *The First Grace: Rediscovering the Natural Law in a Post-Christian World* (Wilmington, Del.: ISI Books, 2003).

and morality follow. If teleology can be defended, Hume's objection loses its force. Or at least it begs the question of the truth of teleology. In other words, only if teleology is not true do moral conclusions fail to follow from factual statements. But if teleology is true, then "oughts" do follow from "is" statements in a very powerful sense.

Here is how we can make sense of this from a contemporary philosophical standpoint: first, no one, including Aquinas, believed that there is a relation of strict logical entailment between facts and values. Values do not follow in *deductive* fashion from facts in the same way that "Socrates is mortal" follows from the two propositions "All men are mortal" and "Socrates is a man." Thinking of the relation in strict logical terms is one of the characteristic modern misunderstandings of the is-ought controversy.

A better way to think about the relation between the "is" and the "ought" is to recognize that the human essence is simply a set of innate dispositional properties—tendencies in human nature that can be observed and measured—that unfold and lead to self-actualization (or eudaimonia). These dispositional properties—which include appetites and drives, such as our physical needs for food, shelter, and sex; emotional needs, such as the desire for love; and intellectual needs, such as to seek understanding of the world—are *facts* about our nature. The realization or fulfillment of these dispositions simply is what Aquinas called our *good*. A state or activity is "bad" if, in a general way, it frustrates the development and realization of these innate tendencies. There need not be anything "mystical" about this: the modern psychological idea of self-actualization as the unfolding of human potential is simply a modern way of reconceiving eudaimonia (though there are some important points of difference).[52] The point is that, if we were meant to unfold in a certain way, then that state of progressive fulfillment simply is our good. Modern thinkers have come to be skeptical of this idea of good only because they have grown skeptical that the world is an orderly place. Behind this skepticism, of course, is often skepticism about the existence of God.

One way to respond to the metaphysical objection, then, is to defend teleology along these lines, demonstrating, in essence, that the is-ought objection is simply misplaced. But there has been a second response by natural law thinkers in the past forty years or so. The "new natural law" thinkers—perhaps most famously Germain Grisez, John Finnis, and Joseph Boyle—have proposed a way of thinking about natural law that eschews teleology altogether.[53] John Finnis' groundbreaking work, *Natural Law and Natural Rights*, is the most fully developed of these. Finnis proposes here a post-Kantian account of natural law that avoids any metaphysical claims about essences and final ends and does not depend on teleological assumptions.

The biggest difference between the older and the newer natural law theory can be summarized as follows: the older natural law theory of Aquinas and other Scholastic thinkers depended on a complex conception of metaphysics, including an understanding of essences, ends, and final causation, et cetera. Ethics is ultimately grounded in metaphysics for these thinkers. Since Kant, however, modern philosophy has been supremely skeptical of the idea that metaphysical truths can be known at all. This is one of many developments that led to the modern abandonment of natural law theory. The new natural law of Grisez, Finnis, and others takes metaphysics out of the picture entirely. Finnis argues that there are seven "basic goods" we intuitively know and act upon without the need for any complex metaphysical theory. These goods are each basic in the sense that they are nonderivative of other goods (they are the fundamental things that we innately seek) and are incommensurable with one another (no one good can be reduced to another; there is no lowest common denominator of ethics).

The seven basic goods are (1) life (living, health, and procreation), (2) knowledge, (3) play, (4) aesthetic experience, (5) friendship or, more generally, sociability, (6) practical reasonableness (which, for Finnis, means having a coherent and well-integrated plan of life that comports with the moral good), and (7) religion or holiness. These goods are constitutive of human flourishing. In other words, they are aspects of human flourishing that motivate and make intelligible human action. The realization of these basic goods contributes to

[53] Germain Grisez is usually credited with having first defended an interpretation of Aquinas now associated with the new natural law. Germain Grisez, "The First Principle of Practical Reason: A Commentary on the *Summa Theologiae*, 1–2, Question 94, Article 2", *Natural Law Forum* 10 (1965): 168–201. Also see, Finnis, *Natural Law and Natural Rights*.

integral human fulfillment, Aristotle's eudaimonia in modern terms. Actions and states of affairs are good to the extent that they contribute to the attainment of these goods and are bad to the extent that they frustrate the realization of these same ends. Finnis' reconstruction, finally, avoids the Humean charge that we cannot go from an "is" to an "ought" by arguing that we know these goods intuitively without recourse to the "is" of complex facts about essences, ends, and human nature. We simply know these goods by living and experiencing what gives us happiness and meaning.

While natural law thinkers are divided over the defensibility of the "new natural law"[54] of Grisez and Finnis, their work has revitalized natural law itself and remains one avenue of response to the objection from metaphysics.

The liberal objection: A third objection to natural law theory claims that natural law will ultimately lead to an antiliberal conception of life and society. Because natural law theory holds that the chief function of law is to assist in making men virtuous,[55] it leads to an overly interventionist, even oppressive, role for government. And because it assumes that there is a limited set of human ends, it is anathema to a liberal, pluralistic society in which all are free to choose their own ends and to live as they wish, consistent with the same right for all others.

We should be clear at the outset that the liberal objection does not say that natural law theory is wrong as such, but simply that its acceptance leads to certain conclusions that some may find politically unpalatable. Still, this may be enough for some to want to avoid the theory. In practice, of course, the liberal objection is usually combined with the metaphysical objection since liberal theory has been antiessentialist in orientation almost from its inception.

There are two kinds of problems with the liberal objection. First, liberals are inconsistent in making the charge. As has been shown over and over again, no political theory is morally neutral. Liberal theory typically couches its morality in terms of an equality of rights

---

[54] See, e.g., Russell Hittinger, *A Critique of the New Natural Law Theory* (Notre Dame, Ind.: University of Notre Dame Press, 1987).

[55] See Robert P. George, *Making Men Moral: Civil Liberties and Public Morality* (New York: Oxford University Press, 1995).

rather than in terms of directing individuals to certain life choices, but liberal theory is every bit as "moralistic" in this sense as natural law theory. Every theory validates certain kinds of activities while placing other activities off-limits. The modes and reasons for intervention may be different, but the progressive liberal government can be just as interventionist as one based on the natural law.

The second response (and the two are not mutually exclusive) is that Thomas Aquinas and other natural law thinkers have consistently pointed out that, while the function of laws is to help create good citizens and persons, it is futile and even dangerous to attempt to push too hard against the tendencies of human nature. Aquinas recognized that "human laws do not forbid all vices ... but only the more grievous vices, from which it is possible for the majority to abstain, and chiefly those that are to the hurt of others."[56] This final and further qualification makes clear that he saw that there is sometimes little point in criminalizing victimless crimes, crimes that are "of no hurt to others". To do otherwise would be to invite rebellion and a general devaluing of all laws.

In sum, natural law theory does not lead in the direction of an oppressive political ethic. Indeed, if it is the correct understanding of reality, embracing natural law should lead to a much happier human existence than that which is engendered by more recent political theories grounded on amoralistic assumptions.

Conclusion

This completes our discussion of the "external" side of the classical worldview involving the moral and physical order of the world. But classical thought had a profound conception of the inner person—a conception that, to this day, continues to sustain our moral and political values. We turn to the classical conception of the person in the next chapter.

---

[56] Thomas Aquinas, *Summa Theologiae* I-II, 96, 2.

4

The Classical Conception of the Person

[T]o have a self, to be a self, is the greatest concession made to man, but at the same time it is eternity's demand upon him.

— Søren Kierkegaard

Introduction: The Significance of the Self

No idea is more foundational to our deepest moral, political, and legal values than the concept of the soul, the self, or the human person. *Everything* depends on who we are, how we are made, whether we are truly free and responsible, and whether there is a foundation for human dignity and equality that transcends each individual's material talents and capacities.

What we mean by "the self" is a matter of the greatest contention, philosophically, but minimally the idea of a core self seems to require at least three things: first, that the self is a *real thing*, that it is not merely a metaphor, a reification, or a social construct, but that it exists in a real sense; second, that the self is *active* in a philosophically significant sense to be explored shortly; and, third, that there is something morally significant about selfhood, personhood, or humanness that makes each human being worthy of special treatment and that distinguishes us from other animals.

For the self to be real—for it to be more than a way of speaking—it must possess a unity of its own and persist through time. To say that the self is a unity is to say that human personality is not hopelessly fragmented, that there are not "plural" selves, that there is some centralized locus of identity, decision making, and action that

Søren Kierkegaard, *The Sickness unto Death*, trans. Alastair Hannay (New York: Penguin Classics, 2004).

serves to bind the person into a whole. It is to say that there is an integrated foundation underlying the tensions we commonly experience between conflicting reasons, desires, and emotions. It is to point to a moral, psychological, and ontological center of gravity in the person—that which gives us our identity and makes us responsible for our actions.

This unity must also persist through time. The self is the psychological or ontological thread that runs through our lives connecting the person I am today with the person I was yesterday, and again with the person I will be tomorrow. In what sense am I the same person I was twenty years ago if every cell in my body has been replaced, and when many of my interests, tastes, and dispositions have fundamentally changed since then? How can I be held responsible for the actions taken by the person I was ten years or five minutes ago? To be responsible for past acts and to make conscious provision for the future is to assume that we are, in some morally and ontologically significant sense, the same person through time.

The position one takes on this first issue concerning the reality of the self has decisive implications for a second set of issues concerning the active powers and capacities of the self. To be active, the self must be the source of its own decisions and actions. Our choices and actions must not simply be products of some constellation of external influences—biology, environment, et cetera—that make us behave as we do. Rather, they must emanate from something internal. Making sense of what this means—parsing the more authentic or intrinsic aspects of human individuality from the external influences that shape us—has been no easy matter for modern philosophers and psychologists. Minimally, however, for us to be active agents in the sense we are speaking of, there must be a self from which our decisions and actions flow. This active conception of human personality has profound consequences for our deepest moral and political values, for our concepts of freedom and responsibility, praise and blame, merit and punishment.

The third important dimension of the self or the person concerns the moral status of human beings. The classical account teaches that the line between men and lower animals is not one of degree but of absolute distinction. There is an *ontological* divide—a difference of *kind*, not simply complexity—between man and beast. The classical conception of the person is the only possible foundation for equality, human dignity, and the sanctity of human life. These values can be grounded only on what we will call a "substantial" conception of humanness, a conception fundamentally at odds with the modern "functional" view of personhood.

In the following sections we will continue to use the terms *self* and *soul*, but they are not interchangeable. The term *self* will refer to the psychological aspects of human identity and personality, whereas the *soul* will refer to the metaphysical foundation for the self. One central question that we will explore is how body and soul are related to each other. The following section explores the opposite views represented by materialism and Platonic dualism. The section after that will develop Aristotle's and Aquinas' understanding of the soul—a theory that avoids the contrary extremes of materialism and dualism.

The Materialist and Platonic Theories of the Soul

Before Plato, the Greeks did not conceive of the self or soul, as we do today, as a kind of thing—a substance or psychological locus of personal identity. They did not attach definite or indefinite articles to the self, speaking of *a* self or *the* self. Homer, who lived around 800 B.C., used no words that could readily be translated into our terms for *mind* or *soul*, designating a psychological center of gravity within the human personality. When we find the term *psyche* used in the *Iliad* and the *Odyssey*, it means not the thinking, feeling mind, let alone the spiritual soul, but rather the life force, something the Greeks closely associated with the breath.[1] Psyche was what animates the living and what leaves the body at death.[2] The Homeric Greeks thought that the shades of the underworld linger on in a lamentable,

---

[1] Charles Taylor, *Sources of the Self: The Making of the Modern Identity* (Cambridge, Mass.: Harvard University Press, 1989), 113.

[2] Though modern translators often translate *psyche* as "soul", it did not have its own modern connotation as a spiritual or mental substance. In the *Iliad*, for example, Achilles remarks that he is constantly risking his soul in battle, and Agenor says that even Achilles has only one soul to give in war. Homer, *Iliad* 9.322, 11.569. See also Bruno Snell, *The Discovery of the Mind: The Greek Origins of European Thought* (Oxford: Blackwell, 1953), chap. 1.

shadowlike existence drained of all vitality—alive but literally soulless, since the life force has left them.

By the time Plato and Democritus came on the scene some four centuries later, philosophers had come to associate the soul with considerably more than the life force. The soul was now regarded as the personal and intrinsic aspect of each individual's personality. When Anaxagoras (d. 427) first distinguished *nous* (mind) from *hyle* (matter), associating the human nous with the divine and opening up the possibility of man's immortality, he set the stage for philosophy's perennial debate between materialism and dualism. The materialists argued that the soul was made up of a gossamer network of atoms that dissipates

> at death as when the bouquet of wine floats off,
> or breath of perfume is wafted to the winds.[3]

As we will see later, modern materialists go much further than their ancient precursors. The moderns deny the existence of the soul altogether, and many deny that the mind has any real metaphysical reality. Not only is there no soul to survive the death of the body, but the very notion that men have freedom must be seriously revised, if not altogether rejected. The ancient materialists such as Democritus and Epicurus would have been scandalized by the modern rejection of the soul. Though they denied that the soul was an expression of the divine and immortal nous, they venerated the soul no less than Plato did. Democritus regarded the body as little more than a vessel for the soul and believed that the soul was the seat of reason, the source of true happiness, and the fount of virtue. Epicurus went so far as to argue that there is an ineffable aspect of the soul that cannot be described in purely physical terms.[4] In these respects, the ancients

---

[3] Lucretius, *On the Nature of Things* 2.221–22.

[4] Epicurus wrote that the soul is a body of fine particles dispersed throughout the entire organism that has the nature of a mixture of heat and wind. Yet there is a part of the soul that is very different even from these and is therefore more interactive, or more in sympathy, with the rest of the organism. All this is made evident by the powers of the mind, its feelings, its mobility, and those faculties of which we are deprived when we die. Epicurus, "Letter to Herodotus", in *The Essential Epicurus: Letters, Principal Doctrines, Vatican Sayings, and Fragments*, trans. Eugene O'Connor (Amherst, N.Y.: Prometheus Books, 1993), 32–33. Lucretius, too,

stopped short of drawing the ultimate consequences of materialism in a way that their modern followers have not.

Plato conceived of the soul, on the other hand, as an immaterial presence inhabiting the body. In the *Phaedo*, he argued that souls transmigrate from animals to people and back again in accordance with the moral behavior of the person during life (e.g., the gluttonous and selfish return as donkeys, the lawless as wolves, etc.).[5] In other ways his description strikingly adumbrates the Christian conception of purgatory and heaven. The good soul passes to a realm "pure and everlasting and immortal and changeless", where it exists, with other souls like itself, in "the presence of the good and wise God".[6]

Plato taught that the soul was absolutely simple, since all composite things are destined to disintegration. Though it is "divine and immortal", intelligible, uniform, and indissoluble, it can be "drawn away by the body into the realm of the variable", so that it "loses its way and becomes confused and dizzy".[7] Plato even proposed that, at death, the soul is led by a guardian spirit to a place "where all must assemble and from which, after submitting their several cases to judgment", they set out for a purgatory-like place where they undergo "the necessary experiences" and remain "as long as required". Plato's Socrates even explains the appearance of ghosts as souls that have been weighted down by their association with the body, which makes them visible and hover about graveyards.[8]

Plato observed that the soul consisted of three elements—reason, the passions (which he associated with the spirited and honor-loving

---

declared that mind and soul atoms are composed of air, heat, and warmth, yet there is something else—a fourth element, "more mobile or tenuous", which he could not name:

> We find that soul, then, has a threefold nature
> And yet all three cannot create sensation,
> for none of these conceivably could cause
> sense-bearing movements.

Lucretius, *On the Nature of Things* 2.237–43. It was the capacity for sensation, the "felt aspect"—what contemporary philosophers refer to as "qualia", the qualitative aspect of self-consciousness—as well as the active capacities of reason that these early materialists could not describe in the crude language of atoms and the void.

[5] Plato, *Phaedo* 76–77, 79d.
[6] Ibid., 79d, 80d.
[7] Ibid., 80b.
[8] Ibid., 107d, e, 81e.

aspect of personality), and the appetites (for food, sex, etc.). Yet he sometimes spoke of the soul as that which is over and above the three elements and "directs all of the elements of which it is said to consist, opposing them in almost everything all through life, and exercising every form of control".[9] But he often simply associated the ruling aspect of human personality with reason, comparing reason to the driver of the human chariot, while the passions and the appetites are the horses, in other words, the motive forces in human personality.[10] Only reason can provide unity, equanimity, and self-possession, which are the marks of the integrated soul.[11] When personality is under the sway of the passions and the appetites, on the other hand, the person lives a turbulent, disordered, and divided existence. Plato compared the desire-driven personality to a nation torn by civil war. But the soul in which reason governs reflects its own internal justice. The just man is fully integrated; he has "bound all three together and made of himself a unit, one man instead of many, self-controlled and in unison". The resulting order conduces to virtue, "which is a kind of health and beauty and good condition of the soul".[12]

Plato's is the first *strong dualist* conception of the person in Western philosophy. It is *dualist* in the sense that the soul and the body are two distinct principles, in other words, mind is not reducible to matter, as it is for materialists. It is a *strong* form of dualism in that it exaggerates the divide between mind and body in ways that have raised difficult problems for the defenders of strong dualism. One problem, known to philosophers as the problem of interactionism, is that it is not clear exactly how mind and body (which are two entirely distinct substances) interact: How does an immaterial thought cause a physical movement of the body? And how do changes in the physical body (becoming intoxicated, for example) cause changes in the immaterial mind or soul? We will examine modern responses to this problem in chapter 6, when we discuss Descartes' return to strong dualism.

The second problem is that strong dualism tends to relegate the body to a kind of secondary status. Strong-dualist conceptions of the soul valorize the mind over the body and reason over the emotions

[9] Ibid., 94c.
[10] Plato, *Phaedrus* 246b.
[11] Taylor, *Sources of the Self*, 116.
[12] Plato, *Republic* 4.443e, 444e.

and other nonrational aspects of the mind. Strong dualism views the human person as a "ghost in the machine", a soul using the body. The relationship between mind and body is one of controller-controlled rather than a holistic, synergistic interaction between soul and body. The real person is identified with the mind (or soul or reason), and the body is its instrument. This "captain of the ship" theory of the person often leads its adherents to an overly ascetic view of human existence, one that fails to celebrate the beauty of the body and the wonders of our embodied existence. The body becomes a weight, something to be subjugated, and the emotions are to be subordinated to reason. For example, St. Augustine, who was heavily influenced by Plato, defined the soul as "a substance endowed with reason and fitted to rule the body" and the human person as "a rational soul using a mortal and material body".[13]

Aristotle and Aquinas offered a third conception of the soul and, with it, a middle way between the extremes of materialism and Plato's strong dualism.

The Hylomorphic Theory of the Person

As we saw in chapter 2, Aristotle taught that all things were substances, composites of matter (*hyle*) and form (*morphe*). According to this hylomorphic theory of the world, form *prefigures* matter: it is the organizing principle that makes each thing what it is essentially. Substances exist in themselves in the world, in other words, they are self-contained units of reality that persist through time on their own. As one recent philosopher has summarized it, the idea of a substance has four characteristics: (1) it has the capacity to exist in itself and not as part of another thing; (2) it is the unifying ontological center of gravity that ties the various properties and capacities of a thing together

---

[13] Augustine, *De Quantitate Animae* 13, 22; *De Moribus Ecclesiae Catholicae* 1, 227, 52. But Augustine occasionally took a position closer to the hylomorphic ideal, to be discussed next. For example, he wrote in *The City of God* that man is "animated earth". Augustine, *De Civitate Dei*, trans. Henry Bettenson (New York: Penguin Books, 1972), 20, cited in Gilbert Meilaender, "Terra es animate: On Having a Life", in *Defining the Beginning and End of Life: Readings on Personal Identity and Bioethics*, ed. John P. Lizza (Baltimore: Johns Hopkins University Press, 2009), 62.

at any given point in time; (3) it is what unifies a thing through time, the ontological foundation that remains the same as a thing's properties and attributes change; and (4) it has "an intrinsic dynamic orientation" toward self-development and self-expression, in other words, substances unfold themselves progressively through time.[14]

The concept of substance proves crucial to Aristotle's and Aquinas' hylomorphic theory of the human person. Aristotle proposed that the soul is the *substantial form* of the body. The soul is to the body as form is to matter in all other things. The soul prefigures, informs, and animates the body. It is considerably more than the mind and its faculties, as it was for Plato (and as it would become, again, for Descartes). To use a contemporary metaphor, the soul is the patterned information—the software, the active blueprint, the spiritual DNA—that governs the physical growth and mental development of the whole person. It is both a principle of life (the Greek term for soul, *anima*, is the root of our term *animate*) and the bearer of our physical and intellective capacities.

A human person is thus an integrated composite of soul and body. The soul and the body are not two distinct substances that interact with each other. Rather, the whole person is a substance composed of form (soul) and matter (body). Aristotle and Aquinas taught that animals and plants, too, have souls. The function of a plant's soul is primarily nutritive; it seeks nourishment from soil and sun and unfolds the structure of the plant. The animal soul has a sensory function that encompasses the lower vegetative function of plants but adds another layer of existence: the ability of animals to move and to respond to their environment. The human soul possesses these two elements and adds a third, intellective aspect. Aristotle argued that the soul proceeds developmentally through the nutritive and sensory stages, culminating, finally, in the intellective soul. Each higher form of the soul replaces the lower form in a manner that almost anticipates an evolutionary conception of human development—ontogenetically if not phylogenetically (i.e., in the individual, if not across species).[15]

---

[14] W. Norris Clarke, *Explorations in Metaphysics* (Notre Dame, Ind.: University of Notre Dame Press, 1994), 105, cited in Francis J. Beckwith, *Defending Life: A Moral and Legal Case against Abortion Choice* (New York: Cambridge University Press, 2007), 132.

[15] Aristotle, *De Anima* 3.

Crucially, Aquinas followed Aristotle in making one important concession to strong dualism. Both argued that only the intellective part
of the soul is immortal since this is the only part of the soul that they
thought could be immaterial.[16]

The hylomorphic conception of the soul provides a sound response
to the materialist and Platonic extremes. Contrary to the materialists,
we are not simply composed of matter. And unlike the strong dualism of Plato and Descartes, the soul is not "in" the body as a sailor
is in a ship. Nor does the soul causally interact with the body as
two distinct things interact, as Descartes later taught. Soul and body
are not two distinct substances at all; they are complementary, inter-
related components of the human person: the soul *informs* the body.

Aquinas found, in the hylomorphic ideal, not only an answer to
the philosophical problems raised by Plato's theory of the soul, but a
way to resolve what seemed to represent the Bible's tension between
materialism and dualism. Genesis seems to support a materialist
account where God tells fallen Adam, "[Y]ou are dust, and to dust
you shall return."[17] Yet other passages appear to endorse dualism. In
Ecclesiastes it is written that at death, "the dust returns to the earth
as it was, and the spirit returns to God who gave it"; and the Gospel
of John declares: "That which is born of the flesh is flesh, and that
which is born of the Spirit is spirit."[18] Aquinas thought these passages
could be harmonized by following Aristotle's hylomorphic idea of
the person.[19] There are two principles in reality, but the whole person is a composite of both.

The hylopmorphic conception of the person provides a needed
corrective both to the ascetic, Platonic idea of the soul and to the
materialist's dismissal of the soul. As against the Platonic idea, Aquinas concluded that the body is not a hindrance to the soul; it is the

---

[16] If the intellective soul were physical in nature, it would perish with the body. But this
means that the intellective soul does not develop naturally as a successor to the nutritive (vegetative) and sensitive (animal) souls. Rather, though it completes and supersedes the nutritive
and sensitive soul, it is given directly by God "at the end of human generation". Thomas
Aquinas, *Summa Theologica* I, 118, 2. We have to be careful not to confuse the intellective part
of the soul with mere rationality in its modern sense, i.e., the calculative function of thinking,
or that capacity that picks out means to desired ends. The intellective principle embraces our
capacity for self-consciousness and all of the powers related to cognition—thinking, feeling,
desiring, hoping, imagining, intending, etc.

[17] Gen 3:19.

[18] Eccles 12:7; Jn 3:6.

[19] Eleonore Stump, *Aquinas* (New York: Routledge, 2003), 192.

physical manifestation of the soul and thus an affirmatively good and beautiful thing in its own right. Aquinas understood that God made the material world and our bodies: "Our body's substance is not from an evil principle, as the Manichaeans imagine, but from God. And therefore we ought to cherish the body by the friendship of love, by which we love God."[20] Sexual appetite, in particular, is not a weight on the soul but, within the bounds of marriage, a good and fully natural part of human life.[21] It not only expresses the nature of each spouse but, like all teleological processes, leads the parts to a more integrated whole expressed in the two-in-one union of the flesh.[22]

Indeed, Aquinas argued that the soul and the body *need* one another. The body requires the soul to make it human, but the soul also needs the body to actualize itself in the physical world. In contrast to the Platonic Idea, the soul is not a separate substance on its own.[23] Only the body and soul together are a substance. Aquinas here again drew explicit support for his conception from the Bible, which teaches that we do not exist simply as souls in the afterlife, but that the resurrection of the person is a true resurrection of the material body.[24] The soul without the body is incomplete. Aquinas conjectured that the soul yearns for the body in the interregnum between death and resurrection. Body and soul are so closely intertwined that they come into being together:

> If the soul is united to the body as its form and is naturally part of the human nature, then it is completely impossible [for the soul to be created before the body].... Since the soul is a part of human nature, it does not have its natural perfection unless it is united to the body. And so it would not have been fitting to create the soul without the body.[25]

---

[20] Thomas Aquinas, *Summa Theologica* I-II, 25, 5, cited in Robert Barron, *The Priority of Christ: Toward a Postliberal Catholicism* (Grand Rapids, Mich.: Brazos Press, 2007), 152.

[21] "Natural inclinations are present in God, who moves all things. So it is impossible for the natural inclinations of a species to be toward what is evil in itself. But there is in all perfect animals a natural inclination toward carnal union. Therefore, it is impossible for carnal union to be evil in itself." Thomas Aquinas, *Summa Contra Gentiles* III, 126.

[22] For an excellent discussion of the implications of the hylomorphic idea for sex and marriage, see Patrick Lee and Robert P. George, *Body-Self Dualism in Contemporary Ethics and Politics* (New York: Cambridge University Press, 2009), 176–217.

[23] Thomas Aquinas, *Summa Theologica* I, 1, 29, reply to obj. 5.

[24] Joseph Cardinal Ratzinger, *Introduction to Christianity* (San Francisco: Ignatius Press, 1990), 347–59.

[25] Thomas Aquinas, *Summa Theologica* I, 90, 4, cited in Stump, *Aquinas*, 207.

As against materialism, the hylomorphic idea provides an explanation of our sense of ourselves as unified persons—as free, enduring selves through time. The concept of substance on which it is based helps to answer what it is about our sense of personal identity that remains the same through time even as many of our physical attributes and qualities change. It explains why I am the same person I was when I was a child, notwithstanding the fact that not a single molecule in my body is the same from that time to now. Thus, the problem of personal identity became a problem only when modern philosophers, beginning with John Locke, dispensed with the idea of substance (see chapter 5). Nor is materialism consistent with human freedom, as we will see in chapter 6. The hylomorphic account entails that we do indeed live through our physical bodies—that our soul is not a ghost in the machine that operates from beyond the veil of physicality. What the hylomorphic idea adds to the materialist explanation is that man is an active, integrated whole, that our rationality and will operate in a top-down holistic way rather than deterministically, as materialists believe.

The hylomorphic idea of the human person also avoids another pitfall of modern ideas of personhood. Because we are human substances, our humanness and the moral respect that attaches to our humanness do not depend on our having certain functional capacities, such as advanced rationality. As modern thought has abandoned the concept of substance, we have been led intellectually to think of things only in terms of their properties. This "property view" of the world has flattened our ontology and impoverished our moral sensibilities. As we will see later, for example, contemporary ethicists frequently argue today that the human fetus is of less moral worth than a full-grown man.[26] This radical moral inversion is possible only

---

[26] Bentham declared that a full-grown horse or dog is far more rational than an infant and opined that they, too, should be protected in the same way that people are. Jeremy Bentham, *Introduction to a Theory of Morals and Legislation* (1789), chap. 7, sec. 1. His modern followers—most notoriously, Peter Singer—have argued that infants do not have a right to life at all until they reach the stage at which they are capable of being a "subject of a life". More recently, Singer has revised his view, claiming that infants should be protected only after they have reached twenty-eight days. Peter Singer, *Practical Ethics*, 3rd ed. (New York: Cambridge University Press, 2011); Peter Singer, *Rethinking Life and Death* (New York: Macmillan, 1996).

An infant has less moral worth than an adult horse. Bentham's modern followers, such as Peter Singer, make similar arguments today. Helga Kuhse and Peter Singer, *Should the Baby Live?: The Problem of Handicapped Infants* (New York: Oxford University Press, 1988).

because modern thinkers reduce each thing in the world—the infant and the dog—to its present capacities while ignoring the substantial differences among the species. Without the concept of substance, many modern philosophers see the world almost exactly as Heraclitus did twenty-five hundred years ago—as the coming into being and perishing of one evanescent, substanceless process after another.

The hylomorphic idea of the human person has been largely lost to modern thought. Indeed, it is strange that most educated people today do not even recognize this conception of the person, though they recognize the Platonic and materialist alternatives. Modern defenders of the hylomorphic idea can accept with equanimity the findings of modern neuroscience, which show the ways in which physical influences shape our mental life. What the hylomorphic account adds to the materialist's interpretation of these findings is that brain processes do not operate entirely deterministically and solely from physical causes. The soul informs the body and so, too, provides the organizing template for our dynamic moral and spiritual development through life. It also accounts for that most essential aspect of human personality—freedom.

St. Augustine and Free Will

Virtually the defining criterion of having a self and of being a human person is to have the capacity to make decisions and to act upon them. As Aquinas wrote, men are rational substances that "have dominion over their own actions; and which are not only made to act; like others; but which can act of themselves."[27] Our choices and actions must flow from the self in some metaphysically significant sense—in a sense that distinguishes the causality of human action from the network of cause and effect that governs the rest of the natural world. But how is this possible?

As we saw briefly in chapter 1, materialists hold that all human acts follow in the same cause-and-effect manner as all other natural causes in the world. The causes and conditions that precipitate our acts may be more complex than other natural causes, but human acts follow from the same network of causes and conditions, and with the

[27] Thomas Aquinas, *Summa Theologiae* I, 29, 1.

same necessity, as do all other things in the universe. If this is true, it is difficult to see how we can have freedom of the will. What the traditionalist calls an act of "will" is, for the materialist, simply the way in which the background causes of human behavior—biology, environment, upbringing, and conditioning—eventuate in particular behavior. Philosophers use the term *determinism* to describe this cause-and-effect view of the world. Determinism is as old as materialism. Democritus himself declared that all things happen by necessity and that human choice is an illusion.

Now, as it turns out, the problem of freedom and determinism is related to how we think about the self. What it means to be free in the fullest, metaphysical sense is for our actions to flow from the internal sources of the self rather than from such external causes as our biological background and environment. These biological and environmental conditions, in one sense, constitute us. They are part of our background and who we are. Yet they are external in the sense that they are *given* to each individual as part of his background. They are not chosen. But the materialist claims that this is *all* that each of us is; in other words, that we can be summed up by looking at these background conditions. What is left, the materialist asks, after we account for all these background causes that make each of us who he is? Nothing. In sum, the materialist's attack on freedom of the will goes hand in hand with an attack on the concept of the metaphysical self. In contending that there is nothing left in the core identity of a person after we have accounted for these background causes, the materialist is claiming that these conditions fully constitute human personality. There is no self in the metaphysically robust sense we have claimed, in which case freedom of the will is a metaphysical impossibility.[28]

Plato and Aristotle rejected determinism. They were metaphysical libertarians. Each believed, in his respective way, that there is a soul not reducible to the matter of the body. Both recognized that there must be some power or inner capacity that moves human behavior. Plato came closer to the truth in concluding that this capacity must

[28] For a modern version of the libertarian conception of free will and the self, see C. A. Campbell, "Has the Self Free Will?", in *On Selfhood and Godhood: The Gifford Lectures Delivered at the University of St. Andrews during Sessions 1953–54 and 1954–55* (New York: Macmillan, 1957).

stand above the flux of desires, passions, and appetites that often drive behavior. It was the concept of the will he was groping for when he said that there is an aspect of the self that "directs all of the elements of which it is said to consist [reason, the passions, and the appetites], opposing them in almost everything all through life, and exercising every form of control".[29] Aristotle agreed that this "something" could not be reason since intellect alone "moves nothing".[30] But he backtracked from Plato's conception somewhat by calling this volitional feature of human personality "desiderative reason" or "ratiocinative desire", desiring reason or rational desire, in other words, a mixture of reason and desire.[31]

But it was St. Augustine who uncovered our idea of the free will as a separate faculty distinct from reason and desire. Augustine (354–430) was born in the Roman province of Numidia (now Algeria) to a Christian mother (St. Monica) and a pagan father, who converted to Christianity shortly before his death. The young Augustine was brilliant, passionate, but, by his own account, drawn to intellectual prestige, fame, and the accompanying worldly rewards. At sixteen he went to Carthage to study rhetoric, and there he soon took a mistress, who bore him a son, Adeodatus (gift of God).

In due course Augustine's search for truth led him to Manichaeism, then the chief rival to Christianity in the postpagan world. The Manichaeans taught that the world was the scene of an eternal conflict between two opposed powers—a principle of goodness, light, and order, and the other of evil, darkness, and chaos. This cataclysmic conflict between good and evil cut right through the center of human personality: the soul was born of the principle of light, while the body came from the principle of darkness. The goal of life was to escape the bondage of the body. Ascetic practices, including celibacy and vegetarianism, were prescribed for the elect. For Augustine, Manichaeism held one chief intellectual advantage over Christianity: Christianity could not, as he then thought, reconcile an omnipotent, omniscient, and supremely good God with the existence of so much pain and evil in the world, whereas the Manichaeans explained evil in terms of one of the two basic forces in the world.

[29] Plato, Phaedo 94c.
[30] Aristotle, Nicomachean Ethics 6.2.1139a31, 35.
[31] Ibid., 1139b4–5.

At the age of twenty, Augustine opened a school of rhetoric in Carthage, but his quest for fame as an author, poet, and rhetorician, along with his growing disgust for the unruliness of his students, led him to greener pastures—first to Rome and then to Milan. His faith in Manichaeism had already begun to give way to a general skepticism when in Milan he met Bishop Ambrose, whose brilliance, erudition, and goodness impressed him far more than the Manichaean teachers he had known in Carthage. When Augustine was in his late twenties, his intellectual peregrinations led him to neo-Platonism, which served as a kind of philosophical dynamite, removing the remaining intellectual impediments to his acceptance of Christianity. From the neo-Platonic authors he learned how to conceive of immaterial reality, clearing the way for his understanding of the soul. He also absorbed the neo-Platonic understanding of evil as a privation, permitting him to reconcile the goodness and omnipotence of God with the evil in the world. Evil was not a real *thing* at all; it was instead the absence of Being.

With these intellectual obstacles to Christianity removed, Augustine became acutely aware of a deeper moral conflict within himself. It was his will, not his intellect, that prevented him from accepting the truth he had so passionately sought. At this stage in his spiritual development, he *understood* but could not bring himself into conformity with this understanding without a total conversion. As he put it, there had to be a "turning around" of the soul from the things of the world to the things of God. It was in his garden in Milan in the summer of 386, when he heard a child on the other side of a wall incanting, "Tolle lege! Tolle lege!" (open it and read). He opened his Bible to a passage in Romans and lit upon the first words that he saw: "[L]et us conduct ourselves becomingly as in the day, not in reveling and drunkenness, not in debauchery and licentiousness, not in quarreling and jealousy. But put on the Lord Jesus Christ, and make no provision for the flesh, to gratify its desires."[32] The passage went to the heart of what had prevented him from accepting the Christian doctrines he had already begun to embrace, if only in an intellectual way. This sealed his conversion. He was thirty-one.

Augustine's personal struggle led to a realization that there are nonrational obstacles to knowledge, faith, and the good life, a

---

[32] Rom 13:13–14; Augustine, *Confessions* 8.8–12.

fundamental tendency in each personality to be drawn in one of two directions. He poeticized this insight, conceiving of the moral orientation of every soul as the "weight" of one's love. In one of the most celebrated passages in his *Confessions*, he wrote, "My weight is my love; wherever I am carried, it is my love that carries me there."[33] This weight draws the lover in the direction of his goals and desires—either back to himself and to a self-centered embrace of the things of the world or to an orientation to others and to the things of God.[34] This weight (and the direction it leads us) is wholly within our power. Indeed, it is the primary power of the self, a power Augustine identified as the will.

Though Augustine undoubtedly loved reason with the intensity of anyone who has searched for truth as ardently as he had, he argued that the true captain of the ship of the soul is not reason, as Plato and Aristotle thought, but the will. The will is a power that stands above the flux of desires, passions, and appetites and that guides and is guided by reason. The will's power of *liberum arbitrium*, or freedom of decision, is a genuine, self-moving human capacity to choose good or evil. But how is this possible? How can the will, will itself when all other things are caused by previous events and conditions in nature?

Augustine, who did more than anyone else in history to associate the soul with the inward orientation of the self, recognized that the powers of reason and will operate in a reflexive manner: they can operate on themselves as well as on external things. The intellect knows itself in a direct act of apprehension. That the self exists is the one thing we cannot be wrong about. It is the one essential piece of knowledge God has given us with certainty. We know that we exist in the very act of questioning our existence. Twelve hundred years before Descartes declared, "I think, therefore I am", Augustine said it first: "Even if I am deceived, *I am*. For he who does not exist cannot be deceived."[35]

Just as the soul knows itself in the very act of thinking, so, too, the will *wills* itself: "So do not be surprised that, even though we use other things by free will, we also use free will itself by means of

---

[33] Augustine, *Confessions* 13.9.

[34] Aristotle presages this insight as well. It is essential to our freedom, for "good action and its opposite, cannot exist without a combination of intellect and character." Aristotle, *Nicomachean Ethics* 6.2.1139a30–35.

[35] Augustine, *City of God* 11.26.

free will, so that the will that uses other things also uses itself, just as the reason that knows other things also knows itself."[36] Thus, in contrast to all natural things that are brought about by previous causes, the will is self-moving. It causes its own actions. Men share with God alone this nonnatural power to bring about their own actions, which are not caused by previous causes. Herein lies the essence of human freedom.

Our will moves us, then. It is the motor of human action. But it is also a fundamental orientation of one's self that colors everything else, including our knowledge and our understanding. In contrast to rationalist philosophies that hold that will is the mere instrument of reason (i.e., that we understand first and then will in accordance with our beliefs), Augustine taught that will *precedes* intellect in an important way. True understanding requires a commitment—indeed, an investment—in which those in search of truth must, in a sense, "pay it forward" by making a prior commitment that may not be fully supported by the evidence as it appears at present. "Unless you believe," Augustine wrote, "you will not understand."[37] Knowledge and understanding supersede mere belief, but *belief*, a disposition of commitment, is a prerequisite to true understanding.

Augustine recognized that will and intellect have a reciprocal relationship in the process of human decision making. Each has a certain influence over the other. Our decisions and actions emanate from the synergistic relationship of will and reason. Yet it was Thomas Aquinas who melded Augustine's conception of the will with Aristotle's teleological understanding of human action to produce the most complex understanding of human decision making ever achieved by philosophy.

Aquinas' Theory of Decision Making

No thinker before or since has provided as painstakingly precise a reconstruction of the mechanism of human choice as Thomas

---

[36] Augustine, *On Free Choice of the Will* 2.19. In the very act of willing the Good, moreover, we attain a certain kind of happiness that is the direct result of our willing it: "It follows that all who will to live upright and honorable lives, if they will this more than they will transitory goods, attain such a great good so easily that they have it by the very act of willing to have it." Ibid. 1.13.

[37] Ibid., cf. Is 7:9.

Aquinas. His moral psychology is a tour de force of philosophical synthesis and introspection. Because the world operates teleologically, not deterministically, men act from final causes. We are moved by the desires and loves before us, not pushed from behind by a plethora of deterministic causes. Human acts must be understood within the framework of Aristotle's four causes—the material, efficient, formal, and final causes.

Aristotle taught that when a person executes a choice deliberately through a volitional decision, he acts as the efficient cause of his action.[38] The efficient cause is nothing but the choice made, the act of executing the decision. But all action is directed toward a goal, a purpose—the final end that motivates the act. We eat because we are hungry or read Plato to attain wisdom. But human action is mediated by formal causes as well. In human behavior, the formal causes that motivate us are none other than our needs and desires, appetites and dispositions, which emanate from our essential constitution (our first nature) and drive us toward achieving our telos, or final end. Our needs and dispositions are shaped and influenced by our culture and environment (our second nature) and by our previous choices, which grow into our character. The material causes, finally, are the physical means of attaining our ends.

Imagine a simple case of preparing a meal. Hunger (the formal cause existing as an appetite or need) causes an actor to envision getting something to eat (the final cause), which motivates him to prepare a meal (the efficient cause) from the food he has on hand (the material cause). Of course, momentary acts can be part of more extended acts over a longer period. For example, a particular act of studying can be described under the aspect of all four causes, but it may also be part of a larger goal—for example, seeking a medical degree (final cause) to satisfy the yearning for knowledge or for success or wealth (the formal cause), which causes the student to make more particular choices using particular material means to obtain the degree (the material and efficient causes). The final cause, in particular, provides the reason for our acts. What makes deterministic accounts of human behavior (for it can be only *behavior* and not true action) so highly implausible is that either these accounts rule out reasons as causes of human action

---

[38] "The origin of action—its efficient, not its final cause—is choice." Aristotle, *Nicomachean Ethics* 6.2.1139a32.

(we eat because of physical conditions in the brain, not because we are hungry) or they must reinterpret reasons as efficient causes, and this raises a host of other problems.

From an internal perspective, human decision making is a function of the interaction of the formal and efficient causes (the way our needs and desires express themselves in our choice making). Aquinas incorporated, but tempered, Augustine's insight that the will colors the intellect. In fact, will and intellect influence each other through a five-stage sequence of interaction that emanates in the decision to act. At each step of the way there is, following Augustine's insight, a paired response between intellect and will.

The first step involves a simple determination by the intellect that a particular end is now desirable, followed by the will's corresponding volition for this end. This volition might be described as a bare longing for the end—a longing that precedes any consideration of how (or whether) it can be achieved. The second through fourth stages involve the selection of the means to achieve the end. Strictly speaking, according to Aquinas' theory, we *intend* the end, but we *choose* the means to achieve our end.[39] At the second stage, the intellect must decide that it is within the actor's power to achieve the end. If the intellect concludes that the end can be achieved, the will then forms the intention to try to achieve it. This act of will spurs the intellect on to the third stage of deliberation, when the intellect picks out various alternative ways to achieve the end (Aquinas calls this act of the intellect "counsel"). But the means picked out must again be acceptable to the will (Aquinas calls this the "consent" of the will). If some of the means are undesirable, they are excluded. In the fourth stage, the intellect selects from among the alternatives the single best possible means to achieve the end; and if the will accepts this alternative, it elects this option (*electio*). Now that the ends and means have been chosen, all that remains is the fifth stage, to perform the action: the intellect commands the action, and the will executes it (Aquinas calls this pairing of acts by the intellect and the will "command" and "use").[40]

[39] Steven A. Long, *The Teleological Grammar of the Moral Act* (Naples, Fla.: Sapientia Press, 2007), 1.

[40] Aquinas' account of human action can be found in the *Summa Theologica* I-II, 6–21. Stump provides an overview of the five stages of action. Stump, *Aquinas*, 287–90.

Several things are important to emphasize about Aquinas' account. First, of course, these stages frequently occur almost instantaneously and, in some cases, various steps drop out (e.g., where there is only one possible means to achieve an end, the third and fourth steps collapse into one). Second, while the intellect is the functional "director" of human action, the will has a kind of veto power in that it must accept the ends and means chosen at each point along the way. The will can also control the intellect by redirecting its focus to other things. Thus, Aquinas' conception of human action falls halfway between Hume's desire-driven psychology (that "reason is a slave to the passions") and Kant's view (that our freest acts are those that are uncolored by desire). Finally, we see here how the orientation of the will enters into the deliberative process. The moral state of the actor is relevant in the selection of both the ends (by coloring the actor's sense of what is desirable) and the means (since a particular means to an end may be acceptable to the bad man but not to the good). Thus, our character, emotions, and moral state influence, and are influenced by, our choices.

What we call "freedom of the will" is the unfolding of the entire five-stage sequence: the intending of ends, the choosing of means, and the commitment that emanates in action. Free will is a property of the twin powers of the self, the will and the intellect, as they function together. Freedom, in fact, is really a power of the entire person as an integrated whole: it is not the will but the entire human person who is free.[41] Aquinas puts special emphasis, however, on the power of *electio*, the fourth of his five stages. Electio is the final election of the will to do the action, the go-ahead that precedes the execution of the action. "Volition is of the end, but choice is of the means."[42] Because electio is the affirmance of our will for a particular action (means and end), it is the fulcrum of our moral responsibility for our actions.

It is truly striking how much of this has been lost in modern accounts of decision making, influenced as they are by materialistic

[41] Stump, *Aquinas*, 297.

[42] Thomas Aquinas, *Summa Theologica* I-II, 13, 3. Intention and volition are each primarily concerned with ends in Aquinas' theory. But intention is the final end, the object of the act that motivates the choice of means, whereas volition is the efficient cause that executes the particular means chosen to obtain the end.

assumptions. By denying the self, the will, and final causes, materialism has desperately impoverished our moral psychology, and by impoverishing our moral psychology, it has rendered plausible a theory that no one could otherwise take seriously—the claim that we do not really choose freely.

The Care of the Self: Moral Virtue and the Psychological Integration of the Person

One last essential element of the classical conception of the person remains for us to discuss, but it may be the most important part as a practical matter. Modern thought has largely divorced our morality from our psychology. According to most modern views, to be psychologically healthy is one thing; to be morally good and socially responsible is quite another. Indeed, for some modern thinkers, to be healthy may require that we overcome our moral sensibilities.

The sources of this peculiar modern attitude are so numerous that they are hard to catalogue, but a brief representative sampling may do for now. Modern thinkers have claimed that human beings operate inevitably from egoism and self-interest, so that altruism is a metaphysical impossibility (Mandeville, Hobbes), that man in the state of nature is inherently beneficent and that society makes us vicious and cruel (Rousseau), that duty and desire are regularly in conflict (Kant), that the pursuit of true love threatens the strictures of the social bond (Romanticism), that society saps our individuality (Mill), that the will to power is the mark of psychological health rather than the height of self-absorption (Nietzsche), and that the saintly soul is often affirmatively sick (Freud).

Nothing could be further removed from this modern dis-sensibility than the classical view of human nature. Plato, Aristotle, Augustine, Aquinas, and many others asserted again and again that the moral and psychic well-being of the person, his capacity to achieve true happiness, depends on self-integration and that genuine self-integration is impossible for the selfish, the nonvirtuous, and the affirmatively wicked.[43] In a world that is teleologically ordered, goodness and

---

[43] This view is at the heart of Plato and Aristotle's moral psychology. Plato, *Republic* 9.571–80; Aristotle, *Nicomachean Ethics* 9.4.

health should run hand in hand. In simple Christian terms, the true self can develop only in the soil of goodness—a soil that only God can water and nourish.

A few schools of modern thought still cling to aspects of this essential human insight. Humanistic psychology, for example, teaches that self-actualization requires the full integration of human personality.[44] But what modern thought leaves out is that this integration must be more than the achievement of a purely *internal consistency* between our thoughts, beliefs, desires, and actions. We can imagine an internally consistent Nazi, or mass murderer or heroin addict, for that matter—someone who has carefully integrated his system of beliefs and desires into a coherent but evil or self-destructive life pattern. This person might act *authentically* in the sense that his spontaneous responses to the world reflect the internal consistency of his system of beliefs and desires, and his chosen pattern might even prevent a certain amount of internal conflict, but internal consistency is not enough for true human flourishing. True integration requires more than internal coherence.[45] It requires a life lived virtuously in accordance with our human telos, which is inherently relational, bound up with the good of others.

We can summarize the classical understanding of our moral psychology with three theses.

Conscience and the reality of moral knowledge: First, and most fundamentally, human beings possess an inherent noetic capacity to recognize the difference between right and wrong. We intuitively know that murder is wrong just as we intuitively know that two plus two equals four, though both forms of knowledge must be actualized by experience (i.e., we are not born with mathematical or

---

[44] See, e.g., Rollo May, *Love and Will* (New York: Norton, 1968); Abraham Maslow, *Toward a Psychology of Being* (New York: Van Nostrand Reinhold, 1968).

[45] In fact, classical thinkers from Plato to Aquinas would point out that full internal consistency is not even possible if one is not living in accordance with his true nature. The reason for this is that the wicked or nonvirtuous life prevents a person from achieving his true nature or identity. The wicked person lives in conflict not only with others but ultimately with himself. An internal consistency of unhealthful or positively evil desires and beliefs will always chafe against the call of one's unrealized nature. Thus, there will always be something incomplete, unfinished, in the consistently wicked individual. One reason for the impossibility of a fully integrated wicked personality has to do with the central importance of the virtue of prudence. Prudence, or practical wisdom, is a powerful integrating force in human personality, but the development of prudence depends on living in accordance with virtue.

moral knowledge, but we gain this knowledge upon being presented with the facts). In the case of moral knowledge, our understanding can be thwarted by dysfunctional circumstances or by a bad character (another example of Augustine's insight that the orientation of our character colors our moral understanding). Nevertheless, a true understanding of the Good is there in latent form waiting to be actualized in every human person.

We commonly call this capacity "conscience". The etymology of the term is significant, for conscience is literally *con-science* (knowing with): we know with others, and with God, the distinction between good and evil.[46] Aquinas used the term *synderesis* to refer to the innate, unrealized potentiality to know and do the Good.[47] Conscience is, in contrast, the way in which synderesis is (more or less well) expressed in particular individuals.[48] Conscience can be deformed by bad culture or character, and this explains why people can authentically express conflicting opinions based on conscience. Thus, synderesis does not err, but conscience can. It is synderesis that grasps the natural law as a universal proposition of practical reason ordered to action.[49] Nevertheless, Aquinas taught that even the erring conscience binds us—that we must follow it as best we can under all circumstances.[50]

Only this conception of conscience can justify modern ideas of liberty of conscience: if what we now call conscience is simply the individualized recrudescence of socialization, as most schools of modern psychology teach, it is difficult to understand why liberty of conscience should be so important. If moral knowledge is put into

---

[46] Conscience is to have "this mind ... which was in Christ Jesus" (Phil 2:5).

[47] Aquinas thought of synderesis as a "natural habit" inclining us to the Good. Since both reason and the will incline toward the Good as reason understands the Good, synderesis is not just knowledge. It is an inclination to the Good implanted in our practical reason. It inclines the will as well as the intellect. Thus, goodness is connatural with our desires, a natural bent to know and to do the Good. Thomas Aquinas, *Summa Theologiae* I, 79, 12. Cf. Aristotle, *Ethics* 6.6.

[48] Strictly speaking, synderesis is not a power, but an act. Thomas Aquinas, *Summa Theologiae* I, 79, 13. It is the way in which synderesis is expressed in the knowledge of a particular individual, more or less distorted by culture, character, and circumstance.

[49] William E. May, "Contemporary Perspectives on Natural Law", in *St. Thomas Aquinas and the Natural Law Tradition: Contemporary Perspectives* (Washington, D.C.: Catholic University of America Press, 2014), 133.

[50] Thomas Aquinas, *Disputed Questions on Truth*, qq. 16 and 17.

us by our cultural influences (some better than others), it is not at all clear why there should be anything special about these, as opposed to other, forms of social influence on our behavior.

Choice and the constitution of our character. The second tenet of the classical understanding of our moral psychology is that our choices are literally self-constituting. Choices are not simply separate and distinct points along the course of life's trajectory. They set a certain course for the future, not simply by committing us to certain actions but, more fundamentally, by depositing a kind of moral residue, a propensity for doing good or evil, in the will of the chooser. This was Aristotle's point in saying that we become good or bad by choosing good or bad actions.[51] In making these choices, as Augustine would say, we create the bent or inclination of our will. We are thus responsible for our character and for the kind of person we become. Aristotle explicitly denied that a person can be excused for acts that flow from an ill-formed character since "men make themselves responsible for being unjust or self-indulgent" by habitually acting in an unjust and self-indulgent manner.[52]

Each choice and every action, then, coalesce into our character. This observation is the source of the oft-repeated wisdom that good thoughts produce good choices, that good choices emanate in good actions, that good actions grow into fruitful habits, that fruitful habits produce the virtues, and that the virtues flower into noble character.[53] But there is a dark flipside as well: bad choices and actions metastasize into vices that generate destructive and often compulsive

---

[51] Aristotle, *Nicomachean Ethics* 5.3.5.1114a1–25. Robert George puts this beautifully: "Choices [for good or evil] shape the character of the choosing person by integrating the moral good or evil of this choice into his will. In this sense, morally significant choices are self-constituting: they persist in the character and personality of the chooser beyond the behavior that carries them out." Robert George, *Making Men Moral: Civil Liberties and Public Morality* (New York: Oxford University Press, 1995), 18.

[52] Not to know that our character will take on the quality of our choices is "the mark of a thoroughly senseless person". The man who has made himself unjust or immoral is like the man who has made himself ill by incontinent living. Both have "thrown away [their] chance, just as when you have let a stone go, it is too late to recover it.... So, too, to the unjust or self-indulgent man, it was open at the beginning not to become men of this kind, and so they are unjust and self-indulgent voluntarily; but now that they have become so it is not possible for them not to be so." Aristotle, *Nicomachean Ethics* 3.5.1114a1–25.

[53] "[W]e rejoice in our sufferings, knowing that suffering produces endurance, and endurance produces character, and character produces hope" (Rom 5:3–4).

character traits over time. Vicious decisions and actions become not simply part of our history, *but part of who we are going forward.*[54] It is a further testament to the state of the human condition that, like walking up and down a hill, it may well be easier to undo the virtuous disposition than to set aright the vicious.

This picture of human responsibility might sound harsh to the modern ear, particularly in light of our understanding of the formative effects of social conditions on the human psyche. Persons who grow up in bad environments, whose options might be limited, or whose biological endowment predisposes them to unhealthy or bad behaviors (e.g., alcoholism) face greater challenges than those from happier circumstances. And though it is true that we are all affected in many ways by our background and environment, no one can claim that there is a cosmic equality, that everyone's burden in life is equal. This, however, is precisely where several Christian and humanistic doctrines mitigate the (potentially) draconian nature of the second core truth of moral psychology.

That we are subject to influences that shape our outlook, that we may be placed in circumstances not of our own making, that only God knows what is in our hearts when we act, that justice without mercy is blind—each of these serves to deepen our understanding of the enigmatic interrelation between the self, the world, and God's grace. Even Aristotle recognized that equity is essential in softening the unbending rules of justice. In sum, that we build our character through choices does not mean that we should ignore the ways in which the world makes each of us the person he is. But neither should our awareness of the ways in which responsibility can be mitigated by circumstance mean that we do not choose and act freely within the constraints set by our condition in the world.

At the end of his life, even Plato was tempted to write that it often seems that "each of us living creatures is a puppet made by the gods, possibly as a plaything, or possibly with some more serious purpose." We are moved this way and that by the cords of our emotions, manipulated perhaps by the gods. But there is also another cord—the

---

[54] In this vein, St. Augustine wrote, "The truth is that disordered lust springs from a disordered will; when lust is pandered to, a habit is formed, when habit is not checked, it hardens into compulsion." Augustine, *Confessions* 8.5.

"golden cord" of reason, which is "softer and more flexible" than the others. Freedom lies in yielding only to the tensions of this cord "if the gold in us is to prevail over the other stuff".[55]

The virtues as an integrative force in human personality: The third tenet of the classical understanding of moral psychology has to do with the importance of the virtues in guiding human behavior and our development. Human personality is integrated by making a consistent pattern of choices over time. These choices coalesce into more or less enduring character traits. It is thus quite literally true that we *become* what we *do*. Depending on whether these choices are good or bad, the resulting character traits will embody virtues or vices. Aristotle observed that virtues are *powers*—capacities of the soul built up from habits (*habitas*). By *habits*, moreover, we mean considerably more than a learned pattern of activity. When a habit is formed, it reflects a change in the self—a conversion in the orientation of the will and the disposition of the soul.[56]

The virtues have three functions in fine-tuning human action to the Good. They permit us, first, to act *consistently* over time, integrating our singular acts into a coherent, integrated pattern of behavior.[57] Second, they permit us to act *readily and spontaneously*—without excessive deliberation or delay.[58] Third, virtues *make virtuous action pleasant*, even joyful.[59] Thus, genuinely virtuous behavior is anything but conformity to externally imposed standards and mores. Once

---

[55] Plato, *Laws* 1.644e, 7.803d.

[56] Romanus Cessario, *The Moral Virtues and Theological Ethics*, 2nd ed. (Notre Dame, Ind.: University of Notre Dame Press, 2009), 35n10. *Habitas* influences the whole person, moreover. It affects reason and the appetites, and it influences (and is influenced by) the orientation of the will. Ibid., 43.

[57] "For what rests on the action alone changes easily if it has not been stabilized by a dispositional inclination." Thomas Aquinas, *Disputed Questions on Truth* Ic, cited in Robert Pasnau and Christopher Shields, *The Philosophy of Aquinas* (Boulder: Westview Press, 2004), 230.

[58] "For unless there is a disposition inclining the rational power in one direction, then, whenever we have to take action, we will have to take up first an inquiry into the action." Aquinas, *Disputed Questions on Truth* Ic. To put it in Augustine's terms, virtues change the orientation of the will to more fitting objects of action.

[59] Virtues permit us to "complete our perfect action pleasantly, something that occurs through a disposition." Aquinas, *Disputed Questions on Truth* Ic. One of the striking contrasts between Aquinas and Kant is that Aquinas believed that good acts performed from a desire to perform them are better, more virtuous, than virtuous actions performed from duty alone. Kant, on the other hand, thought that any emotional inducement to action undercut the moral autonomy of the actor and the goodness of the action.

established, virtue is the true fount of human authenticity. Though
Aristotle or Aquinas would not quite put it this way, consistency,
spontaneity, and pleasure in our actions are the real marks of authenticity—of behavior that emanates from the self, rather than from
externally imposed sources of authority. In this way, virtue is constitutive of (and not merely instrumental to) our well-being.

Plato, Aristotle, and later Christian thinkers recognized four cardinal virtues: prudence (or practical wisdom), fortitude (the capacity
to persevere in difficult situations), temperance (moderation in one's
appetites, desires, and even attitudes), and justice (basic fairness toward
others).[60] To these, Christian thought has added the three theological
virtues of faith, hope, and love.[61] Virtues are attained through human
effort but also through divine grace. As Aquinas said, God "binds us up
by law and supports us by grace".[62]

Of the four moral virtues, prudence is the most important. In fact,
it is the key to achieving all the other virtues. Prudence has a rational,
a volitional, and a more broadly psychological function. As it concerns reason, prudence is not mere foresight or shrewdness. Its real
function is to align the moral understanding of the person with the
objective moral truth.[63] As it concerns the will, prudence is a practical power that facilitates *doing*—a power to put ethical knowledge
into action, to choose the appropriate act under the circumstances.
Prudence prevents the passions from hijacking our moral commitments. But prudence also has a reflexive, psychological component.
By conforming our reason and will to the objective moral order—by
knowing and seeking and doing the Good—prudence facilitates our
genuine self-integration. Herein lies the true meaning of authenticity, of which the Romantics had only a partial understanding. True
authenticity is not simply acting spontaneously from our established
pattern of personality. It is acting spontaneously, and in our individualized ways, from the fully integrated self, the self that acts in accordance with the objective moral order.

---

[60] Plato, *Republic* 6.6.

[61] "[T]he greatest of these is love" (1 Cor 13:13).

[62] Aquinas, *Summa Theologica* I-II, 90, prologue.

[63] As one influential commentator recently put it, the function of prudence is to "ensure
that there exists between the intelligence of the moral agent and the truth of the moral law an
authentic and intrinsic conformity". Cessario, *Moral Virtues and Theological Ethics*, 9.

We have the capacity to know the Good, then. We form our character, and indeed our self, through our choices. We become fully integrated, authentic, and psychically healthy by bringing ourselves into conformity with the moral order. To put it in modern terms, the virtuous life leads to true self-actualization. In this we can see that our noblest modern personal and political values—freedom, responsibility, merit, liberty of conscience, authenticity, self-expression, and self-actualization, among others—have no foundation in the absence of a real, metaphysical self.

But the metaphysical self makes sense only in the context of a broadly teleological view of the world. When early modern thinkers in the fourteenth century began to chip away at this two-thousand-year-old edifice, the self and its attendant social ideals were placed in jeopardy.

Part II

The Moral and Political Consequences of the Decline of the Classical Worldview

5

The Birth of the Modern:
Four Seminal Thinkers

We should not take it upon ourselves to believe that God could take us into his counsel.

—René Descartes

Within a generation or two of Thomas Aquinas' death, the classical worldview began to come under attack from Christian thinkers who had grown skeptical of Plato's universals and Aristotle's essences. The Protestant Reformation of the sixteenth century accelerated the reaction against Roman Catholic theology and the Aristotelian philosophical system with which it had been associated. Luther, Calvin, and other leading Protestant thinkers labored mightily to oust what they regarded as pagan and rationalistic influences in Christian thought. By the late seventeenth century the teleological understanding of the world teetered on the brink of dissolution, the targets of attacks from Protestant theologians on one side and skeptical philosophers on the other.

Within a century, Protestant theologians and skeptical philosophers, once allies in opposition to teleology, became bitter enemies. Those who held a more scientific and increasingly materialistic worldview attacked the core theological assumptions of Christianity, and Christian thought itself seemed driven down the middle. One group reacted against science, typically reverting to literalist interpretations of the Bible. The second group was drawn toward deism, a philosophy that essentially accepted the scientific worldview in toto, rejecting

René Descartes, *Principles of Philosophy* 1.28.

revelation, miracles, and the divinity of Christ while consigning God to the role of the remote Designer of the world. Without the teleological system that had once bridged the gap between the realms of theology and science, the two worlds drifted increasingly apart.

This chapter explores the thought of the four thinkers who did more than any others to usher in the modern age: William of Ockham, René Descartes, John Locke, and Thomas Hobbes.

William of Ockham and the Rise of Nominalism

Fewer than fifty years after Aquinas, William of Ockham (1287–1347) challenged the Aristotelian basis for Aquinas' conception of the natural law. Ockham, an English Franciscan who studied at Oxford, became embroiled in controversy with Pope John XXII over the meaning of apostolic poverty.[1] Ockham and several others were summoned before a papal council at Avignon. Fearing imprisonment and possible execution, they fled in 1328, taking refuge with Holy Roman Emperor Louis IV, who was embroiled in his own dispute with the Pope. Ockham was excommunicated a few days after he took flight (though he was rehabilitated shortly after his death).

Perhaps in response to his excommunication, Ockham wrote a series of works arguing that ecclesiastical and secular powers flowed from God in different ways and that secular rulers were in no way subject to the authority of the Pope. Ockham's political theory, though not entirely new, was perhaps the best developed philosophical defense of political secularism at the time. His political theory included a novel defense of natural rights, including the right to property and the right to revolution. In both his epistemological views and his political theory, he was a precursor to John Locke.

Ockham is best known for his attack on the Aristotelian system on which Aquinas based his theory of natural law. He was, before

---

[1] Ockham defended the Franciscan position that Christ and the disciples had given up all property. He argued that the Pope was in error in claiming that they retained property and that property ownership was not inconsistent with discipleship. Paul Vincent Spade, introduction to *The Cambridge Companion to Ockham*, ed. Paul Vincent Spade (New York: Cambridge University Press, 1999), 3; Frederick C. Copleston, *A History of Philosophy* (New York: Image Books, 1993), 2:44.

all other things, a logician with a passion for ontological parsimony. *Ockham's razor* is the term given for his principle that, as between two alternative explanations of a particular phenomenon, the simpler or more elegant is preferable. He insisted that "what can happen through fewer [principles] happens in vain through more."[2] Partially on this ground, Ockham reduced Aristotle's ten categories of Being (i.e., the ten kinds of things that can be said to exist)[3] to two: all that exists in an absolute sense, he concluded, are individual things (this tree or that person) and qualities (redness, largeness, intelligence, etc.) He argued, moreover, that even qualities exist as individual things. In other words, there is no "redness" in the abstract, only this or that instance of redness.[4] What "exists" is what can be signified with a name (a subject or a predicate).

All the other categories of Being that Aristotle and Aquinas had accepted as real parts of reality—space, time, numbers, and relations—were, according to Ockham, merely "connotative" in nature. They are simply ways of talking about what really exists. Thus, space does not really exist, nor does time. These are simply constructs we use for relating two or more concrete individual things that do exist. There is this rock and that rock, but the concept that there are *two* of these things adds nothing over and above the existence of the things themselves. Thus, mathematical entities do not really exist. Similarly, John Kennedy and Robert Kennedy were real people, but the relation "being the brother of" is not a real thing, as Aristotle thought. Only things exist, not the relationships between and among them.

Perhaps the most important upshot of Ockham's theory was his denial of universals. There are individual trees but no form of the

---

[2] To similar effect, he wrote, "Plurality is not to be posited without necessity", and "When a proposition is verified of things, more [things] are superfluous if fewer suffice." These quotations and references are collected in Paul Vincent Spade, "Ockham's Nominalist Metaphysics: Some Main Themes", in *The Cambridge Companion to Ockham*, 101.

[3] The ten categories include substance, quantity, quality, relation (e.g., being greater than or being the brother of), place, time, position (i.e., where a thing sits relative to other things), state or condition, actions (i.e., to act on something else), and affection (i.e., to "suffer" change by being acted upon). Aristotle, *Categories* 1.4.

[4] Whereas Aristotle or Aquinas would have said that the same quality, "redness", exists in each instance of redness in particular things (i.e., that it is the same "red" in the fire engine and in the apple), Ockham thought that there are as many instances of redness as there are red things. Ockham's ontology flattened the world at the level of categories, but flooded reality with an almost infinite plethora of individual things.

tree that unites and defines all particular trees. Similarly, among the qualities of things, there is no universal "redness" that inheres in all red things, only a plurality of individual instances of redness. Ockham is thus remembered as the father of modern nominalism, the doctrine that only individual things exist.[5]

Ockham's reduction of the world confronted him with some serious difficulties. He had to admit that things were positioned in space and ordered in time, but he denied that space and time existed. He recognized that one thing causes another but denied that causation itself is real. He recognized that Caesar lived before Jesus even though he would not admit that the relational predicate "lived before" is real.

The problem with Ockham's position is that, in each case, the truth value of propositions will depend on the truth value of entities that he thought were not real. It is true that Caesar lived before Jesus, and it is false that he lived after Jesus. "Living before" and "living after" are what philosophers call "truth-functionally" significant— the truth of these statements depends on them. In what sense, then, could relations and numbers not be real? He had no satisfying answer

[5] If nominalism is simply the denial of universals, Ockham was a nominalist in the wider sense of the term. In fact, however, Ockham took a middle position, known as conceptualism, between Aquinas' moderate realism and the true nominalism of later thinkers such as Thomas Hobbes. Moderate realists, including Aristotle and Thomas, held that species are real, that they reflect realities in the world. This entails, among other things, that there are real natures to things—that things of the same class have essential similarities. At the opposite extreme, nominalism is the view that names arise through language (i.e., that we arbitrarily place labels on things and class them into categories but that each class is simply an artificial construction of language). Conceptualism is an intermediate position. It holds that concepts are neither in the world nor merely a function of language. Rather, they arise through an operation of the mind. Ockham was a conceptualist in this respect. In fact, Aquinas' view is closer to Ockham's than is sometimes thought, for Aquinas did not believe in universals in the world. He thought they arise from an abstraction of the mind, but he was closer to Aristotelian realism because he believed that universals reflected objective truths in the world. Robert Pasnau and Christopher Shields, *The Philosophy of Aquinas* (Boulder: Westview Press, 2004), 73–75. In its wider sense, however, nominalism was a movement that drove a "wedge ... between philosophy and theology, and which broke apart the synthesis achieved in the thirteenth century. The nominalist spirit ... was inclined to analysis rather than synthesis, and to criticism rather than to speculation. Through their critical analysis of the metaphysical ideas and arguments of their predecessors the nominalists left faith hanging in the air, without (so far as philosophy is concerned) any rational basis." Copleston, *A History of Philosophy*, 3:11.

to this question. Ockham was able to salvage his ontology only by giving these other entities a second-class status, distinguishing real things and connotative terms, which turn out to be indispensable to language after all.[6]

His denial of universals had even more profound metaphysical and theological consequences. It meant that we could not speak of essences in the traditional sense: there is no human nature, for example, but only individual men and their qualities. This, in turn, made it more difficult to understand how men could share a common telos. Since there is no shared human nature, the idea of a shared human end becomes obscure. Ockham retained much of the earlier language of forms and ends, but they begin to lose their significance as supports for the teleological framework. An increasingly mechanistic understanding of reality crept into his thought as final causes gave way in his philosophy to purely efficient causes: he waffled notoriously, for example, about whether final causes were necessary to explain natural phenomena at all.[7] Even in the realm of human action, he sometimes seems to have conceived of final causes as reason-driven efficient causation—a very modern idea in philosophy.[8] He retained Aristotle's hylomorphic understanding of nature as being composed of form and matter, but since he rejected a shared nature common to all things in a species, he denied that they were two separate principles that can exist apart from one another.[9]

One principal effect of Ockham's metaphysics was to deny the claim, central to metaphysics from Plato's time on, that there are *degrees* of Being, greater and lesser gradations of reality in things. For

[6] Spade, "Ockham's Nominalist Metaphysics", 108.

[7] In one place (*Quodlibetal Questions* 4.1.297, 299–300) Ockham rejects teleological thinking in nature as a "category mistake" and argues that all natural phenomena can be explained by efficient causality alone—that we need not posit teleological ends to explain the phenomena of nature. But in another (*Expositio in Libros Physicorum* 2.12.11–12; 2.13.7) he concludes, perhaps with some reluctance, that the reality of final causes in nature is "true but not evident". See Marilyn McCord Adams, "Ockham on Will, Nature, and Morality", in *The Cambridge Companion to Ockham*, 249–50.

[8] We are not simply "drawn forward" by our natural human ends (since these do not exist) but, rather, are moved in an efficient way by reasons. Adams, "Ockham on Will, Nature, and Morality", 249–51.

[9] André Goddu, "Ockham's Philosophy of Nature", in *The Cambridge Companion to Ockham*, 147–49. Goddu concludes that Ockham remained an Aristotelian but that Aristotle "gets bent to Ockham's own purposes". Ibid., 155.

Aquinas, as for Plato, some things are literally more *real* than other things. Substances have greater reality than their properties because properties depend on substances for their existence: the redness of an apple, for example, cannot exist independently of the apple itself. Men are substances but, having their being in and through God, have a lesser degree of reality than God, who is the only necessary and purely actual thing in the world.

Ockham's denial of universals made it impossible for him to make sense of this idea that there are degrees of Being. He admitted that there was a hierarchy of *excellence* among things, from natural things to men to God, but he denied that any existing thing could be more real than any other existing thing. Existence itself became a binary concept: a thing either exists or it does not, and anything that exists is as real as anything else that exists. Thus, God Himself is no more real than the things of the created world—a Being among beings, rather than the Ground of all Being (though Ockham was careful to add that God was the only infinite and necessary Being). This utter flattening of the metaphysical landscape led the way back to the anthropomorphism of more primitive conceptions of God. If God is simply another thing (even an infinite and necessary thing), rather than the Ground of all Being, He had to be conceived as a spiritual *thing* of some sort. It was but a short step from Ockham's nominalization of God to Hobbes' contention, three centuries later, that if God exists, He must be physical and extended in space.[10]

In the long run, nominalism has similar consequence for how we think of the soul. Whereas Aristotle and St. Thomas defended the sophisticated idea that the soul was the substantial form of the body (Ockham himself defended a version of this), the latent thrust of nominalism led the way back to Plato's more primitive view of the soul as a ghost in the machine that interacts with the body. This led, in Descartes' and Locke's philosophies, as we will see shortly, to a dualistic conception of the person—a conception that quickly

---

[10] "[A] man can have no thought, representing any thing, not subject to sense. No man can conceive anything, but he must conceive it in some place, and indeed with some determinate magnitude." Thus, as he says a few lines earlier, "the Name of God is used, not to make us conceive Him [for He is incomprehensible] but to honor Him." Thomas Hobbes, *Leviathan*, ed. C. B. Macpherson (New York: Penguin Books, 1968), 99.

collapsed, in Hobbes and later eighteenth-century thinkers, into simple materialism.[11]

Beyond his ontological parsimoniousness, Ockham also had a theological objection to the teleological framework of Aristotle and Aquinas. He found in the doctrine of fixed forms and essences a pagan distortion of Christian theology. The problem was that essences impose limits on God's freedom to create as He wills. God's omnipotence cannot be cabined by fixed natures and specific ends. His freedom and omnipotence entail that He can create in any way He chooses and that He cannot be limited by the species of things that were, again, tied to human reason through the Aristotelian essences. God's sovereignty requires, he thought, that we abandon the doctrine that all things have fixed natures.

This emphasis on God's sovereignty, omnipotence, and absolute freedom led Ockham, finally, to argue that morality depends simply on God's will, not on the realization of our human telos. Recall that Plato had asked in the *Euthyphro* (chapter 3) whether something is "good" because God has declared it so, or whether God declared it so because it is good. Is murder wrong because God has commanded us not to murder, or has He commanded us not to murder because it is (intrinsically) wrong? Plato answered that God prohibits things that are wrong and looks with favor upon things that are right because they *are* wrong or right. Acts such as murder are wrong in themselves, wrong "by nature".

But Ockham was suspicious of making God's commands dependent on moral principles that are independent of God's sovereignty and freedom. Plato's ethical naturalism seems to make God's will depend on independent moral standards, rather than these standards depending on God's will. Ockham thought that

---

[11] Once it is maintained that only individual "things" exist, it is difficult to see how something can be a "thing" without being a material thing. To exist is usually thought to mean that something has a spatial and temporal location, i.e., that it exists in space and time. But anything that exists in space and time is material. Thoughts, for example, must then either be physical processes in the brain or be entirely banished from the materialist's ontology. On the other hand, to maintain that a nonmaterial thought is a "thing" raises questions about whether other nonmaterial things—numbers, relations, laws of nature—exist. But these notions have been notoriously difficult to unpack without reverting to some conceptions of universals. See, e.g., Bertrand Russell, *The Problems of Philosophy* (New York: Barnes and Noble, 2004), 63–76.

this compromised God's omnipotence. In fact, Ockham insisted that God could command actions normally thought to be wrong (e.g., murder) or forbid acts normally thought to be required (e.g., He could command that we hate Him).[12] Thus, all moral standards are based on God's will, not on God's reason—a doctrine known as moral voluntarism.[13]

Ockham's moral voluntarism emphasized the importance of the will from the human side as well. Particular actions (e.g., murder or theft, on the one hand; self-sacrifice, on the other) are morally neutral, he argued. Ockham pointed out that a physical movement can be good or bad depending on the intention with which it is performed (e.g., pushing an old lady is a noble act if the actor is pushing her out of the path of an oncoming bus but an evil act if he is pushing her into the bus' path).[14] Thus, it is not the nature of the act but the character of our *willing*—the motives and purposes for which we act—that defines the moral quality of an act, according to Ockham. (Aquinas would have agreed but would have insisted that the intention is part of the act—that pushing an old lady out of the way is a different act from pushing her into the path of the bus.) At any rate, what makes an act "good" for Ockham is not that the act itself is good but that we act in ways that conform to the will of God—*because* it is the will of God. The highest pitch of human moral motivation is to love God above all else, and "to love God above all else is this: to love whatever God wants to be loved."[15]

---

[12] William of Ockham, *Commentary on the Sentences of Peter Lombard* 4.16.352. God can will anything but a contradiction, according to Ockham. Adams, "Ockham on Will, Nature, and Morality", 259.

[13] Recall that, for Aquinas, "good" and "bad" are reflections of God's eternal nature. Moral goodness and badness do not, therefore, depend on a specific act of God's will, nor would God violate His nature, or reason, by willing in contradiction to the Good. The natural good is a reflection of God's eternal goodness—a goodness that is not subject to change. See chapter 3 for a discussion of this.

[14] Recall that Aquinas recognized this feature of human action and defined *act* in a way that included the object of the action. An act, in other words, is the physical act along with the specific intention motivating the act. This has the added advantage of being consistent with the hylomorphic idea that the person is not split between two substances, physical and mental. An action is not simply a physical movement. It is a physical movement motivated by a specific intention. Two excellent treatments of these issues are Steven A. Long, *The Teleological Grammar of the Moral Act* (Naples, Fla.: Sapientia Press, 2007) and Romanus Cessario, *The Moral Virtues and Theological Ethics* (Notre Dame, Ind.: University of Notre Dame Press, 2008).

[15] See Peter King, "Ockham's Ethical Theory", in *The Cambridge Companion to Ockham*, 137.

To love God is to follow His will, and to follow His will is to fol-low His commandments.[16]

This was a fateful move in moral theory. By shifting the focus of morality away from the nature of our actions and onto the will (God's and ours), Ockham began to drive a wedge between nature and morality. It was the internal character of our will—and here we find something of Augustine's old notion that the will inclines either toward the things of God or the things of the world—that mattered most. The problem with this, from a natural law perspective, was that, pushed far enough, voluntarism drains the natural sources of our moral knowledge—especially our reason and *synderesis*—of all power to help us discern right from wrong. Natural law thinkers from Cicero to Aquinas pointed out that even the pagan knows that mur-der is wrong, independently of knowing anything about God's will. But if our knowledge of right and wrong depends on our knowledge of God's will, it becomes difficult to understand how we can possess any moral knowledge without this theological knowledge.

All of this had a profound effect on the postclassical understand-ing of the sources of moral knowledge. Faith and revelation slowly replaced reason and synderesis as conduits of moral knowledge: "Only faith gives us access to theological truths", Ockham declared. "The ways of God are not open to reason since God has freely chosen to create a world and establish a way of salvation within it apart from any necessary laws that human logic or rationality can uncover."[17] Ockham was thus the first to detach the moral law from the natu-ral order. In this respect, he was the intellectual ancestor of Hume and Kant, even as his theology foreshadowed that of later Protestant thinkers such as Luther and Calvin.

All of this proved immensely destructive of the natural law tradi-tion. For one thing, if God's moral order is solely a matter of what He

---

[16] Voluntarist conceptions of morality thus have a moral deontological focus. They tend to make the fundamental moral categories "right" and "wrong" rather than "good" and "bad". The "rightness" of an action is a matter of aligning one's act or one's will with the law, or with a command, whereas moral naturalism holds that goodness and badness are intrinsic to certain acts and are themselves linked to the achievement of some human good. Recall that Aquinas had argued that following God's will and pursuing the human good are consistent. But since Ockham thought that moral acts are themselves neutral, the focus of morality must be on the will, not on the act, and on the rightness, rather than the goodness, of our acts.

[17] Dale T. Irwin and Scott W. Sunquist, *History of the World Christian Movement* (Maryknoll, N.Y.: Orbis Books, 2001), 1, 434.

wills—and if, indeed, God can change His mind and will that murder or rape is good, for example—then morality becomes a highly mercurial affair subject to the changing whims of the divine Legislator. Reason is defenseless in a world of such mutable truths. If God can make murder morally good simply by willing it, nothing short of direct access to His will on every moral question, and at any given point (since He can always change His mind) will tell us what our obligations are. For us to be able to reason about morality, there have to be principles of good and bad intrinsic to moral actions themselves, principles that even the atheist can glean from the order of things in the world.

Not only does voluntarism undercut any human claim to be able to know and reason about moral truth without direct revelation, however; it also plays havoc with what it means to *do* the Good. It can lead away from an ethic of love and virtue and toward a narrow legalism, a morality of rule following.[18] Paradoxically, for a thinker such as Ockham, whose focus was always intensely on the rectitude of the will, voluntarism can lead less subtle minds toward a shallow pharisaism.

Ockham did not draw some of the more radical conclusions from his rejection of essences and universals, but others, beginning from similar assumptions, would. His denial of universals thus not only began a radical transformation of metaphysics; it powerfully influenced successor theories of morality and law.[19]

---

[18] Romanus Cessario, *The Moral Virtues and Theological Ethics*, 3. An ethic of rules, in turn, changes the nature of how we think about what it means for morality to be objectively knowable: if doing the Good was about rule following, rather than acting from our inward sources of virtue and goodness, knowing the Good also meant having a system of determinate rules and conclusions. This, perhaps ironically, drove modern moral thought into its equal but opposite extremes—moral rigorism (which requires that, to be "objective", moral conclusions must follow with deductive precision from a system of moral rules) and moral skepticism (which concludes that morality cannot be objective because no such deductive system of rules and conclusions exists).

[19] The voluntaristic cast of modern legal thought is also evident in modern attitudes to the validity of legal rules (i.e., to be "valid", a legal rule must issue from the will of the sovereign). Legal positivism was the successor to natural law theory in the nineteenth century. Legal positivists think of law as a system of rules. These rules, in turn, need not be reasonable or morally defensible to be legally valid. Rather, the essence of law was, as John Austin put it, "a command of the sovereign backed by threats". John Austin, *The Province of Jurisprudence Determined* (London: John Murray, 1832; Indianapolis: Hackett, 1998). Law is a function of political will, not reasonableness or goodness. When voluntarism is secularized, "the state becomes good and its positive will becomes the supreme norm of justice, admitting of no appeal." Heinrich Albert Rommen, *The Natural Law: A Study in Legal and Social History and Philosophy* (Indianapolis: Liberty Fund, 1998), 77.

Descartes: Between Two Worlds

Some trace the birth of modern philosophy to the night of November 10, 1619. On that evening, when shut up in a tiny, oven-heated room, the twenty-three-year-old French mathematician René Descartes (1596–1650) had three terrifying dreams. The night was the vigil of the feast of St. Martin of Tours, and Descartes, a devout Catholic, was on military campaign in northern Germany shortly after the onset of the Thirty Years' War. Descartes had been a sickly child and probably saw no fighting, helping out as a military engineer and writing mathematical and philosophical papers between military engagements. For several days he had been lamenting the "disunity and uncertainty" of the state of knowledge, suffering what he described as an escalating state of intense agitation and a "steady rise of temperature" in his head. He shut himself up in the room to warm himself and to meditate, but after a period of intense concentration, he fell asleep and had the three dreams in quick succession.

In the first, he was assailed by phantoms, thrown around violently by a whirlwind. He was plunged through the abyss of infinite space with no place to land—as if all his foundations had been cut out from beneath him. Suddenly he found himself on solid ground and was presented with a strange melon from an exotic land. The wind then abated, and the dream ended. Was the melon an offer of the fruit of modern science, or was it instead the gift of religious salvation? Descartes could not be certain.

In the second dream he found himself back in his room surrounded by thunderclaps with electrical sparks flying all around him. He found no peace, but there was exhilaration even as he was terrified. In the third and most provocatively allegorical dream, he found himself again in his room, this time in a quiet and contemplative mood. Two books were open before him: a dictionary and a compendium of poetry. His eyes glanced down at a verse in the second book and lit upon the question: "Quod vitae sectabor iter?" (Which path shall I take in life?) The dictionary seemed to represent the assembled facts of the sciences arranged in a cold but orderly fashion before him, whereas the book of poetry was the pursuit of wisdom and inspiration, the life of the spirit rather than matter. A stranger appeared and recited yet another verse: "Est et non" (yes and no). Descartes attempted to show the stranger the other question, but the book kept disappearing and reappearing until he woke up. More agitated than before, he began to pray and promised to go on a pilgrimage to Notre Dame de Lorette in Italy, a trip he took four years later.

Descartes interpreted his three dreams as an illuminated prediction, a divine prompting. The sparks and thunderclaps of the second dream represented intuition and inspiration, the stuff of poets, mystics, and religious visionaries. But this was not enough to give him true knowledge of the deepest mysteries of human life. What was needed was a unifying philosophy that could bridge what was even by his time the widening gulf between science and religion. He was convinced, as was Aquinas, that the two worlds could be united under one rationally knowable set of philosophical principles. He decided that his three dreams were sent to urge him to devote his life to working out a new unifying paradigm.[20]

Descartes lived during the greatest period of "disunity and uncertainty" in two thousand years. He was still an adolescent when, in 1610, Galileo published his defense of the heliocentric view of the solar system based on his observations with the newly invented telescope.[21] This flatly contradicted the geocentric view of the universe dominant since Aristotle's time. But, worse, it seemed to imperil the entire teleological theory of the universe.

Aristotle had concluded that all things in the universe were drawn to their "natural place", that solid bodies were drawn to the ground and gasses moved upward. Thus, he reasoned that the earth must be at the center of the universe, since objects naturally moved downward toward the earth, while the planets and stars revolved around it in a series of concentric circles. His geocentric theory of the universe

---

[20] Desmond M. Clarke, *Descartes: A Biography* (New York: Cambridge University Press, 2006), 58–59.

[21] Copernicus had begun the speculation in the late sixteenth century. He assumed that the world operated in teleological fashion but agreed that the Aristotelian-Ptolemaic system was much too complicated to be correct. In 1609, Johannes Kepler published his first two laws of planetary motion, rejecting Aristotle's geocentric theory and supporting the Copernican heliocentric theory. Perhaps ironically, Kepler attacked Aristotle's theory, not because he wanted to dispense with teleology but because he assumed that God's order had to have a simpler explanation. He quoted Plato to the effect that God was a geometer and argued that a heliocentric understanding of the solar system provided a far more elegant explanation of the movement of the sun and the planets. Galileo confirmed this with observations made with his telescope a year later. Edwin A. Burtt, *The Metaphysical Foundations of Modern Physical Science* (New York: Harcourt Brace, 1927), 53–54.

seemed consistent with astronomical conclusions at the time, but subsequent astronomers, including the second-century Egyptian Ptolemy, were forced to amend Aristotle's theory with an increasingly ponderous and ad hoc set of "epicycles" to make the theory conform to more recent observations. By the sixteenth century, the geocentric theory was laden with increasingly improbable amendments and assumptions. Galileo's discovery, built on the speculations of Copernicus and Kepler before him, ended these attempts to salvage the earth-centered universe.[22]

But the rejection of the geocentric theory had deeply philosophical and theological, as well as scientific, consequences. That the earth was not at the center of Creation seemed to challenge the very notion that man had a central place in the created order and that mankind was the defining achievement of God's plan. The more direct effect of Galileo's observations, however, was to throw into question Aristotle's entire theory of the world. If his physics was incorrect, why should we retain his metaphysical system, which was based, after all, on the same teleological assumptions?

Of course, the teleological view of the world did not depend on Aristotle's physics or the geocentric picture of the universe. God can operate through final causes without the earth being at the physical center of the universe. The assumption that mankind could be at the center of Creation only if the earth was at the physical center of the universe was the product not only of ignorance but of hubris.[23] Indeed, Aquinas doubted the Aristotelian-Ptolemaic model, insisting that it "falls short of a convincing proof, for possibly the phenomenon might be explained on some other supposition".[24]

---

[22] The second-century Egyptian astronomer Ptolemy introduced "epicycles", in which the celestial bodies traveled around the earth, as Aristotle thought, but also traveled in smaller cycles around the trajectory of their larger orbits—circles within circles—which harmonized the geocentric theory with astronomical observations.

[23] As the psalmist declares:

> When I look at your heavens, the work of your fingers,
>   the moon and the stars which you have established;
> what is man that you are mindful of him,
>   and the son of man that you care for him?

Psalm 8:3–4.

[24] Thomas Aquinas, *De Coelo*, II, 17. For a discussion on Aquinas' views of the Aristotelian account, see Edward Feser, *The Last Superstition* (South Bend, Ind.: St. Augustine's Press, 2008), 173.

Nevertheless, nominalism and the discovery that the earth was not at the center of God's order contributed to a widening skepticism about the teleological picture of the world. The best thinkers of the time—Kepler, Galileo, and the father of the scientific method, Francis Bacon—continued to cling to the spiritual core of the teleological model but treated its assumptions as a postulate of metaphysics rather than science. Bacon conceded to the older model that "true knowledge is knowledge by causes" and that causes "are not improperly distributed into four kinds: the material, the formal, the efficient and the final".[25] But he also insisted that since the formal and final causes could not be directly empirically observed, scientific inquiry had to bracket them. Descartes, too, accepted the reality of final causes but dismissed their empirical relevance, cautioning, "We should not take it upon ourselves to believe that God could take us into his counsel."[26]

It is little wonder that Descartes' search for truth began with an all-consuming doubt. The physical sciences were undergoing the greatest paradigm shift in history, and philosophy was of no help since, as Descartes lamented, "[I]t has been studied for many centuries by the most outstanding minds without having produced anything which is not in dispute."[27] A kind of revolutionary conservatism took hold of the young mind. Not the attainment of truth, but the avoidance of error, he wrote in the *Meditations*, "comprises the greatest and principal perfection of man".[28] We should accept nothing as true that can be doubted. Only those propositions of which we have a "clear and distinct idea" should form the foundation of our knowledge. Only from these indubitable foundations can we build up our world of beliefs. All propositions must be broken down into their simplest forms, analyzed, and then reassembled as part of our system

[25] Francis Bacon, *Novum Organum*, published as *The New Organon* (New York: Cambridge University Press, 2000), sec. 2.2.

[26] René Descartes, *The Philosophical Works of Descartes*, trans. Elizabeth S. Haldane (Cambridge: Cambridge University Press, 1912), 1:230. Cf. "For what man can learn the counsel of God? / Or who can discern what the Lord wills?" (Wis 9:13).

[27] René Descartes, *Discourse on Method and Meditations*, trans. Laurence J. LaFleur (Upper Saddle River, N.J.: Prentice Hall, 1952), 8.

[28] Descartes, *Meditations on First Philosophy* 4, in Descartes, *Discourse on Method and Meditations*, 117.

of accepted knowledge.[29] The search for knowledge, he said, was like going through a barrel of apples one by one, discarding the rotten ones lest they contaminate the others.

And that one pristine apple from which all hope for real knowledge begins, Descartes was to argue, was none other than St. Augustine's old insight. As Descartes put it, "Cogito ergo sum" (I think, therefore I am).[30] I can doubt the existence of the entire physical world, but even in this act of radical doubt, I cannot be wrong that I exist. With this, Descartes began modern philosophy, inverting the classical understanding of the relationship between metaphysics and epistemology. Aristotle and St. Thomas thought that we must know how the world works before we can understand the mechanism of human knowledge. Descartes began from exactly the opposite direction: we must have clear criteria for truth and knowledge before we can venture out into the world of facts. Here was the defining break with classical philosophy: epistemology is prior to metaphysics, Descartes in effect argued. Before all else, we must have a method, a reliable process for truth gathering. We must know *how* we know before we can know *what* we know.

Descartes is considered the father of modern rationalism, one of two approaches to epistemology that succeeded the Scholastic theory of knowledge. The other approach, empiricism, was championed by John Locke, as we will see in the next section. The essence of rationalism is the belief that there are certain truths that can be known by reason alone, independently of sense experience (which can always deceive us). These truths are built into the very fabric of the intellect. Mathematics was Descartes' paradigm for knowledge since every mathematical truth is known with certainty and is connected to every other mathematical truth by an operation of logic. Descartes' method was an attempt to approximate the same degree of precision as Euclid achieved in his system of geometry. And it led Descartes to some of the most stunning intellectual achievements since Euclid's time.

---

[29] Descartes' method consisted of four rules: first, never accept anything as true unless it is "certainly" and "evidently" true. Second, analyze all problems into their component parts. Third, start with the simplest of these and work through them to the more difficult. Fourth, make enumerations so general and complete that nothing is omitted. Descartes, *Discourse on Method* 2, in Descartes, *Discourse on Method and Meditations*, 15.

[30] Descartes, *Discourse on Method* 4, in Descartes, *Discourse on Method and Meditations*, 25.

In his essay on *Optics*, which he appended to the *Discourse on Method*, he was the first to advance the wave theory of light, a theoretical account of farsightedness and nearsightedness, a theory of lenses, and a theory of the light-gathering powers of the telescope. His was also the first empirically accurate account of space perception. In another appendix, the *Meteorology*, he provided the first scientific outline of meteorological science and advanced the kinetic theory of heat. In the *Geometry*, he single-handedly invented analytic geometry, the most important mathematical discovery since the ancient Greeks.[31] All this came as appendices to his *Discourse on Method*.

Yet rationalism had a darker legacy over the longer haul. It fostered, in more reckless minds, an intellectual subjectivism, a turning away from experience in favor of a world of self-generated truths. That the philosopher can sit in his armchair and arrive at systems of metaphysics and politics without the benefit of empirical experience, especially the accumulated experience of tradition and custom, would have struck Aristotle and Aquinas as both preposterous and dangerous. Rationalism severed reason from the rest of the human personality and sundered the mind from the body. Where the Scholastics saw understanding as a power of the whole person, accomplished by the joint action of sense and reason, body and mind, it became the province of the rational mind alone for Descartes. In this respect, Descartes' theory was one powerful source of the individualism of the coming modern age.[32]

Descartes' second great break with the older Scholastic tradition was in the realm of metaphysics. With Bacon, he insisted that

---

[31] Laurence J. LaFleur, introduction to Descartes, *Discourse on Method and Meditations*, xiv–xvi.

[32] In fact, Descartes' rationalism and Locke's empiricism (as we will see next) each took half of the older Scholastic whole, epistemologically. Understanding was, for Aristotle and Aquinas, a power of the whole person, accomplished by the joint action of sense and reason. In fact, it was Aristotle and Aquinas, and not John Locke, who insisted that knowledge passes through the senses to the intellect. The doctrine of innate ideas seemed to place truth in the mind, rather than in the world. Rationalism and empiricism thus represent a splitting of the mechanism of human understanding as the Scholastics conceived it. Rationalists, including Descartes, Spinoza, and Leibniz, and empiricists such as Locke, Berkeley, and Hume each took half of the older unity—rationalists insisting that knowledge is a feature of reason alone, and the empiricists insisting that it is a feature of sense experience. Rommen, *The Natural Law*, 77, 143–45.

Aristotle's formal and final causes had to be bracketed in the name of science. Where Ockham treaded lightly, Descartes pushed ahead boldly. Nature had to be understood mechanistically—as a system of cause-and-effect occurrences in which everything that happens, happens by necessity. Democritus' old determinism had returned to the world, but it clashed inevitably with the Christian paradigm of free will and responsibility that Descartes explicitly accepted. Confronted with this head-on clash of paradigms, Descartes attempted to split the difference. He accepted the mechanistic explanation of physical phenomena in nature but drew a metaphysical line in the sand, separating the world of Nature from the world of Mind.

Descartes' solution was dualism. He divided the world into two distinct substances—the *res extensa* of the material world, which operates mechanistically, and the *res cogitans* of the free thinking mind. This was a significant departure from Aristotle's and Aquinas' conception that each material thing constitutes a distinct and unique substance composed of form and matter. Descartes retained the word *substance* but fundamentally altered its meaning. Man was not a unified substance of form and matter, soul and body, but two distinct substances—mind and matter—that must somehow interact with each other. Descartes' mind-body dualism led to a plethora of philosophical problems. He could not really explain how the nonmaterial mind causes actions in the physical body. Indeed, in equating the physical with extension in space and distinguishing this from the mental, his theory implied that the mind and its contents did not exist in space at all. How, then, could a thought or intention cause a change in the physical body? There were other problems as well. Descartes' dualism seemed to relegate the body to a kind of second-class status compared with the mind, just as Plato's theory had in antiquity. We will explore the fallout from Cartesian dualism in the next chapter.

But there were even bigger problems—theological problems—for dualism seemed to isolate God from the world in the same way that it insulated the mind from the body. The increasingly mechanistic account of nature explained all natural phenomena as the result of cause-and-effect laws of nature. The more that could be explained in this fashion, the less there was for God to do. As God was no longer needed to explain the immediate physical causes of the world, philosophy lurched toward the deism of the eighteenth century.

Deism came in various flavors. Some, including some of the founders of the United States, continued to think in specifically Christian terms.[33] For others, God was simply the Creator and first efficient cause of the world, and nothing more. The "divine watchmaker" set up the line of dominoes and kicked the first one over but had no reason to intervene after that. He did not answer prayers or perform miracles. Increasingly the central dogma of the Christian religion itself—the Resurrection of Christ—was questioned. God was retained as the distant First Designer of the world, but the substance of Christianity became purely ethical—a religion of good deeds but with little in the way of any genuinely religious content.

Blaise Pascal taunted Descartes with the charge of being a closet deist: "Descartes could not avoid prodding God to set the world in motion with a snap of his lordly fingers; after that he had no use for God." Perhaps for this reason, in part, Descartes compensated by investing God with a self-evidence that went far beyond anything Aquinas could have countenanced. He wrote that "there is surely nothing I know earlier or more easily than facts about God." Whereas Aquinas cautiously asserted that our knowledge of God is derivative of our a posteriori knowledge of the world—that we can deduce God's existence only from the order of the world—Descartes insisted that knowledge of God is innate, a first principle of knowledge. "[T]he existence of God should pass, in my mind, as at least as certain as I have hitherto considered all the truths of mathematics."[34] In this way, that peculiar modern blend of cautious skepticism and reckless intellectual audacity entered the stream of modern thought.

John Locke and the Decline of the Natural Law

There are two contrasting views about John Locke's (1632–1704) place in intellectual history. The first holds that Locke was the last of the premodern thinkers, a philosopher for whom God and the natural law still play a foundational role in moral and political thought.

[33] For a recent discussion of this see, David L. Holmes, *The Faiths of the Founding Fathers* (New York: Oxford University Press, 2006), 39–52.

[34] Descartes, *Meditations on First Philosophy* 5, in Descartes, *Discourse on Method and Meditations*, 120–21.

The second is that he was, with Thomas Hobbes, the first genuinely modern political thinker.

The truth, however, is that Locke was both of these. The *Second Treatise of Government*, which defended limited government, the social contract, and individual rights, is the first genuine exemplar of the modern liberal political tradition. Yet Locke set his liberalism in the framework of theism and the natural law. His *Essay concerning Human Understanding*, his most important philosophical work, is the fount of modern empiricism, yet, throughout the *Essay*, his faith and common sense serve as a counterweight to some of empiricism's more radical conclusions.[35] In general, however, the spirit of his *Essay* runs so entirely counter to the natural law assumptions of the *Second Treatise of Government* that the two can scarcely be reconciled.[36] In fact, Locke became infuriated when a close friend pointed out the inconsistencies, and he responded that the two works must simply be read apart from one another.[37]

Why should such a brilliant thinker have been so notoriously ambivalent? The tensions cannot be explained away by suggesting that Locke changed his mind over time, since he worked simultaneously during the 1680s on both the *Treatises* and the *Essay*, the two being published within a year of each other. The only plausible answer is that Locke was conflicted. The *Second Treatise of Government*, arguably liberalism's founding charter, required Locke to appeal to a skein of natural rights based on some conception of the natural law. But because he was a Protestant, it could not be the *old* natural law that had been used to prop up the divine right of kings and the authority of the Church. A moderate solvent was required. God and *something*

---

[35] Richard Ashcraft, *Locke's Two Treatises of Government* (Boston: Allen and Unwin, 1987), 1. For the view that Locke is among the first of the moderns and, indeed, a radical thinker, see Julian H. Franklin, *John Locke and the Theory of Sovereignty: Mixed Monarchy and the Right of Resistance in the Political Thought of the English Revolution* (New York: Cambridge University Press, 1978). And for the opposite view that he must be seen as the last of the classical thinkers, see James Tully, *A Discourse on Property: John Locke and His Adversaries* (New York: Cambridge University Press, 1980).

[36] As one of the foremost of contemporary Locke scholars has remarked, "It is pointless to look upon his work as an integrated body of speculation and generalization, with a general philosophy at its centre, and as its architectural framework." Peter Laslett, "Locke and Hobbes", in John Locke, *The Two Treatises of Government*, ed. Peter Laslett (New York: Cambridge Univeristy Press, 2009), 87.

[37] Laslett, "Locke and Hobbes", 79–83.

of the natural law had to be preserved, but the appeal to teleology and Descartes' innate ideas had to go.

Descartes, nevertheless, had been an imposing influence in Locke's thought. Locke became familiar with Descartes' philosophy while in exile in France in the late 1670s. He wrote in his journal that it was Descartes who first taught him the love of philosophy, and in many ways he followed Descartes' metaphysical positions, perhaps most importantly Descartes' mind-body dualism.[38] But Locke's chief difference with Descartes concerned their respective understandings of the mechanisms of human knowledge—a difference that had significant religious and political consequences. Descartes, the Catholic, was the father of modern rationalism, and Locke, the Protestant, the father of empiricism. As Locke and the empiricists saw it, Descartes' doctrine of innate ideas retained the lingering vestiges of the older Scholasticism while exaggerating claims that certain metaphysical or theological truths were self-evident, irrefutable, and not subject to the dis-verification of the senses.

Locke's empiricism, however, was an overreaction to Descartes' overreaction. Aristotle and Aquinas would have agreed with Locke that "nothing is in the head that is not first in the senses"—the central assumption of any moderate empiricism. But Locke moved beyond Thomas' moderate empiricism in one direction, just as Descartes went beyond it in the opposite direction. In his *Essay*, Locke maintained not only that all knowledge comes through the senses but that there are no inborn structures of human understanding that precede and mediate our experience of the world. Man is born a tabula rasa, "like a piece of paper" on which the world writes.[39]

Locke's tabula rasa theory of human personality amounted to a rejection not only of Descartes' innate ideas but of Aquinas' synderesis. There is no inborn moral template that, under the right conditions, matures into conscience. At points in the *Second Treatise*,

---

[38] The particulars of Locke's mind-body dualism might differ from Descartes'. Some have argued that he did not believe mind and body were two distinct substances, as Descartes did, since he was skeptical of the idea of substance generally. But, minimally, he believed that mental and physical properties were distinct kinds of properties, making Locke what is known today as a "property dualist". Edward Feser, *The Last Superstition*, 286n23. In the next chapter, we will discuss Locke's conception of substance as it relates to the concept of personhood.

[39] John Locke, *An Essay concerning Human Understanding* 1.2.1.

when he wanted to emphasize the importance of the natural law, Locke reverted to the notion that the moral law was "written on the heart".[40] But these passages are the exception. In the *Essay*, Locke attempted systematically to dismantle synderesis and its corollary doctrines, for example, that knowledge of the natural law can be corrupted or destroyed by bad education.[41] He similarly denied that the natural law inclines us, in our nonrational dispositions, toward the Good. "Principles of action indeed there are lodged in men's appetites, but these are so far from being innate moral principles that if they were left to full swing they would carry men to the overturning of all morality."[42]

Nor, when we look at the practices of men, is there a universal tendency to human decency that should be evident if the natural law were written on the hearts of men. Quite the contrary:

> View but an army at the sacking of a town, and see what observation, or what sense of moral principles, or what touch of conscience, for all the outrages they do. *Robberies, murders, rapes* are the sports of men set at liberty from punishment and censure. Have there not been whole nations, and those of the most civilized people, among whom, the exposing of their children, and leaving them in the fields, to perish by want or wild beasts, has been the practice, as little condemned or scrupled, as the begetting them? Do they not still, in some countries, put them into the same graves with their mothers, if they die in

[40] He wrote, for example, that "Cain was so convinced that everyone had a right to destroy [him] that, after the murder of his brother, every one that findeth me shall slay me, so plain was it writ in the hearts of all mankind." John Locke, *Second Treatise of Government* 11.

[41] His arguments frequently made straw men of the Scholastic understanding of synderesis and conscience. For example, in asserting that it is no defense of synderesis to argue that our natural knowledge can be lost or corrupted, he maintains that, if this is true, we should find the purest expressions of synderesis in children and in the uneducated, whose consciences have not been deformed by poor education. Locke, *Human Understanding* 1.3.20. But Aquinas and other defenders of synderesis were hardly so naive as to assume that a child or a person in the state of nature was inevitably beneficent. Synderesis is like the capacity to do mathematics, Aquinas says. Like the capacity to do complex mathematics, moral reasoning must be honed by education in order to serve its function.

[42] Locke, *Human Understanding* 1.3.3. This may be in tension, again, with Locke's more pacific view of man in the state of nature as portrayed in the *Second Treatise of Government*. There, Locke is hardly as pessimistic as Hobbes in his own account of the state of nature as "solitary, poor, nasty, brutish and short". Man in the state of nature was, for Locke, self-interested but sociable and ultimately reasonable.

childbirth; or dispatch them, if a pretended astrologer declares them to have unhappy stars? And are there not places, where at a certain age, they kill, or expose their parents without any remorse at all?[43]

For Locke, the Puritan, there was little trace of any inborn morality in natural man. Law and human nature are set against one another. The natural law was no longer "in us", an affirmative principle that moves us by love toward our natural end, as it was for Aquinas. For Locke, the natural law was purely external and largely prohibitive in character. It was imposed from the outside, grounded in the commands of God, and buttressed by God's natural sanctions, pain and pleasure.[44]

All this meant that Locke had to stake out a middle ground between the Scholastics, Descartes, and others who held that the moral law is innate, and those, like Hobbes and other materialists, who denied the moral law altogether:

> There is a great deal of difference between an innate law and a law of nature, between something imprinted on our minds in this very original, and something which we being ignorant of may attain to the knowledge of, by the use and due application of our natural faculties. And I think they equally forsake the truth, who running into the contrary extremes, either affirm an innate law, or deny that there is a law.[45]

The natural law is real, but it is "out there" and not "in here". It is something to be learned—by "due application of our natural faculties"[46]—through reason and experience, guided by the natural sanctions of pain and pleasure.

---

[43] Locke, *Human Understanding* 1.3.9.

[44] "But what duty is, cannot be understood without a law," Locke wrote, "nor a law be known, or supposed without a lawmaker, or without reward and punishment." Locke, *Human Understanding* 3.3.12. Locke's voluntarism and his empiricism reinforced each other in this respect. Since there are no innate sources of moral knowledge, and since all moral knowledge comes from experience alone (as empiricism teaches), all moral obligations must arise from external sources, usually expressed in imperative form as commands of the divine will (as voluntarism teaches) and conveyed through pleasurable and painful sanctions (as both empiricism and voluntarism can consistently claim).

[45] Locke, *Human Understanding* 3.3.13.

[46] Ibid., 1.3.13.

But then we find the same ambivalence about reason that we saw in Locke's wavering commitment to human conscience. In the *Second Treatise* reason was "the common rule and measure God hath given to mankind", whereas in his *Reasonableness of Christianity* he lamented that "human reason unassisted failed men in its great and proper business of morality. It never from unquestionable principles, by clear deductions, made out an entire body of the 'law of nature'."[47] Pleasure and pain are the real spurs to human action, and they are also the only worldly criteria by which we can judge good and bad.[48] Had Locke fully worked out a moral theory, it would have been essentially utilitarian with a backdrop of divine command theory. "[V]irtue is approved ... because it is profitable", though, he hastened to add, the ultimate basis for good and evil is God's will.[49]

Locke's most devastating revision of the natural law tradition, however, was the result of his individualism. With Hobbes, Rousseau, and other social contract thinkers, Locke helped invert the classical understanding of the relationship between the individual and the State. The entire classical political tradition from Aristotle on held that "the state is by nature prior to the individual."[50] By this Aristotle had meant that the State was formally prior to the individual, as form is prior to matter. It is the State, conceived as society and all its institutions, that gives us our humanity. But this priority also means that the State is a natural end of the individual, a natural outgrowth of our human essence. Society and its political institutions are an organic expression of the human telos. For Locke and the social contract theorists, on the other hand, the State was artificial, the product of a contract grounded in self-interest. Where

---

[47] John Locke, *The Reasonableness of Christianity as Delivered in the Scriptures* 7.139–40, cited in Peter Laslett, "Locke and Hobbes", 88–89.

[48] Locke, *Human Understanding* 1.3.13.

[49] Ibid., 1.3.6.

[50] Cf. Aristotle, *Politics* 1.2. Aristotle was no collectivist in the modern sense, of course. He thought the State exists for the benefit of creating the conditions of the good life for the individual, but he also taught that the State was prior to the individual in a *formal* sense— that the individual apart from the State is not fully human. Aristotle taught the eminently sensible thesis that our social life is literally *constitutive* of our humanity; the man in the state of nature is less than fully human. To put it in modern terms, we become individuals *by being socialized*. Locke found in the state of nature the kind of individual that Aristotle thought could be found only in civilized society—a rational individual who can be morally bound by his commitments and promises.

classical political thinkers had always assumed that the chief end of
the State was the perfection of man himself, Locke declared that
the chief end of government is the protection of "property", a term
he used to refer not simply to one's estates and possessions but to the
totality of one's individual rights.

These developments represented a hardening of the division
between the individual and the State. The State was to become, in
subsequent liberal theory, a "public" realm divided from the "private" sphere of the individual, the family, and immediate social relationships. Rights came to have a defensive and insulative function
against society and especially the State. Locke and other social contract thinkers inverted the very relationship between the social good
and individual rights. The Good was prior to individual rights for the
Scholastics: a right, for them, was simply any individual claim deriv-
able from the common good. Aquinas used the term *ius*, translated
as "what is just" or "right", to refer to these claims. Ius was not a
moral power of the person, let alone an individual "trump" against
the collective welfare, as rights came to be thought of later in liberal
thought. It was simply any claim that followed from the overall social
order. Since it was wrong to murder an innocent person, the ius
prohibited doing others harm. Rights were simply derivative of "right
order". Scholastic thinkers would have found the modern idea of
having a "right to do what is wrong" impossibly self-contradictory.

This conception of ius began to break down in later Scholastic
and early Enlightenment thought.[51] Though Locke still based rights
on the natural law, reconceived as divine commands, they were for
him *prior to* the overall moral good, rather than being *derived from* the
overall good. They were conceived negatively as limits on the power

---

[51] Late Scholastic thinkers in the sixteenth century, particularly Vitorio, Suarez, and
Vasquez began to think of rights as moral powers of the individual. Elements of Ockham's
voluntarism are apparent, e.g., that original sin had destroyed the natural moral law, making
moral speculation from nature impossible. Rommen, *The Natural Law*, 51–61. Early Enlightenment thinkers followed by detaching moral truth from metaphysics. For some, like Hugo
Grotius, reason assumed an almost autonomous function: moral truth is a feature of reason, not of the world. In fact, moral truth would be exactly the same "even if we should
concede that which cannot be conceded without the utmost wickedness, that there is no God,
or that the affairs of men are of no concern to Him". Hugo Grotius, *On the Law of War and
Peace*, Prolegomena 11. Rommen provides an excellent description of the breakdown of the
older natural law tradition from Grotius in *The Natural Law*, 62–96.

of government. The content of individual rights flowed, moreover, not from the human good but from a principle of self-ownership. Because we are by nature rational, we are morally sovereign over ourselves. Each individual possesses a right of self-ownership and a general liberty of acting from his will that prohibits any other person from compelling or coercing him in violation of his natural rights.[52]

The will—God's will in framing the natural law and man's will in consenting to his social and political obligations—now replaced reason and Nature as the source of all moral obligation. Individual consent, the self-binding of the will through promise making, and not the good of the individual man or society, became the touchstone for political legitimacy. The express or tacit consent of the individual became the cement by which all social and political institutions, from the family to the State, were built up and held together, subject only to the limitation that the individual could not alienate his own natural right to self-ownership. Locke's political thought was a legacy of Ockham's voluntarism and the harbinger of more recent liberalism, which makes personal choice the ultimate foundation for morality and politics.

Thomas Hobbes: The Rebirth of Materialism

Like Locke, Thomas Hobbes (1588–1679) lived during the English Civil War, but Hobbes drew radically different conclusions from the experience than the much younger Locke.[53] He was born in 1588, the year the English burned the Spanish Armada. Though he came from middling beginnings—his father was the vicar of Westport—his genius was recognized early by others. A wealthy uncle sent him at the age of fourteen to Oxford, where he spent the next five or six years. After completing his studies, he became tutor to the son of

---

[52] Locke wrote, "We are born free, as we are born rational." Locke, *Second Treatise of Government* 61.

[53] Hobbes was already fifty-four when the English Civil War broke out. His political opinions, particularly his exaltation of centralized authority, were long formed by this point. The Thirty Years' War on the Continent and the peace forcibly imposed by the Huguenot French king Henry of Navarre were probably more formative of his beliefs about the importance of a strong sovereign. Stephen Priest, *The British Empiricists* (London: Penguin Books, 1990), 17–18.

William Cavendish, the Earl of Devonshire and a leading scientist in his own right. Later he was mathematics tutor to the future Charles II. Everywhere he went, Hobbes found his way into the most influential intellectual circles. He traveled to Italy, where he met Galileo, and returned to England, where he was befriended by Francis Bacon. In the 1640s, he met Descartes, two years before the latter's death.

Unlike Locke, Hobbes was a royalist. In 1640, shortly before the outbreak of the English Civil War, he fled to France, where he remained for a decade. It was toward the end of his stay when he met Descartes. Though Hobbes had written a work objecting to Descartes' *Meditations*, the meeting was apparently cordial. Nevertheless, Descartes thought Hobbes' view of the state of nature much too pessimistic, and Hobbes confided that he thought Descartes a hypocrite for defending religious doctrines he secretly doubted. Hobbes published his most remembered work, *Leviathan*, in 1651, having returned to England after making his peace with the Commonwealth.

A metaphysical radical and yet a political conservative, Hobbes was a monarchist who denied the doctrine of the divine right of kings. His materialism and his support for strong centralized authority sprang from a common root. The human condition was for Hobbes a "warre of every one against every one" in which self-interested individuals, driven by the fear of death and the quest for security and power, clash in a world of limited resources. Human behavior is driven by passion, not reason. With Hobbes, reason began its gradual demotion to instrument of the passions. Hobbes understood all actions as expressions of self-interested desire. Even apparent acts of altruism were disguised expressions of egoism.[54] In this context, only a powerful centralized State could counteract the centrifugal forces of human nature. Hobbes was thus the first of

[54] Indeed, altruism was a metaphysical impossibility for Hobbes, since all actions are produced by egoistic desires. A non-self-interested act was virtually a contradiction in terms since all acts are motivated by desires and all desires have as their focus some aspect of the individual's well-being. In the *Leviathan*, Hobbes describes all motivating factors in human nature as a function of self-seeking appetites and aversions. Hobbes, *Leviathan*, 19. A biographer tells the story of how a clergyman caught Hobbes giving alms to a beggar and accused him of inconsistency. Hobbes responded that he gave the money to the man because it made him (Hobbes) feel better. John Aubrey, *Brief Lives*, ed. John Buchanan-Brown (New York: Penguin Classics, 2000).

several modern thinkers to draw the (potentially) totalitarian consequences from materialism.[55]

Hobbes rejected the teleological worldview root and branch. Philosophy, he said, concerns only the observable physical world and
"excludes theology, I mean the doctrine of God, eternal, ingener-
able, incomphrehensible".[56] He denied, as Ockham, Descartes, and
Bacon did not, the reality of final causes, reducing these to efficient and material causes.[57] He did not disguise his contempt for
all things Aristotelian, dismissing forms, essences, and substances as
pure fictions produced by using language in imprecise and even self-
contradictory ways.[58] Plato's universals were simply produced by
language's tendency to reify things, to turn adjectives into nouns.
Whereas even Ockham admitted the existence of qualities (e.g., the
appearance of red, the smell of a rose, the sound of a bell), Hobbes
denied these "secondary qualities" as projections of the mind that
are not really "in the things themselves".[59] He denied the existence
of relations (e.g., being greater than) and dismissed space and time
as "phantasms" of the mind.[60] All of this was a further extension of
Ockham's nominalism.

Hobbes was, in sum, the first important materialist since Epicurus.
All that exists, he argued, are bodies—corporeal things that have
physical extension in space. The concept of a "spiritual substance",

[55] In fairness to Hobbes, he was not truly a totalitarian in the modern sense, since he recognized that there would be spheres of society left relatively untouched by the State. On the
other hand, his insistence that the sovereign is to be the sole judge of right and wrong, and of
religious orthodoxy, bears the mark of later totalitarian thinkers. Even before Marx's dialectical materialism, agnostic thinkers frequently sought refuge from the vicissitudes of human
nature in the bosom of a strong, centralized State.

[56] Thomas Hobbes, *The English Works of Thomas Hobbes of Malmesbury*, ed. William
Molesworth (London: J. Bohn, 1839), 1:10.

[57] "A final cause has no place except in such things as have sense and will; and this also I
shall prove hereafter to be an efficient cause." Hobbes, "Concerning Body", 2.9.5 in Thomas
Hobbes, *Works* 1.123, cited in Copleston, *A History of Philosophy*, 5:22.

[58] These names, which are "taken up and learned by rote from the schooles as hypostati-
cal [substance], transubstantiation, consubstantiate, eternal-Now and the like: canting of the
schooles." Hobbes, *Leviathan*, 115.

[59] Hobbes, *Leviathan*, 107. Locke called these "secondary qualities", and Hobbes agreed
with Locke that they are subjective in nature, as compared with primary qualities such as the
length or extension of a thing. There is an excellent discussion of the distinction in Edward
Feser, *Locke* (Oxford: Oneworld, 2007), 48–51.

[60] Hobbes, *Leviathan*, 102–3.

as with the Cartesian or Platonic soul, is an oxymoron; it was not so much false as downright *meaningless*. Even God, if He exists at all—and Hobbes frequently made reference to Him, if for no other reason than prudence—must be a physical object, a material body that exists in space.[61] What classical thinkers took for granted as objective and real, Hobbes banished altogether from ontology or placed in the mind of the subject. Bereft of the forms and essences by which human reason participates in the objective world, the very notion of truth fell in upon itself. Truth and falsity, for Hobbes, as for his many modern followers, is not a measure of the correspondence between our subjective judgments and objective facts in the world. "True and False are attributes of Speech", he wrote, "and not of Things."[62]

Hobbes' materialism was a rude rebuke to the classical understanding of the person. Human consciousness was, for him, nothing but matter in motion. As with the materialists of antiquity, he was also a determinist. Everything that happens follows necessarily from prior causes. Given those causes, nothing could occur but the event that does occur. His determinism thus left no room for Descartes' freedom of the will. Nor, as an empiricist, did Hobbes have any sympathy for any occult capacities such as the faculty of the will standing over the flux of passions and desires. What earlier thinkers called the "will" was simply "the last Appetite, or Aversion, immediately

[61] Hobbes was certainly accused of atheism in his own time. In correspondence with Bishop Bramhall, however, he described God as "a most pure and simple corporeal spirit" and as "a thin, fluid, transparent, invisible body". Copleston, *A History of Philosophy*, 5:8. Hobbes' God reminds us of the ancient materialists' view that the gods were made of the finest and most subtle atoms (see chapter 1). At any rate, whether Hobbes was a prudent atheist or simply a very unorthodox theist, though still debated, is less important than the consequences of his argument. Since the idea of an immaterial substance is impossible for him, it appears that there can be no human soul in the Platonic or Cartesian sense. And since Hobbes rejected the entire Aristotelian philosophy, he could not appeal to Aristotle's or Thomas' idea of the soul as the substantial form of the body.

[62] This view of truth makes it difficult to connect knowledge to the real world. Truth was, for Aristotle, Aquinas, and the Scholastics, a correspondence between subjective judgment and objective fact. For Hobbes, truth links only words together. Without the concept of form and essence, which connect (subjective) judgment to (objective) fact, all that was left of truth for Hobbes was the "right ordering" of words. "Truth consisteth of the right ordering of names." Hobbes, *Leviathan*, 105. The problem with this is that it makes all true statements tautologies or forms of question begging. More importantly, the link between subjective judgment and object fact is lost. To say, "It is raining outside" is to make a statement of objective fact, whose truth depends not merely on the ordering of words but on facts as they are in the world.

adhering to the action or the omission thereof". Deliberation was nothing but the clash of desires and aversions that "continue[s] till the thing be done, or thought impossible".[63] After Aquinas' highly nuanced five-step analysis of decision making, Hobbes' explication of the mechanism of human choice represents a catastrophic deflation of the active dimension of human personality.

Hobbes' moral theory, like Epicurus' two thousand years earlier, was a matter of rational self-interest. There are no eternal moral truths. In the state of nature, "every man has a Right to everything, even to one another's body."[64] All morality comes into existence with the creation of the social contract since "where there is no Commonwealth, there nothing is Unjust."[65] The foundation of all morality, moreover, is the making of the contract itself—the binding of oneself by a promise. This promise can have moral effect, moreover, only when there is someone to enforce it. As a radical voluntarist, Hobbes could not even conceive of the *existence* of a moral principle in the absence of its enforceability. "Therefore, before the names Just and Unjust can have place, there must be some coercive Power, to compel men equally to the performance of our Covenants."[66]

Hobbes thus thoroughly secularized the voluntarism of Ockham and later Locke. With both of these thinkers he agreed that there are no duties without law, no law without a lawmaker, and no lawmaker without the power to punish violations of these duties.[67] But where Ockham and Locke believed in a God-made law, Hobbes did not. Moral obligations arise by an act of will, a promise of one man to another, and they are given effect by another act of will—by the sovereign's willingness to enforce the promise of punishment. The State is now the source and support for all morality. It is little wonder that Hobbes refers to the sovereign as "the Mortall God".

Hobbes wrote of the natural law, but he meant nothing like what Locke, let alone Aquinas, had meant by the term. *Natural law*

---

[63] Hobbes, *Leviathan*, 127.
[64] Ibid., 190.
[65] Ibid., 202.
[66] Ibid.
[67] Cf. Locke, *Human Understanding* 3.3.12 with Hobbes: "The desires and passions of a man are themselves no sin. No more are the actions that proceed from those actions until they know a law which forbids them; which till laws be made, they cannot know, nor can any law be made, till they have agreed upon the person that shall make it." Hobbes, *Leviathan*, 202.

referred to the rules of conduct that we construct artificially to quell the "warre of every one against everyone". It is nothing more or less than the rationally derived man-made rules of conduct necessary to preserve social order and peace, given what Hobbes took to be the vicious and self-interested condition of human nature.[68] In stark contrast to Aquinas, or even Locke, Hobbes gave the ideas of right and law contrasting meanings. A right was simply the natural freedom to do what one wants to do, so long as he is able. Thus, "there is nothing to which every man had not Right by Nature." A man has a "right" to take the entire world if only he possesses the strength to do it. Law is what restrains him: it is the system of rules made by the sovereign to constrain the exercise of our "rights".[69]

With Hobbes, Western thought had come full circle from the materialists of antiquity. He agreed with Democritus that all the world was matter in motion. There were no absolute moral truths, just as the Sophists had taught. And, with Epicurus, all moral and legal rules were expressions of utility and simple self-interest. Unlike the materialists of antiquity, however, the materialists who followed Hobbes believed neither in the gods nor the soul nor freedom of the will. The moral, psychological, and political consequences of the theories of those who followed Hobbes would come to be far more devastating than those of his predecessors.

---

[68] A law of nature is simply "a Precept, or general Rule, found out by Reason, by which a man is forbidden to do that which is destructive of his life, or taketh away the means of preserving the same". Hobbes, *Leviathan*, 189. Not only are these rules not objective aspects of reality—"natural" in the original sense of the word—but they apply to the individual only, rather than to the common good. Hobbes' individualism and his psychological egoism permeate even his notion of the natural law.

[69] "Right and Law ... ought to be distinguished, because Right consisteth in liberty to do, or to forbear, whereas Law determineth, and bindeth ... so that Law, and Right, differ as much as Obligation and Liberty." Hobbes, *Leviathan*, 189.

6

The Problem of the Disappearing Self

The immortality of the soul is something of such vital importance to us, affecting us so deeply, that one must have lost all feeling not to care about knowing the facts of the matter.

—Blaise Pascal

One of the greatest ironies of our time is that the self has become the defining shibboleth for many of modernity's highest spiritual aspirations at precisely the point in history when most philosophers and psychologists deny its very existence. We valorize self-actualization, self-discovery, self-expression, authenticity (i.e., acting in accordance with one's "true self"), and autonomy (acting from internal sources of freedom, rather than from purely external influences) when the very concept of the internal self is deeply contested.

We saw in chapter 4 that the classical conception of the person consists of three essential features: first, a substantive core, an ontological foundation that lies at the center of human personality; second, the capacities of freedom and rationality; third, moral significance that distinguishes men from lower animals. Together these features entail that personhood is real, that we are responsible for what we do and who we become, and that there is a dignity inherent in the human person that underlies the moral sanctity of every human life.

Aristotle's and St. Thomas' hylomorphic understanding of the human person explains and expresses each of these three features in ways that materialism and substance dualism cannot. The hylomorphic conception of the soul holds that the complete human person is an integrated substance composed of a soul and a body. Soul and

Blaise Pascal, *Pensées*, trans. A.J. Krailsheimer (New York: Penguin, 1995), 427.

body do not interact with each other as distinct substances but are, rather, the equivalent of the formal and the material aspects that together represent the entire human person. Second, the soul is the substantial form of the body. The soul, in other words, is not simply equivalent to the immaterial mind, as it seemed to be for Plato and Descartes. Rather, the soul *informs* the body. It is the template for the unfolding of the complete human being, body and mind. Third, the soul possesses the twin capacities of reason and free will, which together make us morally responsible for our actions.

Under the influence of the regnant materialism of our age, the great majority of modern philosophers and, perhaps more surprisingly, psychologists reject each of these three tenets. Modern philosophy, in particular, jettisoned first the soul, then its secular analogue, the self, and finally the very notion of the mind. Some psychologists continue to use the term *self*, but this mysterious entity is for many of them simply a metaphor, a reification—a way of talking. This chapter traces the disintegration of the concepts of the soul and of the self in modern philosophy and psychology, beginning with Descartes.

Dualism and Its Discontents: Descartes and the Rationalist Tradition

As we saw in the previous chapter, Descartes had no doubt that there was a substantive self; but, in contrast to the hylomorphic idea of the person, he concluded that the mind was an entirely separate substance from the body. Descartes' *res cogitans*, the thinking mind, was nonmaterial and nonspatial. (It had to be, in order for him to exempt mind from the mechanistic laws of physics.) The *res extensa* of the physical world included the body, which functions entirely like a machine, operating on mechanistic principles, while the res cogitans, or thinking mind, controls our voluntary activity.[1] Whereas we could doubt the existence of even our bodies, the existence of the mind was self-evident. In his *Discourse on Method* Descartes wrote, "[T]his

---

[1] "I regard the human body as a machine made up of bones, nerves, muscles, veins, blood and skin such that even without a mind it would do just what it does now (except for things that require a mind because they are controlled by the will)." René Descartes, *Meditations on First Philosophy* 6, in Descartes, *Discourse on Method and Meditations*, trans. Laurence J. LaFleur (Upper Saddle River, N.J.: Prentice Hall, 1952), 138.

ego, this mind, by which I am what I am, is entirely distinct from the body, and is easier to know than the latter, and that even if the body were not, the soul would not cease to be all that it now is."[2]

In one respect, Descartes' notion of the soul was a return to the strong dualism of Plato. In contrast to the Thomistic belief that the entire person was a composite of body and soul, Descartes identified the person with his mental properties. The soul was like a captain of the ship, something that lives within but also controls the material body. Descartes was one of the first thinkers to use the term *mind* and to associate the soul exclusively with the mind or the self.[3] This was not only a retreat from the hylomorphic idea of the person as a composite of body and soul; Descartes' conception of the mind was even more extreme than that of Plato, who sometimes spoke of the soul as something more than human personality.

Descartes' dualism led to two significant problems. First, Cartesian dualism tended to subordinate the material aspects of our nature. Men were not rational animals, as they were for Aristotle and Aquinas, but "thinking things". This implied that the body was something less than the mind, a thing to be "owned" and subjugated by the mind. Though Descartes seemed to recognize and tried to mitigate this picture of the relationship between mind and body,[4] it is fair to say that Cartesian

[2] Descartes, *Discourse on Method and Meditations*, 25.

[3] Raymond Martin and John Barresi, *The Rise and Fall of Soul and Self* (New York: Columbia University Press, 2006), 126. Descartes still associated the mind with the soul, of course, but it was significant that he began to associate the soul with the contents of our consciousness, rather than with the substantial form of the body, as Aquinas and the Scholastics had understood the soul. The move was fateful, for it led later thinkers, beginning with Locke and the empiricists, to associate the mind itself with its contents—the thoughts, feelings, etc. As these thinkers tried to understand the soul in purely empirical or phenomenal terms, there was a progressive narrowing of the modern conception of soul and mind. As we will see in this chapter, this led eventually to the denial of the soul, the self, and even the mind.

[4] In fairness, Descartes sometimes recognized that the body and the mind were connected in ways reminiscent of the Scholastic view:

> Nature also teaches me by these feelings of hunger, pain and thirst, and so on, that I am not only residing in my body, as a pilot is in his ship, but that I am intimately connected with it, and that the mixture is so blended, as it were, that something like a single whole is produced. For if that were not the case, when my body is wounded I would not, therefore, feel pain. I, who am only a thinking being, but would perceive that wound by the understanding alone, as a pilot perceives by sight if something in his vessel is broken.

Descartes, *Meditations on First Philosophy* 4, in Descartes, *Discourse on Methods and Meditations*, 134–35.

dualism contributed to the intellectual objectification of the body. But it also led to the dethronement of the soul. Later thinkers such as Locke began to associate the mind with the contents of our consciousness (i.e., our particular thoughts and feelings and objects of consciousness). As *objects* of consciousness, these thoughts and feelings could not be central to the soul: they are simply what the soul experiences. To put it in post-Kantian terms, our thoughts and feelings are objects, not the subject. But this left nothing of the subject. If the soul were simply the mind, and the mind were simply the objects of consciousness, and these objects themselves were not part of the soul, it is hard to understand what remains of the soul. This was the line of reasoning followed by thinkers after Descartes. Modern thought after Descartes was led along two inconsistent paths—one that placed the body wholly in the service of the mind and one that deconstructed the soul and the mind entirely, leaving only the body.[5]

The second and even more tangible problem with Cartesian dualism is known as the problem of interactionism. Descartes split reality between the res extensa of the material world and the res cogitans of the thinking mind. The material world is extended in space, but the mind does not exist in space at all. How, then, do nonphysical thoughts and intentions interact with the physical body? For example, how can a nonspatial intention trigger the neural processes of the brain that, in turn, move the body? And how can changes in the physical body, as with intoxication or illness, effect alterations in the nonphysical mind?

The problem, in fact, is even more complicated. Because Descartes rejected a teleological account of the world, he could not really explain what role our thoughts and intentions have in bringing about our actions. If they were not formal and final causes, what were they? He could only suggest that our mental intentions must function purely as efficient causes that *precede* and *cause* physical movement, much as one billiard ball moves another by striking it. But how does this interaction occur? And how can a nonphysical thought effect a physical movement? And where, moreover, is the physical locus of

[5] There is a good discussion of the problems related to dualism in Edward Feser, *The Last Superstition: A Refutation of the New Atheism* (South Bend, Ind.: St. Augustine's Press, 2008), 190–97, 204. See also Patrick Lee and Robert P. George, *Body-Self Dualism in Contemporary Ethics and Politics* (New York: Cambridge University Press, 2008).

this interaction between soul and body? Descartes conjectured that it all took place in the pineal gland at the base of the two hemispheres of the brain.

It did not take long for Cartesian dualism to come under attack, and like all good middle-of-the-road attempts to provide a via media between two clashing worldviews, it was assailed mercilessly from both sides. Theologians attacked his concessions to mechanism, while the more scientifically minded argued that Descartes was a halfhearted materialist. Still, some philosophers, especially those associated with the rationalist tradition, attempted to salvage dualism. One group, faithful to Descartes' legacy, argued that God fills the gap between mind and matter. These "occasionalists" proposed that on each occasion that someone wills an action, God sets the physical movement of the body in motion.[6]

A second group tried to preserve dualism while avoiding the problem of interactionism altogether. But this solution would take thinkers even further afield metaphysically. The Dutch Jewish philosopher Baruch Spinoza (1632–1677) argued that there is only one great substance, which he called "God" but which was simply the world in its totality. Mind and matter are but two of the numberless "modes" of this one infinite substance that unfold in parallel with one another. Thoughts do not *cause* physical actions but occur simultaneously with them. Each was, he argued, a different manifestation of the one all-embracing substance of which we all are a part.

Though Spinoza was not a materialist (since he did not insist that matter was the basic constituent of reality), his philosophy had many of the same practical moral consequences as materialism: he denied free will, rejected the existence of a nonmaterial soul, and equated God, as the Stoic pantheists had, with the world as a whole. Men are part of the natural world and, as such, are just as determined by the

[6]Perhaps the most famous of these was the French priest, physiologist, and philosopher Nicolas de Malebranche (1638–1715). Malebranche argued that spirit cannot move matter and, thus, that mind and body do not interact. God causes everything in the universe, including every human movement, but men are still free and responsible since God moves our limbs in accordance with our free volitions. Father Copleston describes Malebranche's view as a form of mind-body parallelism, though this term might be better reserved for Spinoza and Leibniz since Malebranche taught not that mind and body move together simultaneously but that God causes bodily movements in accordance with human volition. Frederick C. Copleston, *A History of Philosophy* (New York: Image Books, 1993), 4:188–96.

laws of necessity as every other natural thing in the world. In making this point, he famously declared that if

> a stone, while continuing in motion, should be capable of thinking and knowing that it is endeavoring, as far as it can, to continue to move ... [it] would believe itself to be completely free, and would think it continued its own motion solely because of its own wish. This is that human freedom which all boast that they possess.[7]

Our freedom is nothing more, he thought, than being aware of, and accepting, the causes that move us—a version of the old Stoic idea of human freedom.

The German rationalist philosopher and mathematician Gottfried Wilhelm Leibniz (1646–1716), who discovered calculus simultaneously with Newton, also proposed a parallelist solution to the mindbody problem. Whereas Spinoza proposed that mind and matter are distinct attributes of the whole, Leibniz concluded that every elemental thing in the universe had both a material and a mental aspect. Everything in the world is, in a sense, conscious in at least a rudimentary way. Leibniz called these most basic units of reality "monads", which he described as simple, nonspatial, nonmaterial substances. Every man is a monad, but so are other substances in the world. Monads follow a template that God established at the beginning of time. Nature as a whole is, he said, the *horologium Dei*, the "clock of God", and every monad unfolds according to the divine plan. Thus, whereas parallelism led Spinoza to pantheism, it led Leibniz to panpsychism, the still stranger notion that the most basic constituents of reality (including nonliving things) have a kind of basic consciousness and knowledge of the preestablished order, which they must faithfully follow.[8]

These doctrines might seem bizarre to us, but their defenders were among the most brilliant thinkers of their time—men who advanced

---

[7] Baruch Spinoza, *The Ethics and Selected Letters*, trans. Samuel Shirley (Indianapolis: Hackett, 1982), letter 58, 250. Accordingly, Spinoza's idea of freedom is similar to the Stoic ideal. We are determined to act as we do, but by coming to understand that the world operates deterministically, we can accept and even embrace it rationally.

[8] An excellent recent treatment of Leibniz's life and thought can be found in Robert Merrihew Adams, *Leibniz: Determinist, Theist, Idealist* (New York: Oxford University Press, 1994).

science and mathematics even as they attempted to develop a post-teleological philosophy. That they went to such lengths to avoid the problem of interactionism makes clear how devastating the problem was. Modern philosophers have been correct to reject Cartesian dualism, but unfortunately, rather than turning back to the classical, teleological conception of the world, most have moved from the well-intentioned halfway house of Cartesian dualism to the streets of materialism.

Dissolving the Substance of the Person: Locke, Hume, and the Empiricist Tradition

Beyond the problem of interactionism, a second trend contributed to the erosion of the classical conception of the person. It was John Locke, the father of modern empiricism, who took the next step, raising doubts about the very idea of substance upon which the classical idea of the person was based.

Recall that Aristotle had shown how the concept of substance gave metaphysics a middle way between the claims of idealists such as Plato, who denied the reality of material things, and the claims of materialists who maintained that particular things are nothing but the sum of their atoms. The idea of substance is crucial in explaining the unity of a thing over and above its parts and properties and in showing how particular things can retain their identity through time notwithstanding changes in their accidental properties. St. Thomas adopted Aristotle's hylomorphic conception of the person as a unified substance composed of form and matter, soul and body. Descartes, as we have just seen, distilled the person into two distinct substances, mind and body, which he thought must interact. But Locke's empiricism made it difficult to make sense of the idea of substance at all.

In contrast to rationalists such as Descartes, Spinoza, and Leibniz, who held that we have innate ideas that give us knowledge independently of our sense experience, Locke concluded that all knowledge is built up from simple ideas that are derived from the senses. We see the apple and sense its redness, taste its sweetness, feel its roundness, et cetera. Each of these is a simple idea we derive from sensation.[9] All knowledge is built up from these ideas. Crucially, Locke thought that the mind "perceives nothing but its own ideas".[10] Whereas the Scholastics taught that we know the world directly through the senses and the intellect, which intuits the form of each object, modern epistemology has largely followed Locke in asserting that what we know is ultimately only "in the head".[11]

Locke's empiricism made it difficult for him to justify the concept of substance. We can know the phenomenal properties or qualities of things—the redness, roundness, sweetness, solidity of the apple— but what is this thing called the "substance" of the apple? How is it known? Locke thought of substance—incorrectly—as a kind of underlying "substratum" of a thing, an ontological pincushion in which the properties of a thing inhere.[12] He described the idea of

---

[9] A simple idea is one that "contains in it nothing but one uniform appearance, or conception of the mind". John Locke, *An Essay concerning Human Understanding* 2.2.1. Simple ideas are to knowledge what Locke thought atoms were to the material world—the simplest building blocks from which all complex ideas are constructed.

[10] We can know the outer world "not ... immediately, but only by the intervention of [our] ideas". Locke, *Human Understanding* 4.4.3.

[11] This epistemological trend is just one source of our modern subjectivism and skepticism. According to Aristotle's account, we can have objective knowledge because the form of the object is identical to the form as it exists in the mind. According to the modern account, on the other hand, because we can know only our ideas, we never have direct access to the world itself. Human knowledge, Locke thought, is always mediated by our ideas. Nevertheless, Locke was a "representative realist". He believed that our ideas more or less accurately represent the things of the real world. As Edward Feser notes, however, there are at least two problems with this account. First, it is not clear how our ideas can "represent" something entirely external and unknowable. Secondly, there is no way to know—even on principle— that our ideas do reflect the external object, since we can never really get to that object in itself. Edward Feser, *The Last Superstition*, 200. Moreover, starting from similar premises, other thinkers were more skeptical about whether we could ever know the world itself. Some, like Berkeley, doubted the existence of the external world, while Kant thought that we can never know the "thing in itself"—the world as it really is in some unvarnished, objective sense.

[12] Locke did not have a completely accurate understanding of Aristotle's concept of substance. He thought of substance as a kind of substratum, an underlying aspect of a thing in which the thing's properties inhere—almost as a pincushion holds its pins. He notes that "the true import" of substance is "*standing under* or *upholding*". Locke, *Human Understanding* 2.23.2 (my italics). One problem with this is that a substance is not entirely distinct from all of a thing's properties. Some properties are internally related to the substance, and others are accidental. Aristotle thus distinguished essential and accidental properties. The redness of an apple is accidental since the same apple may have previously been green. But the solidity of an apple is part of its intrinsic nature. An apple cannot be a liquid or a gas. The point is that substances are logically but not metaphysically distinct from their essential properties. For an excellent discussion of this, see D. Q. McInerny, *Metaphysics* (Elmhurst, Pa.: Priestly Fraternity of St. Peter, 2004), chap. 9.

substance as a "something ... we know not what", yet he could not bring himself to exile substance entirely from his philosophy. He continued to think of substance as the Scholastics had, as the ontological center of gravity that unites the qualities of a thing into a unified whole that persists through time.[13]

Yet Locke was not entirely comfortable with the concept of substance either. Throughout his discussion in his *Essay concerning Human Understanding* there appears a distinct note of vacillation as his empiricism collided with his Christianity and with his more practical sensibilities. He observed, skeptically, that "*our specific ideas of substances are nothing else but a collection of simple ideas considered as united in one thing*", and he concluded that the concept of substance is one example of "where we use words without having clear and distinct ideas".[14] Yet he recognized that there cannot simply be free-floating properties that exist *independently of some particular thing*. He ultimately grudgingly recognized that we do not seem to be able to do without the concept of substance in metaphysics, concluding that there must be both physical and spiritual substances, for "*we have as clear a notion of the substance of spirit as we have of body.*"[15]

Locke had to retain the concept of substance for a second reason as well: to prevent his empiricism from collapsing into the kind of extreme idealism into which George Berkeley later fell. Locke naturally assumed that material objects really do exist "out there" in the world, yet his empiricism made it difficult to understand how we can be sure of this since, once again, we can know only our *ideas* of the world, not the world itself. When we perceive objects, Locke argued, we perceive their qualities—primary qualities such as shape, size, and solidity, and secondary qualities such as color, feel, and taste. But for us to perceive a quality such as the sweetness or redness of an apple, there must be an inherent "power" in the apple itself. This power, Locke assumed, was caused by the apple's chemical structure, which produces the sweetness or the sense of redness as the light strikes

---

[13] Locke, *Human Understanding* 2.23.2.

[14] Ibid., 2.23.14, 2.23.2 (italics in original). The idea to which we give the name "substance", he wrote, is "nothing but the supposed, but unknown, support of those qualities we find existing, which we imagine cannot subsist *sine re substante*, without something to support them". Ibid., 2.23.2.

[15] Ibid., 2.23.5. Locke also thought that things have essences that can be discovered through empirical investigation. For an excellent discussion of these issues see Edward Feser, *Locke* (Oxford: Oneworld, 2007), 56–66, 79–87.

our eyes. But for there to be such an inherent power, there must be an *underlying something* out there in the world that has this power to cause our ideas. Thus, in order for physical objects to exist independently of our minds, there must be something deeper in which qualities inhere, and this *something deeper* is a thing's substance.[16]

Most importantly for our purposes here, the concept of substance is necessary to make sense of the classical conception of the person as a unified, enduring entity through time. Here, too, however, Locke was torn between his empiricism and his commitments to common sense and Christianity. Just as his empiricism led him in his skeptical moments to reduce material substance to a mere collection of a thing's properties, so in discussing the problem of personal identity he declared that the concept of a "person" is "merely a forensic term appropriating actions and their merit".[17] The concept of a person, in other words, is a term we use conventionally to unify the disparate thoughts and actions of a distinct man. The implication is that there is nothing deeper that unifies the person. Locke's response here strikingly anticipates the views of contemporary agnostics who deny the existence of a deeper personal unity.[18] This view, however, obviously did not sit well with his Christian sensibilities. It is hardly possible to believe in personal immortality and the Last Judgment if there is nothing deeper uniting a person

[16] Some scholars have argued that Locke advanced a second position on substance later in the *Essay*. In discussing the concept of essence, Locke distinguished the nominal essence from the real essence. The nominal essence is simply the collection of simple ideas that we associate with a thing; e.g., the nominal essence of the apple is its color, roundness, sweetness, etc.—all the properties by which we nominally classify apples from other things. The nominal essence is a human construction; it is the name we give to a class of objects in virtue of its shared properties. We distinguish apples from oranges in virtue of their different tastes, shapes, colors, etc., but this distinction is not innate but only a matter of human classification. The "real essence" of a thing, on the other hand, is the "real, internal ... constitution of a thing". This real essence is essentially a thing's atomic structure, "that on which all the properties of the species depend". Locke, *Human Understanding* 3.5.14, 15. Locke subscribed to a corpuscular theory of matter analogous to atomism, and he assumed that what makes an apple an apple in a deeper, more substantial sense was simply its atomic structure—which can be scientifically investigated. For a discussion of this distinction, see Feser, *Locke*, 56–66. The deepest problem with associating a substance with its atomic structure, however, is that the atomic structure can also be unpacked in terms of the quantifiable properties of the thing.

[17] Locke, *Human Understanding* 2.27.26.

[18] A good contemporary example of this skeptical view of the person is Derek Parfit, *Reasons and Persons* (Oxford: Oxford University Press, 1984).

throughout his life and uniting him with the resurrected person whom God will judge.

So how did Locke resolve this conflict? He reinterpreted along empiricist lines the dualism he inherited from Descartes. Just as there is body and mind, so there is a distinction between asking what makes someone the same man and asking what makes him the same *person* over time.[19] A man is unified over time by having the same material structure, even if all the particular atoms of which his body is composed change over time.[20] But the unity of personhood consists in the unity of our consciousness preserved by our memory of ourselves. It is our memory of ourselves "that makes everyone to be what he calls self.... Personal identity [exists] as far as this consciousness can be extended backwards to any past action or thought."[21]

But is there anything of the person beyond memory and matter? Locke could not say that there was anything "deeper" consistent with his empiricism, yet he concluded in the end that there must be a spiritual substance, an underlying self or soul. The very experience of seeing and hearing indicates not only that there are material things "out there" in the world but "that there is some spiritual being within me that sees and hears. This, I must be convinced, cannot be the action of bare insensible matter; nor ever could be without an immaterial thinking being."[22] In the end, Locke's Christianity won out over his empiricism, but this did not satisfy later empiricists who accused Locke of inconsistency.

The next important empiricist, George Berkeley (1685–1753), an Irish Anglican bishop, thought that he could save philosophy from religious skepticism, dissolve the problem of interactionism, and purify Locke's empiricism—all in one fell swoop. Locke had not pushed his empiricism far enough. "The same principles which at first view lead to skepticism," Berkeley wrote, "pursued to a point, bring men back to common sense."

Berkeley was the first modern defender of philosophical idealism, which falls at the opposite end of the spectrum from materialism.

---

[19] It is "one thing to be the same substance, another to be the same man and a third to be the same person." Locke, *Human Understanding* 2.27.7.

[20] Ibid., 2.27.9.

[21] Ibid.

[22] Ibid., 2.23.15.

Whereas materialists hope to reduce mind to matter, Berkeley wanted to reduce matter to mind: he accepted in principle Locke's account that all knowledge comes through the senses and that we know only our own ideas directly. If Locke had had the courage of his empiricist convictions, however, he would have admitted that empiricism prevents us from saying anything about substance. More radically, he would have recognized that it prevents us from being committed to any belief in the objective material world as a whole! Berkeley constructed some rather ingenious arguments to prove that the "objective" material world is simply a projection of mind. He declared, "Esse est percipi" (To be is to be perceived.) Nothing exists but that which is perceived (either by us or by God). The idea of an external physical world that exists independently of the mind, and that must be discovered by the mind, is an illusion.

Yet the soul does exist, Berkeley insisted, and he argued in terms reminiscent of Descartes that there cannot be a thought without a thinker, a perception without a perceiver. "If I should say that I was nothing, or that I was an idea, nothing could be more absurd than either of these propositions." The terms *soul*, *spirit*, and *substance* have real referents. They "are neither an idea nor like an idea, but that which perceives ideas, and wills, and reasons, about them".[23] Berkeley's idealism meant that mental substances exist, but physical substances do not. The material world is an illusion of the mind. As radical a solution as this obviously was, it permitted Berkeley to claim to have solved Descartes' old problem of interactionism: there is a mind, but there simply is no body for the mind to interact with. All that exists is the mind. All physical things, including the body, are nonexistent.[24] Berkeley's system was philosophically ingenious— and totally unbelievable. Dr. Johnson famously kicked a rock and declared, "I refute it thus."

Later empiricists followed the logic of Locke's empiricism but, untempered by his Christianity (and his common sense), drew

[23] George Berkeley, *The Principles of Human Knowledge with Other Writings*, ed. G.J. Warnock (London: Collins, 1975), 139.

[24] "In short, if there were external bodies it is impossible we should ever come to know it; and if there were not, we might have the very same reasons to think that there were that we have now." George Berkeley, *Philosophical Writings* (Cambridge: Cambridge University Press, 2008), 90.

progressively more radical conclusions. It was the Scottish skeptic David Hume (1712–1776) who brought the empiricist tradition to its startling denouement. Hume attacked Berkeley where Berkeley had attacked Locke, charging that the bishop was as inconsistent in holding on to the concept of a mental substance as Locke had been in holding on to the concept of substance generally. Whereas all these earlier thinkers—Descartes, Locke, and Berkeley—were theists who were motivated to salvage God, the soul, and free will, Hume was an agnostic who notoriously refused absolution on his deathbed. With religion out of the way, there was nothing to prevent him from taking empiricism to a crashing crescendo.

Hume argued that we have genuine knowledge of only one thing—our immediate perceptions (he called them "impressions") experienced by our senses. There was nothing more to be said of any "deeper" reality. He called the idea of material substance an "unintelligible chimera".[25] And if material substances have to go, so, too, must mental substances. Where Descartes and Berkeley assumed that there cannot be a thought without a thinker—that the "I think" implies that there is really an "I" who is doing the thinking—Hume responded that there is no reason to assume the existence of the thinking subject. We simply have no empirical reason for believing that there is a perceiver, since all we can sense directly is the perception itself.

What earlier philosophers called "the self" Hume called a fleeting "bundle of perceptions". The self is nothing but the stream of consciousness as it unfolds in our awareness. We cannot even say that it unfolds "in the mind" for this simply reintroduces the substantial notion of the mind. Just as there exists no substance underlying the phenomenal properties of material objects, Hume contended, so there is no mental substratum—no substantial self—that underlies and ties together this stream of consciousness. In one of Hume's most famous passages he declared:

> For my part, when I enter most intimately into what I call myself, I always stumble on some particular perception or other, of heat or cold, light or shade, love or hatred, pain or pleasure. I never catch

[25] David Hume, *A Treatise of Human Nature* 1.4.3.

myself at any time without a perception, and never can observe anything but the perception.[26]

All that we can truly say exists are the same ideas or impressions
with which Locke began. Hume's position was later known as "neutral monism", since it entails that what exists is one thing and this
one thing is neither mental nor physical: there are no subjects, and
there are no objects. All that remained of reality when the empiricists
were through was *experience itself.*

From the Spiritual Soul to the Secular Self

By the late eighteenth century, the attack on substance and the growing materialism of the age resulted in a profound shift in focus from
metaphysics to psychology and from the soul to the observable contents of consciousness. Descartes had already been among the first
to begin using the term *mind* as a synonym for the soul and to begin
thinking about man as a thinking machine. Two newer traditions
now converged to replace the metaphysical soul with a glossier, if less
substantive, notion of the self.

Immanuel Kant (1724–1804), a German savant of Scottish descent,
was perhaps the last major philosopher to refuse to relinquish God,
freedom, and immortality, yet as a philosopher he was supremely
sympathetic to the skepticism of the age. He declared that reading
Hume had "awakened him from his dogmatic slumber" and wrote in
the introduction to the second edition of his *Critique of Pure Reason*
that it was "necessary to deny knowledge to make room for faith".[27]
Kant's thought represents the culmination (and perhaps the perfection) of the era begun by Locke, when religion still functioned as a
ballast for philosophy and where philosophy taught us more about
the limits of our knowledge than about the limits of Being.

Kant was sympathetic to Hume's contention that we cannot
know the true self directly, but unlike Hume, he insisted that there
is something real at the center of human identity, after all. From

---

[26] Ibid., 1.4.6.

[27] Immanuel Kant, *Critique of Pure Reason*, trans. J. M. D. Meiklejohn (New York: Barnes
and Noble, 2004), xxxviii.

Descartes and the rationalists he took the idea that all experience is self-reflexive, that with each thought or feeling there is an "I think" that is the logical subject of the thought or experience. From Leibniz he borrowed the term "the transcendental unity of apperception" to describe this persistent sense of self. He called this core of human identity the "noumenal" self, distinguishing it from the "phenomenal" contents of our consciousness (i.e., thoughts, feelings, and other objects of consciousness that Hume thought exhausted the contents of the self). We cannot know the noumenal self directly since, as Hume pointed out, we have direct access only to our phenomenal impressions, thoughts, and feelings, but we see *through* the self to the contents of our consciousness. The self is like a movie projector through which the data of the world (the film of our raw experience) is projected onto the screen of consciousness. We can infer the existence of the self only by making a "transcendental deduction" from our empirical experience. Thus, Kant argued, we must posit the existence of the self as a "regulative idea", a concept necessary to make sense of our experience of ourselves as autonomous agents who exist through time.[28]

In sum, Kant had *faith* that the soul exists but thought the noumenal self was as close as we could come to knowing that the soul exists. The soul stands entirely behind the realm of knowledge. Our reason and our autonomy (i.e., our capacity to give ourselves a rule to live by), are essential attributes of this self. In virtue of these attributes, Kant argued, each person is worthy of dignity and respect. Thus, one version of his categorical imperative, which is binding on all rational creatures, is that we must "always treat humanity, whether in your own person or in the person of any other, never simply as a means, but always at the same time as an end".[29]

Though he accepted God, freedom, and immortality as necessary postulates, Kant's thought reflects a significant departure from classical thought in at least one respect. While he agreed with classical thinkers that men possess reason and a capacity for freedom, which he called autonomy, Kant concluded that *there is no human nature*: we possess no essence, no telos and, crucially, no built-in ends to

---

[28] Ibid., 61–66.

[29] This is the second formulation of Kant's categorical imperative. Immanuel Kant, *Groundwork of the Metaphysics of Morals*.

guide our lives. The greatest human capacity—autonomy—is living in accordance with a rule—a rule we give to ourselves. Freedom as self-creation became a central value for Kant and for the liberal tradition he so powerfully influenced.[30]

In modern ethical thought, Kant has come to be associated with the idea of *personhood*, the notion that what makes us special as human beings is our rationality and autonomy—our capacity to give ourselves a rule to live by and to follow it, unperturbed by the potentially destabilizing influences of our emotions. This capacity for autonomous reason grounds our commonality as persons. It is what undergirds the modern values of equality and human dignity (see chapter 9). But a second tradition arose within a generation of Kant that held up a set of contrasting ideals—those rooted in spontaneity, authenticity, and individuality. These writers exalted not personhood but *selfhood*.[31]

The greatest exemplars of this tradition were the Romantic writers and thinkers of the nineteenth century, including Johann Wolfgang

---

[30] Kant thought that, in one respect, all individuals are essentially the same: at our core, we share the basic attributes of rationality and autonomy. Because all persons are rational and capable of autonomy, each of us is worthy of being treated as an end, rather than as a mere means to the purposes of others. It was here that Kant found the source of the values of human dignity and equality. But because, in another respect, we are each unique insofar as we must choose our own ends, the value of freedom is essential. Kant's conception of the self is thus one of the most important philosophical expressions not of traditionalism but of the liberal tradition. His moral thought also influenced liberalism by rejecting utilitarian approaches to justice and rights. Both aspects have influenced the liberalism of thinkers such as John Rawls and Ronald Dworkin. See, e.g., John Rawls, *A Theory of Justice* (Cambridge, Mass.: Harvard University Press, 1971); Ronald Dworkin, "Liberalism", in *A Matter of Principle* (Cambridge, Mass.: Harvard University Press, 1985), which are examples of Kantian-influenced liberalism. As reactions to utilitarian strands of liberalism, the popularity of Kantian-inspired ideas of justice promised to preserve human rights against the utilitarian's demand for maximizing principles.

Nevertheless, Kantian liberalism had been criticized by communitarians and others who have recognized that the empty Kantian self is problematic for liberalism. See, e.g., Michael J. Sandel, *Liberalism and the Limits of Justice* (Cambridge: Cambridge University Press, 1982). Sandel criticized the "unencumbered self" of Kantian metaphysics, which conceives the self as something completely prior to, and independent of, its social commitments and obligations. This natureless, empty self that freely chooses its own ends, Sandel argued, in fact cannot generate the kind of motivation necessary to justify the choice of any particular ends. In other words, there is no reason for the unencumbered self to choose one set of ends rather than another. All values and choices are ultimately arbitrary.

[31] Personhood and selfhood as ideals are discussed in various places, including George Kateb, "The Value of Association", in *Freedom of Association*, ed. Amy Gutmann (Princeton, N.J.: Princeton University Press, 1998), 48.

van Goethe, William Wordsworth, Samuel Taylor Coleridge, Lord Byron, John Keats, William Blake, Mary Wollstonecraft Shelley, and Percy Bysshe Shelley. The Romantics were anti-Kantian to the core. They valorized emotion over reason, the natural over the conventional, and the aesthetic over the ethical dimension of human existence. They hated conformity, social convention, business, and all things routine and bureaucratic. Their commitment to our individual uniqueness over our commonality meant that they prized most highly a life of authentic self-expression over the sterner, Teutonic virtue of autonomous Kantian rectitude. If Kant was the moralist, the Romantics were the sensualists. If Kant's ideas are today associated with the Apollonian virtues of rationality and order, the Romantics valued the more Dionysian values of play, spontaneity, and self-transcendence. Romanticism was nothing if not a sentimentalized and secularized recrudescence of religion and a reaction to the rationalism of the Enlightenment. In lieu of God they offered Spirit; in place of the immortal soul, the authentic self.

By the mid-nineteenth century, Romanticism had crossed the Atlantic and influenced American thought, including transcendentalism. Writing in the 1840s, Ralph Waldo Emerson, who had given up his Unitarian ministry to embrace a mixture of Romanticism, German idealism, and Buddhism, gave wing to these instincts in his essay "Self-Reliance":

> To believe your own thoughts, to believe that what is true for you in your private heart is true for all men—that is genius. Speak your latent conviction, and it shall be the universal sense, for the inmost in due time becomes the outmost, and our first thought is rendered back to us by the trumpets of the Last Judgment.[32]

What lies within is what is true, and what is true is consistent with our nature and our happiness: "I must be myself", Emerson wrote. "I will not hide my tastes or aversion. I will so trust that what is deep is holy.... You will soon love what is dictated by your nature as well as mine, and if we follow the truth, it will bring us out safe at last." He exhorted his hearers, "[I]nsist on yourself, never imitate.... Every

---

[32] Ralph Waldo Emerson, "Self-Reliance", in *Selected Essays, Lectures and Poems* (New York: Bantam Books, 1990), 148.

great man is a unique."[33] There was a self, after all, but it is given to us neither by God nor by society. It is at once a discovery and a creation—of ourselves, by ourselves.

The authentic self is Romanticism's most powerful legacy to modern thought and especially to modern liberalism. Liberalism's greatest thinker, John Stuart Mill (1806–1873), refashioned the classical liberal tradition, transforming its basic outlook and assumptions into modern progressive liberalism. Mill is most remembered today for his essay *On Liberty*, a work that exalts to previously unknown heights the values of selfhood and individuality. Whereas Locke based the case for liberty on natural rights, and Bentham on utilitarian principles, Mill argued in *On Liberty* that the case for freedom rests crucially on the idea of self-individuation, a state of character in which the individual develops his personality in accordance with the inner springs of his unique nature.

The spiritual heart of *On Liberty* is chapter 3: "Individuality as an Element of Well-Being". Here Mill virtually apotheosized the self, writing that "among the works of man which human life is rightly employed in beautifying and perfecting, the first in importance surely is man himself."[34] Self-development, individuality, and genius were largely coextensive, realized in pursuit of one another. "Individuality is the same thing with development and ... it is only the cultivation of individuality which produces, or can produce, well-developed human beings."[35] This cultivation of individuality depends on the ability of every individual to discover and develop his true, authentic self, the real self that lies beneath the welter of social influences and ordinary moral commitments. Freedom was both a means to, and a constitutive element of, this process of self-individuation.

Sounding considerably more like Aristotle than his mentor, Jeremy Bentham, Mill wrote in *On Liberty* that "human nature is not a machine to be built after a model, and set to do exactly the work prescribed for it, but a tree, which requires to grow and develop itself on all sides, *according to the tendency of the inward forces which make it a*

---

[33] Ibid., 168.

[34] John Stuart Mill, *On Liberty*, ed. Gertrude Himmelfarb (New York: Penguin Classics, 1985), 124.

[35] Ibid., 128.

living thing."[36] One must follow his own impulses, not those imposed by society:

> A person whose desires are his own—are the expression of his own nature, as it has been developed and modified by his own culture—is said to have a character. One whose desires and impulses are not his own has no character any more than a steam engine has a character.[37]

Crucially, freedom of choice is not simply a means to an end, a way of satisfying particular desires. Choice making has intrinsic significance; our choices are the means by which we constitute ourselves:

> The human faculties of judgment, perception, discriminative feeling, mental activity and even moral preference are exercised only in making a choice. He who does anything because it is the custom makes no choice. He gains no practice either in discerning or in desiring what is best. The mental and the moral, like the muscular powers, improve only by being used.[38]

There is something here of Aristotle's and Aquinas' teaching that we form our character and literally become what our choices make us. But Mill parted ways with classical thinkers by exaggerating the tension between tradition and individual choice. Against the conservative view that time-tested customs and mores provide a ballast for self-formation, Mill sided with the Romantics when he concluded that custom and tradition are the enemy of true selfhood. Fearing that social influences inevitably rob us of our individuality, he wrote, "It is not by watering down into uniformity all that is individual ... but by cultivating it and calling it forth ... that human beings become a noble and beautiful object of contemplation."[39]

Mill drew the political consequences of the Romantic's quest for individuality by linking freedom to the values of self-discovery,

[36] Mill, *On Liberty*, 123 (emphasis mine). The authentic self, however, is a gentle reed easily overwhelmed by the forces of social conformity. Only by discovering, protecting, and nurturing this core essential identity can we truly achieve freedom. Only by preserving a broad sphere of personal liberty, Mill argued, can government foster this process of self-individuation.

[37] Ibid., 125.

[38] Ibid., 123–24.

[39] Ibid., 127.

self-development, and self-expression. These values, he argued in *On Liberty*, require a broad sphere of personal freedom in which the individual is free to perform "experiments in living". In *The Subjection of Women* he argued that women will be free to develop their true selves only when they are freed from their traditional role as wives and mothers. In each respect, society, custom, and tradition became the nemesis of the self.

How strange it is that liberal political thinkers began to embrace the self at precisely the point in history when philosophers and psychologists—including Mill (in his more academic writings)—were preparing to dispense with the self entirely.

Dissolving the Secular Self

By the time Mill wrote *On Liberty* in the 1850s, even the authentic self of Romanticism was living on borrowed time. For well over a century, materialists had been busy resurrecting the old Democritean doubts: if only material things exist, what could the self be other than physical states in the brain?

Mill was torn between his Romanticism and his materialism. The Mill of *On Liberty* needed the self, yet the Mill of *A System of Logic*, perhaps his most important philosophical work, defended a cautious version of materialism:

> According to this theory, one state of mind is never really produced by another; all are produced by states of body. When one thought seems to call up another by association, it is not really a thought which recalls a thought; the association did not exist between the two thoughts, but between the two states of the brain or nerves which preceded the thoughts.... On this theory the uniformities of succession among states of mind would be mere derivative uniformities, resulting from the laws of succession from the bodily states which cause them. There would be no original mental laws, no Laws of Mind ... and mental science would be a mere branch, though the highest and most recondite branch of the science of Physiology.[40]

[40] John Stuart Mill, *A System of Logic: Ratiocinative and Inductive* 6.4, in *The Collected Works of John Stuart Mill*, ed. J. M. Robson (London: Routledge, 1974), 7:850.

If this were true, then the traditional view of the self (whether Aristotle's, Descartes', or Kant's), which holds that the mind is in control of the body, would be radically wrong. As physical processes, our brain states unfold deterministically in accordance with the laws of neurophysiology. As with all other things in nature, Mill insisted, "the law of causality applies in the strict sense to human actions."[41] He sometimes drew a verbal distinction between *moral* and *physical* causes—the causes of human behavior and the causes of physical phenomena—but, in the end, Mill admitted that moral causes had to be a special case of physical causes.[42] Thus, Mill was a determinist. He denied free will as an illusion, but, as we will see in the next chapter, he attempted to cabin the consequences of his position with a verbal dodge.[43]

But how can the self that Mill virtually apotheosized in *On Liberty* be squared with a materialist account that rejects mind and free will? What becomes of those "inward forces" of the self upon which Mill laid the groundwork for modern liberalism? How, moreover, are we to distinguish one's "authentic" desires from those that are merely the product of biology or social conditioning? What makes one desire genuinely "internal" and another socially implanted? And if the authentic self must be abandoned, what becomes of the case for liberty?

Here Mill was frankly perplexed. In his most detailed treatment of the concept of the self, his *Examination of Sir William Hamilton's*

---

[41] Ibid., 1.413. Mill elaborated:

> The doctrine of Physical Necessity is simply this: that given the motives which are present in an individual mind, and given likewise the character and disposition of the individual, the manner in which he will act may be unerringly inferred; that if we knew the person thoroughly, and knew all the inducements which are acting upon him, we could foretell his conduct with as much certainty as we can predict any physical event.

Ibid, 1.414.

[42] "A volition is a moral effect which follows the corresponding moral causes as certainly and invariably as physical effects follow their physical causes." Mill followed Hume in doubting that there is any true *necessity* connecting causes and effects, adding, "Whether it *must* do so, I acknowledge myself to be entirely ignorant.... All I know is that it always *does*." Ibid., 1.446–47.

[43] Mill was a "soft determinist" or "compatibilist", whose position purports to make freedom and determinism compatible. We will discuss the problems with compatibilism in the next chapter.

Philosophy, he vacillated, as Locke had 150 years earlier, between his empiricism and his common sense. He was tempted by Hume's "bundle of perceptions" theory but observed, "our notion of Mind . . . is the notion of a permanent something contrasted with the perpetual flux of the sensations and other feelings or mental states which we refer to it; a something which we figure as remaining the same while the particular feelings through which it reveals its existence, change."[44] But here Mill came to the final stumbling block—a vicious circularity in the Humean picture of the self:

> If, therefore, we speak of the Mind as a series of feelings, we are obliged to complete the statement by calling it a series of feelings which is aware of itself as past and future: and we are reduced to the alternative of believing that the Mind, or Ego, is something different from any series of feelings . . . or of accepting the paradox that something which is, *ex hypothesi*, but a series of feelings, can be aware of itself as a series.[45]

Mill recognized what Augustine had many centuries earlier—that the intellect knows itself just as the will can will itself. Either each thought and perception must somehow possess a germ of self-awareness that transcends itself, or the self must be distinct from the bundle of perceptions that it experiences. Mill's intellectual honesty compelled him to counsel caution: "I think by far the wisest thing we can do is to accept the inexplicable fact without any theory of how it takes place, and when we are obliged to speak of it in terms which assume a theory, to use them with a reservation as to their meaning."[46] There is something more than the contents of consciousness, but, as good empiricists and scientists, we cannot say what it is. This, he concluded, is "the final inexplicability" of the self.

If Mill found the self inexplicable, others tried to explain it in a thousand ways. Most led in the direction of an antirealist conception

[44] John Stuart Mill, *An Examination of Sir William Hamilton's Philosophy and of the Principal Philosophical Questions Discussed in His Writings*, in *The Collected Works of John Stuart Mill*, ed. J. M. Robson (London: Routledge, 1974), 9:189.

[45] Ibid., 194.

[46] Ibid., 225–26. As G. W. Smith, a thoughtful Mill scholar put it, Mill's concept of the self is "a void at the center of his philosophical system". John Gray and G. W. Smith, eds., *J. S. Mill* On Liberty *in Focus* (London: Routledge, 1991), 255–56.

of the self. One route was to reconceive the self not as a substance but as a *process*. Johann Fichte (1762–1814), a German idealist influenced by Kant who nevertheless abandoned the noumenal side of Kant's philosophy, dismissed the soul as "a bad invention" and rejected Kant's noumenal self as a vestige of Christianity. Yet, like many after him, Fichte wanted to save the self *in some sense*—as the vehicle for human freedom. The self, he argued, is simply *pure activity*. The "I" of self-awareness is prior to the empirical personality. It "must exist before it is determined—it must have an existence independent of its determinacy."[47] The "I", in other words, is pure freedom. It spins out the empirical personality by which the world knows us in a continuous act of free activity. Presaging Jean-Paul Sartre and the existentialists, Fichte was saying that existence precedes essence: we freely create ourselves, but in so doing, we leave behind the ossified remains of this activity in the patterned persona we present to the world (and to ourselves). Yet the "remains" of our past activity threaten to entrap our present freedom. True freedom requires that we continue to spin the self out authentically at each moment, never to be enmeshed in the previous *excreta* of the living self. Fichte's idea of freedom as authenticity profoundly influenced the Romantics.

A second route was to abandon all metaphysical speculation and to think of the self in purely relational terms. G. W. F. Hegel (1770–1831), who followed Fichte in the chair of philosophy at the University of Berlin, proposed that the self is simply the product of social and historical forces that unfold in a dialectical sequence through history. Each self is a facsimile of the unfolding of the Absolute Spirit at a particular moment in history. We become a self only by understanding that there are other selves and that we are an object for them, just as they are an object for us.

Hegel's concept of the self was the grandfather of all social-relational ideas of the self that were to become popular in the twentieth

---

[47] This "I" arises, Godlike, from itself. "The concept of the 'I' arises through my own act of self-positing, by virtue of the fact that I act in a way that reverts back upon myself." Johann Fichte, *Foundations of Transcendental Philosophy*, trans. Daniel Breazeale (Ithaca, N.Y.: Cornell University Press, 1992), 112. This pure, essenceless "I" is in contrast with the "not I" of the objective world, which has a nature. Among the contents of the "not I" of the world are the empirical aspects of human personality—our thoughts, inclinations, beliefs and patterns of behavior, etc. See Martin and Barresi, *The Rise and Fall of Soul and Self*, 186.

century.[48] Each self is the product of its own self-interpretation. This self-interpretation is itself the residue of its relational status with others. Philosopher Charles Taylor recently defended a version of the relational idea of the self: "To ask what a person is in abstraction from their self-interpretation is to ask a fundamentally misguided question."[49]

> I am a self only in relation to certain interlocutors, in relation to those conversation partners who were essential to my achieving self-definition.... A self exists only within what we call webs of interlocution.[50]

A third approach was simply to explode the self entirely. In this spirit, Friedrich Nietzsche (1844–1900) found at the foundation of the self nothing but Heraclitus' flux of experience. Just as we never step into the same river twice, Nietzsche concluded, "the assumption of one single self is perhaps unnecessary; perhaps it is just as permissible to assume a multiplicity of subjects." Internal tension and conflict suggest that "the subject is multiplicity".[51]

More recently, postmodern pragmatist Richard Rorty rejected both the true self of classical thought and the modern secular self in one fell swoop as an untenable fiction.[52] Michel Foucault derided

[48] See, e.g., George Herbert Mead, *Mind, Self, and Society from the Standpoint of a Social Behaviorist*, ed. Charles W. Morris (Chicago: University of Chicago Press, 1934).

[49] Charles Taylor, *Sources of the Self: The Making of the Modern Identity* (Cambridge, Mass.: Harvard University Press, 1989), 34.

[50] Ibid., 36.

[51] Friedrich Nietzsche, *The Will to Power* (1901), no. 490. "[W]hen we desire to descend into the river of what seems to be our own most intimate and personal being, there applies the dictum of Heraclitus: we cannot step into the same river twice." Friedrich Nietzsche, *Human, All Too Human: A Book for Free Spirits*, trans. R.J. Hollingdale (Cambridge: Cambridge University Press, 1996), 267–68. In fact, Nietzsche went so far as to declare that "the concept of substance is a consequence of the concept of the subject, not the reverse. If we relinquish the soul, 'the subject,' the precondition for substance in general disappears." Friedrich Nietzsche, *The Will to Power*, no. 485.

[52] He wrote:

> I think conservatives are wrong in thinking that we have either a truth-tracking faculty called "reason" or a true self that education brings to consciousness.... But I think the radicals are wrong in believing that there is a true self that will emerge once the repressive influence of society is removed. There is no such thing as human nature, in the deep sense in which Plato and Strauss use the term. Nor is there any such thing as alienation from one's essential humanity due to societal repression.... There is only the shaping of an animal into a human being by a process of socialization, followed (with luck) by the self-individualization and self-creation of that human being through his or her own later revolt against that very process.

Richard Rorty, *Philosophy and Social Hope* (New York: Penguin Books, 2000), 117–18.

belief in the self and its active powers as the "anthropological preju-dice" and punned that the term *subject* accurately captured its function as an internalized form of social subjection.[53] Thus, the self became a burden to modern thinkers. Freedom, it is increasingly contended, requires a total rejection of the unified self. Once there seemed to be no turning back, others pushed the deconstructive tenor of modern thought as far as it could go. Only when we become "intentionless phenomena", announced the postmodern anarchists Gilles Deleuze and Félix Guattari, will we be truly liberated.[54]

The Self in Modern Psychology

Modern psychology, too, was virtually born in the ruins of the sub-stantial self. It might seem strange that psychologists found it difficult to resist these same intellectual currents—psychology was, after all, the study of the self, the mind, or the mental system—but psychol-ogists were motivated powerfully by a desire to gain acceptance as a real science. To do this, they had to conform to the prevailing standards of positivism and materialism that shaped modern science generally. This placed modern psychology in a strange predicament since it seems to entail that psychology's ultimate success must bring about its extinction as a distinct science. If psychology could be reduced to biochemistry or physics, nothing would remain of the original subject matter of the discipline.

Near the dawn of modern psychology, perhaps the greatest Amer-ican philosopher-psychologist, William James (1842–1910), struggled with this problem. In his classic two-volume *Principles of Psychology*, published in 1890, James began (promisingly enough) by insisting that the study of the self must be the central pursuit of modern psychol-ogy. No respectable theory of human psychology "can question the

---

[53] The term *subject* captures this double meaning; the "subject" is "subject to someone else by control and dependence, and tied to … [one's] own identity by a conscience or self-knowledge." Michel Foucault, "The Subject and Power", in *Michel Foucault: Beyond Structur-alism and Hermeneutics*, edited by Hubert Dreyfus and Paul Rabinow (Chicago: University of Chicago Press, 1982), 212.

[54] They offered a process they called "schizoanalysis" designed "to dissolve the ego and the superego and liberate the pre-personal realm of desire". Gilles Deleuze and Félix Guattari, *Anti-Oedipus: Capitalism and Schizophrenia* (New York: Penguin Classics, 2009), 362, 368.

existence of personal selves".[55] But what is this self? James quickly jettisoned the traditional alternatives. The soul of classical metaphysics and the noumenal self of Kantian thought were both, he said, "merely attempts to satisfy the urgent demands of common sense".[56] But common sense is misleading. Sounding rather more like Hume than Kant, James wrote, "[W]henever my introspective glance succeeds in turning round quickly enough to catch one of these manifestations of spontaneity in the act, all it can ever feel distinctly is some bodily process, for the most part taking place within the head."[57]

The unity of the self "is only potential, its centre ideal, like the center of gravity in physics". Indeed, there are many selves—an empirical self, a spiritual self, and as many social selves as there are people with whom we interact. The self includes all that we own or feel connected with—possessions, relationships, et cetera—fading gradually into the not-self at some indeterminate point. The self, in sum, is a way of organizing our experience, a pragmatic conception that serves the "urgent demands" of our ordinary sense of ourselves as unified beings with enduring, core identities. But this one true self is simply an illusion.

Perhaps the most well-known of all psychological theorists was Sigmund Freud (1856–1939), the inventor of psychoanalysis. To put it mildly, Freud's conception of the self was in every way antithetical to the classical idea. The human psyche was, in his view, hopelessly fragmented, causally determined, irrational, largely unconscious, and deeply antisocial at its core. Freud's self was splintered among its three components—the id, the ego, and the superego—which are in constant conflict in a battle for psychic preeminence. Of these three parts of the self, only a portion of the ego is conscious. The id and the superego, the true engines of human motivation, are wholly unconscious. Human personality, Freud said, was like an iceberg, the great majority of which exists below the waterline of consciousness.[58] What little remains of the classical idea of the self, the conscious ego,

---

[55] "The universal conscious fact is not 'feelings and thoughts exist' but 'I think' and 'I feel.'" William James, *The Principles of Psychology* (Cambridge, Mass.: Harvard University Press, 1918), 1:226–27.

[56] Ibid., 1:301, 338–39.

[57] Ibid.

[58] On the opening page of one of his most important books, he warned his readers against the Cartesian assumption that all mental states are, by definition, conscious thought. Unconscious states are exactly like conscious states in a functional sense—in the sense that they

was, in Freud's view, beset on all sides by forces more powerful than it—the all-desiring, all-consuming id; the aggressive and often self-destructive superego (the internalized autocratic parental figure); Eros and Thanatos (the life and death instincts); and the demands of the external world. Between these forces, the hapless, partially conscious ego is condemned to mediate.[59]

Freud compared the conscious ego to a rider on a runaway horse who cannot slow the beast but at best can prod it in a particular direction. Not only are we not free, however, but we normally do not even recognize our own real motives for our behavior. Freud would have regarded even the gloomy determinism of the Stoics, who thought that we can attain a measure of freedom by under-standing and accepting the causes and conditions that determine our behavior, as hopelessly optimistic. Reason is a slave to the passions, but in an even more pernicious way than Hume would have imag-ined. The ego must, it seems, remain convinced of its own autonomy as it carries out the imperatives of the id and the superego. At best, the ego is like "a constitutional monarch without whose sanction no law can be passed, but who hesitates long before imposing his veto on any measure of Parliament".[60] We do not live, Freud declared, "but *are lived* by unknown and uncontrollable forces".[61]

Freud was also profoundly pessimistic about the possibility of human happiness as extolled by Aristotle, Aquinas, and other classical thinkers. Whereas Aristotle and the classical tradition held that man is born for happiness, that social life is a natural state for him, and that he has an inherent tendency toward goodness, Freud rejected each of these ideas in no uncertain terms. "Happiness, in the reduced sense in

---

mediate human behavior. They simply lack the quality of consciousness that was, in his view, a more or less accidental property of mental states. Sigmund Freud, *The Ego and the Id*, trans. Joan Rivierre (New York: W.W. Norton, 1961), 3.

[59] The ego's role, Freud thought, was "to bring the influence of the external world to bear upon the id and its tendencies and endeavors to substitute the reality principle for the pleasure principle that reigns supreme in the id". Freud, *The Ego and the Id*, 19. The ego thus faces three dangers—from the external world, from the libidinous impulses of the id, and from the aggression of the superego, each of which corresponds with three distinct types of anxiety. Sigmund Freud, *Moses and Monotheism*, trans. Katherine Jones (New York: W.W. Norton, 1960), 26.

[60] Freud, *The Ego and the Id*, 57.

[61] Ibid., 17.

which we recognize it as possible, is a problem of the economics of the individual's libido. Every man must find out for himself in what particular fashion he can be saved."[62] He called the idea of an inborn tendency toward moral perfection a "benevolent illusion" and wrote that, to the extent that this tendency develops in a few isolated saints, it is the result of a process of instinctual repression.[63] Men, he wrote,

> are not gentle creatures who want to be loved, and who at the most can defend themselves if they are attacked; they are, on the contrary, creatures among whose instinctual endowments are to be reckoned a powerful share of aggressiveness. As a result, their neighbor is for them not only a potential helper or sexual object, but also someone who tempts them to satisfy their aggressiveness, to exploit his capacities for work without compensation, to use him sexually without his consent, to seize his possessions, to humiliate him, to cause him pain, to torture and to kill him. *Homo homini lupus.*[64]

Freud did not have much regard for the masses or, for that matter, democracy. Because of the inherent limits of rationality in most men, "the masses are lazy and unintelligent." Thus, it is "only through the influence of those who can set an example and whom the masses recognize as their leaders that they can be induced to do the work and undergo the renunciation on which the existence of civilization depends."[65] Freedom, it seems, requires true reason and autonomy, but these are virtues beyond the ken of most men. Whereas the classical tradition teaches us that society is our true earthly end, Freud insisted that "every individual is virtually an enemy of civilization".[66]

A second important school of modern psychology, behaviorism, made an even more radical departure from the classical understanding of the person—as difficult as that might seem. Whereas James thought the self the primary datum of psychology and embraced the importance of introspection as a methodology, and whereas even Freud

[62] Sigmund Freud, *Civilization and Its Discontents*, trans. Joan Rivierre (New York: Vintage Books, 1963), 34.

[63] "What appears in a minority of individuals as an untiring impulsion toward further perfection can be easily understood as a result of the instinctual repression upon which is based all that is most precious in human civilization." Sigmund Freud, *Beyond the Pleasure Principle*, trans. James Strachey (New York: W. W. Norton, 1961), 42.

[64] Freud, *Civilization and Its Discontents*, 68–69.

[65] Sigmund Freud, *The Future of an Illusion*, trans. James Strachey (New York: W. W. Norton, 1961), 7–8.

[66] Ibid., 6.

emphasized self-analysis as a means to psychological health—each of which reflected a "mentalistic" approach to psychology—behaviorism sought to escape these remaining vestiges of a "prescientific" psychology. Desires, motivations, thoughts, and beliefs—whether conscious or unconscious—had no significance whatsoever under the behaviorist paradigm: either they do not exist at all, or they simply have no functional role in generating human actions.[67] One of the most influential early behaviorists, John Watson, once boasted that he could take any newborn infant and turn him into any kind of person he wished—a saint or a psychopath, a concert pianist or a skid row bum—simply by arranging his early environment in a way conducive to the development of any particular character type. All there was to the self was the residue of one's environmental influences.

The philosophical upshot of behaviorist theory is to reduce all inward mental states to descriptions of external behavior. Watson's most illustrious student, B. F. Skinner, attempted to demonstrate that all mental states are at best dispositions to behave in certain ways. Thoughts and desires, beliefs and intentions do not *cause* any particular behavior. They must be written off as side effects of our conditioning. Skinner argued, for instance, that beliefs are simply predispositions to act in a certain way. To believe that it is cold outside is nothing more than to have a disposition to put on heavy clothing, for example. Similarly, to have an intention to do something is simply a "report of strong covert behavior likely to be emitted publicly when the occasion arises". Whereas earlier materialists such as Hobbes had reduced deliberation to the play of desires, Skinner and other behaviorists sought the complete erasure of the mental. To deliberate and to make a choice was, for them, simply to perform the chosen act.[68] Skinner similarly described wishing, mnemonic search and recall, selective attention, problem solving, and creative behavior in the same reductive behavioral terms.[69]

---

[67] In general, behaviorists attempted to reduce all mental states to dispositions to behave in certain ways. B. F. Skinner, *Beyond Freedom and Dignity* (Indianapolis: Hackett, 2002), 3–25 (describing the reasons for adopting this position). Philosophers at one time attempted to give the "methodological behaviorism" of psychologists such as Skinner a firmer philosophical grounding. See, e.g., Gilbert Ryle, *The Concept of Mind* (Chicago: University of Chicago Press, 1949).

[68] B. F. Skinner, *About Behaviorism* (New York: Alfred Knopf, 1974), 19, 27–28, 113.

[69] Ibid., 58, 108–18.

What counts, for the behaviorist, are the observable "inputs" and "outputs" of behavior—the conditions and environmental contingencies and their resulting behavioral responses. These are the only things, after all, that can be sensed, gauged, and measured. There is no character from which behavior flows, only probabilistic statements about human behavior. A person simply *is what he does*. There obviously was no point in retaining the self as anything other than a way of speaking about human behavior. Thus, "the self is not essential", Skinner concluded, but "is simply a *device for representing a functionally unified system of responses.*"[70] In other words, the self is a way of talking, a concept we use to organize our experience of ourselves as more-or-less unified psychophysical entities.

Like Freudianism, behaviorism has been almost universally discredited as a philosophy of mind, though methodological behaviorism (the study of behavior as a response to reinforcement) remains an important approach to psychology today. But Skinner's definition of the self has won important converts among contemporary philosophers. Echoing Skinner, John Searle called the self a "purely formal entity" for organizing our subjective experience.[71]

We have had the space here to discuss briefly only a few representative theories of modern psychology, but if we were to elaborate, we would find that the problems we have discussed run through other variants of contemporary psychology as well. Modern psychology rejects not only the soul of classical metaphysics but the secular self of Kantian and Romantic thought. By the twentieth century, all that was left for modern philosophy to challenge was the concept of the mind itself.

The Triumph of Materialism?

It is one thing to deny the existence of the soul, or even the secular self. It is quite another to insist that the mind, thoughts, and consciousness are illusions. Yet once modern thinkers took these

---

[70] B. F. Skinner, *Science and Human Behavior* (New York: Free Press, 1953), 285 (emphasis in original).

[71] John R. Searle, *Freedom and Neurobiology* (New York: Columbia University Press, 2007), 33.

previous steps, they began to see that there was no logical stopping place short of an uncompromising materialism. That our most influential *thinkers* were now denying the very existence of *thought* might seem paradoxical—but the paradox became a standard position among twentieth-century philosophers.

Philosophy had moved steadily in this direction from Hobbes' time. By the seventeenth century, Descartes' dualism and Hobbes' materialism were, for most thinkers, the only two plausible philosophical options. But the problems with Cartesian dualism soon left only the alternative of materialism. Among academic philosophers today, even the charge of dualism is enough to elicit a hush of astonished embarrassment from the crowd. As Daniel Dennett, a contemporary materialist bluntly put it: "[D]ualism is not a view to contend with, but rather a cliff over which to push one's opponents."[72]

In 1748, the French physician and philosopher Julien Offray de La Mettrie argued in *L'homme machine* (*Man the Machine*) that our mental states could be explained in purely materialistic terms. He singled out for special contempt Descartes' attempt to preserve a realm of human freedom from the otherwise physical world and drew all the usual consequences: there is no soul or substantial mind independent of the body, and human behavior is entirely determined by physical causes. Moreover, "from animals to man there is no abrupt transition." Anticipating Darwin by more than a century, he wrote that man is to the ape as the most advanced planetary pendulum of the time is to a watch—more complex, but not different in kind.[73]

La Mettrie influenced subsequent secular materialists, including Paul-Henri d'Holbach (1723–1789). In 1770, d'Holbach anonymously published *The System of Nature*, a thoroughgoing materialist account of the world in which he attacked Christianity, defended atheism, and argued that if happiness should conflict with virtue, we should prefer happiness.[74] The work was so radical for the time that

---

[72] This is cited in Charles Taliaferro, *Consciousness and the Mind of God* (New York: Cambridge University Press, 1994), 6.

[73] "We have the ideas of matter and thinking, but possibly shall never be able to know whether any mere material being thinks, or no." Locke, *Human Understanding* 4.3.6.

[74] "It would be useless and almost unjust to insist upon a man's being virtuous if he cannot be so without being unhappy. So long as vice renders him happy, he should love vice." Henri d'Holbach, *System of Nature* 1.109.

even deists such as Voltaire denounced it. In 1795, Pierre Cabanis (1757–1808) argued for the first time that the brain was the physical organ of consciousness. By 1874, T. H. Huxley, who had defended Darwin against his religious critics and invented the term *agnosticism*, argued in a widely read essay that consciousness was purely the result of molecular activity in the brain.[75]

But all of this raised an obvious question: If materialism were correct, what were we to make of our mental states? We *have* thoughts. We *are* conscious of our world and of ourselves. Not only do we ordinarily think that our intentions and decisions cause our behavior, but there is a felt aspect to many of our mental states. We *experience* pain and pleasure. We *feel* sadness and joy. This felt aspect, which modern philosophers refer to as "qualia", cannot be cashed out in purely material terms, as Descartes saw. They are not "in space" in the same sense that physical objects are. In surveying the brain, we can see and measure neural processes, the physical states of the brain, but not feelings, thoughts, and beliefs. My thought of my mother is not located anywhere in a spatial sense, even if the physical processes of the brain are. In sum, my thoughts exist but not as physical things. What was the modern materialist to say of this?

Nineteenth-century materialists such as Mill and Huxley took a kind of middle-way position concerning this problem. Their brand of materialism, known among contemporary philosophers as "epiphenomenalism", "nonreductive materialism", or "supervenience" theory, concedes that mental entities have a kind of shadowy existence apart from the physical brain states on which they depend. They are epiphenomena, occurrences that float above the surface of physical reality. Mental states *supervene* on brain states much as the reflection of a face in a mirror supervenes on the actual face. They exist in some sense but, crucially, *they play no causal role whatsoever in our behavior:* there is *something* to feelings, desires, and thoughts, but they are the flotsam and jetsam of the noneliminative materialist's ontology, apparently having no function whatsoever in mediating human actions.[76]

But what *is* this mysterious something? How could the noneliminative materialists consistently claim that only physical things exist,

---

[75] Martin and Barresi, *The Rise and Fall of Soul and Self*, 202–5.

[76] Edward Feser, *Philosophy of Mind* (Oxford: Oneworld, 2006), 53–57 (comparing supervenience theory to the fully reductionistic theories of the eliminative materialist).

that mental states are not physical and that they (nevertheless) exist in some sense? The position struck more radical thinkers as a halfhearted materialism. In response, twentieth-century philosophers have developed a second and even more extreme materialist position known as "eliminative" materialism (so called because it seeks to eliminate all mentalistic concepts from our language and self-understanding) or "mind-body reductionism" (because its defenders want to reduce mentalistic concepts entirely to physical concepts). Eliminative materialists claim that feelings, thoughts, beliefs, and even pain *do not exist*—even in the murky, provisional way in which they exist for noneliminative materialists.[77]

Paul and Patricia Churchland, philosophers who have defended eliminative materialism, have argued that it should be the goal of science and philosophy to eliminate entirely all mental language from our vocabulary, at least as anything but shorthand for the more appropriate way of speaking. Paul Churchland stated, for example, that it is always false to say something along these lines: "Campers warm themselves next to the fire and gaze at its flickering flames." This is the stuff of folk psychology, implying that we act intentionally and with purposes in mind. Rather, we should speak of human actions in the passive voice, saying, for example, they "absorb some EM energy in the M range emitted by the highly exothermic oxidation reaction and observe the turbulence in the thermally incandescent river of molecules forced upward by the denser atmosphere surrounding". Similarly, dizziness is "a residual circulation of the inertial fluid in the semicircular canals of the inner ear". And pain is simply a "sundry mode of stimulation in our A-delta fibers and / or C fibers (peripherally) or in our thalamus or reticular formation (centrally)".[78]

---

[77] As William Hasker described the position: "Eliminative materialism is the thesis that our commonsense conception of psychological phenomena constitutes a radically false theory, a theory so fundamentally defective that both the principles and the ontology of that theory will eventually be replaced." William Hasker, *The Emergent Self* (Ithaca, N.Y: Cornell University Press, 2001), 59. The "principles" and "ontology" are nothing short of the way we think about ourselves normally as beings who have thoughts, desires, beliefs, and intentions that we freely act upon to achieve certain ends. Materialists hold that this is simply a grossly inaccurate picture of human reality, so much so that they use the pejorative phrase "folk psychology" to caricature our traditional self-understanding.

[78] Feser has written a hilarious parody of the Churchlands' way of talking about the world. For example, the couple admits they "have exchanged a lot of oxytocin" over the years. Feser, *The Last Superstition*, 229–35.

Reductionistic materialism represents the final materialist assault on the last bastion of personhood. It is a position so radical, and so contrary to our everyday lived experience and understanding of ourselves, that even the materialists of antiquity would have been scandalized by it.[79] Yet the modern rejection of teleology, and ultimately of God, has led modern thought, step by philosophical step, to this inevitable philosophical destination.

The philosophical objections to materialism are formidable. Putting aside its radical discontinuity with our lived experience—its claim that our thoughts and decisions and perceptions and beliefs really have no effect on our actions, that we are complicated automata and, indeed, that the mind and its contents literally do not exist in any significant philosophical sense (and what materialist, in his private moments, really thinks of himself in these terms, after all?)—materialism entails that no one ever eats because he is hungry or runs because he is afraid. Indeed, the materialist position entails that no one ever defends a philosophical position because he thinks that it is true. Materialism is a self-refuting philosophy: the very ideas of believing a true theory, of persuading others, and of accepting theories that make the most sense entails a kind of subjective propositional stance that is incompatible with the eliminative materialist's own theory.

In fact, the materialist's claim that mental states have no causal role in human behavior conflicts with his usual understanding of the mechanisms of evolution: if what we call intentions, beliefs, and decisions are, at best, only side effects of neurological processes that do the real work of producing human behavior, these physical processes in the brain would do exactly the same work they now do, producing

---

[79] For all his insistence that the soul atoms disperse at death, Democritus still thought that, while we live, the soul should be nurtured and cultivated above all other things. Similarly, Lucretius would have thought it absurd to deny that the mind is in control of the body:

> I now declare that mind and soul are joined
> together, and form one single entity
> but the head, so to speak, that rules in all the body,
> is counsel, mind and intellect, as we say,
> For the body obeys the mind and moves to its command
> For mind thinks its own thoughts, knows its own pleasures
> When nothing has stimulated soul or body.

Lucretius, *On the Nature of Things*, trans. Alicia Stallings (New York: Penguin Books, 1977), 2.136–39, 144–46.

the same behavior they now produce, without consciousness at all. If the materialist is correct, consciousness has been irrelevant to the unfolding of the entire course of history. Civilizations would have arisen and decayed exactly as they have in history without the existence of consciousness. Cities would have been built and machines invented; philosophical theories would have been attacked and defended; everything would have occurred exactly as it has occurred in a world of unconscious automata. Why, then, has consciousness evolved as part of the human mechanism? The materialist has no answer to this question.

Conclusion

The dismantling of the teleological conception of the self led, step by step, first to Cartesian dualism, then to the empiricist abandonment of the substantial self, later to the rejection of the secular self, and finally to the denial that the mind exists. These consequences are extraordinarily at odds with how we live (even how materialists live) and what we think about ourselves. But the consequences do not end with the total dissolution of the person. As we will see next, the substantial conception of the person is indissolubly linked to our most important moral and political ideals. Without the substantial self, modern thought has been unable to make sense of freedom, responsibility, equality, and human dignity.

7

Doing without Free Will

It is absurd to say that a man shows his liberality by denying his liberty.

—G. K. Chesterton

Broken Machines

In the summer of 1924, the naked body of fourteen-year-old Robert Franks was found in a culvert about twenty miles south of Chicago. The boy had disappeared without a trace on his way home from school a day earlier. As the investigation unfolded, it led to two boys, seventeen-year-old Richard Loeb and eighteen-year-old Nathan Leopold. Leopold and Loeb knew their victim; they were all neighbors, their families were on friendly terms, and Loeb had even played tennis with the younger boy. Each of the three came from affluent homes near the University of Chicago. Leopold was brilliant but undersized and insecure. He spoke nine or ten languages and was at eighteen already a second-year law student at the University of Chicago. Loeb was athletic, well liked by all who knew him, and a detective-novel fanatic. He had conceived a plan to commit the perfect crime and, with Leopold's assistance, invited the young Franks into Leopold's car on the pretense of driving him home. Within minutes Loeb drove a chisel into the back of Franks' head. The two older boys then serenely drove around the crowded Chicago neighborhoods as the young Franks bled to death. They dumped the body under a railroad track in a remote area where they thought it would not be found for weeks. Then they penned a ransom letter to Franks'

G. K. Chesterton, *The Everlasting Man* (San Francisco: Ignatius Press, 2008), 241.

father asking for ten thousand dollars and followed this up with a hearty meal at a local restaurant.

Leopold and Loeb were apprehended within a few days of the murder—foiled by their note and by their offer to help with solving the crime. After they had been interrogated and ultimately confessed to the crime, their affluent families retained famed defense lawyer Clarence Darrow to defend them. Darrow had already won national attention in the Scopes Monkey Trial. He recounted in his autobiography that he was drawn to criminal law by his fascination with the causes of human behavior. He was also something of a philosopher who accepted a materialistic understanding of the world and incorporated this into his work as a defense lawyer. Like other materialists, Darrow was a determinist. He believed that human behavior must be understood in purely naturalistic, cause-and-effect terms and insisted that what traditionalists regard as free choices are really nothing but the inevitable consequence of heredity, environment, and the panoply of background conditions that operate on each of us throughout our lives with unerring efficacy from moment to moment. As he put it in his autobiography:

> No one attributes freewill or motives to the material world. Is the conduct of man or the animals any more subject to whim or choice than the action of the planets?... We know that man's every act is induced by motives that led him here or there; that the sequence of cause and effect runs through the whole universe, and is nowhere more compelling than with man. While cause and effect are not always easy to discover our observations have been so general that we are warranted in the belief that every manifestation of matter, and what we call mind, is the result of some cause, or causes, most of them fairly obvious but some of them beyond the ken of man. That crime, so-called, stands out alone as an uncaused manifestation of human conduct is beyond the understanding of those who try to study and comprehend.[1]

Darrow put on a defense for Leopold and Loeb that lived up to this worldview. Although humanitarians from the eighteenth century on had frequently argued that the poor or uneducated should be excused for behavior resulting from their inferior socioeconomic

[1] Clarence Darrow, *The Story of My Life* (New York: Grosset and Dunlap, 1950), 76–77.

conditions, Darrow recognized that if determinism were true, it would encompass and excuse *all* behavior—that of the wealthy and indigent, the educated and uneducated, alike. Affluence could be as much a determining factor in the etiology of crime as poverty. Darrow introduced expert psychiatric testimony to show that Leopold and Loeb, though not clinically insane, were "deficient in emotions". They were victims of their own privileged background, which left them, he argued, insouciant to the condition of others. In closing arguments he referred to the two boys as "broken machines". He declared that "this terrible crime was inherent in [their] organism" and that "it came from some ancestor." The judge was not moved. Though he spared the two the death sentence because of their youth, he sentenced both to life in prison.[2]

Darrow's determinism was of a piece with a long philosophical tradition that stretches back twenty-five hundred years to the dawn of Western materialism. Materialism entails that every effect has a material cause, and, given any particular set of causes, *there can be no effect other than the one that actually occurs*. We can call this the "iron law of cause and effect", the idea that there is no "openness" in the fabric of reality and that, given the unchanging laws of science, every event has been predetermined from the beginning of time. The iron law of cause and effect entails that, while our understanding of these laws might be imperfect, with time and the progress of human knowledge we will one day be able to predict and to explain everything that happens with absolute precision. And as this occurs, the truth of determinism itself will be ever more apparent to us.

Determinism is not fatalism. The fatalist picks out some particular significant human event (e.g., Oedipus' patricide and incest with his mother) and shows how free human choices lead to the fated event. Determinism, on the other hand, holds that what the traditionalist calls "choice" is simply the way in which external causes—our biology, background, and circumstances—unfold themselves in human acts. Ultimately, nothing can happen, given the set of causes and conditions that obtain at any given moment, other than what does

---

[2] Loeb was killed by another inmate about ten years later; Leopold was paroled in 1958 after thirty-three years behind bars. The events of the Leopold and Loeb case are described in Darrow, *The Story of My Life*, 226–43.

happen. For the determinist, free will is an illusion. As atheist Sam Harris recently put it, "Our wills are simply not of our own making. Thoughts and intentions emerge from background causes of which we are unaware and over which we exert no conscious control. We do not have the freedom we think we have."[3]

Unless some loophole is found, all forms of materialism inevitably result in determinism because materialism denies that thoughts and desires have any causal role in our behavior. Philosophers refer to this idea as "the causal closure of the physical domain". In simple terms, this means that only physical things (such as brain processes) can have physical effects (such as bodily actions). Since all things unfold in accordance with the physical laws of science, each effect follows *by necessity* from its causes. Each link in the chain of cause and effect unfolds exactly as it must in accord with the unbreakable laws of physics. This is why Descartes had such a difficult time answering the problem of interactionism. A thought is not a physical thing; thus, it cannot bring about any real physical actions, such as my raising my arm.

The causal closure of the physical means not only that thoughts do not cause bodily movements but, as William Hasker stated, that "the mind cannot vary independently of the body."[4] It means that each person's entire mental life, insofar as he seems to be planning his actions and making decisions, is an illusion. One brain process causes another brain process and so forth throughout each person's life. Thoughts and desires and other mental states may flit above the surface of our brain processes like the smoke from a smoldering fire, but they have no effect on our behavior. This means, as we said in the last chapter, that consciousness or human awareness has absolutely no causal role in our behavior. Mind is superfluous (if it exists at all).

---

[3] Sam Harris, *Free Will* (New York: Free Press, 2012), 5. On the following page, and apparently without realizing the contradiction, Harris goes on to say that "a moment or two of serious self-scrutiny and you might observe that you no more decide the next thought you think than the next thought I write." But of course, if we could not decide the next thought we think, Harris would not be able to appeal to our "serious self-scrutiny" as if *this* were not under our control.

[4] William Hasker, *The Emergent Self*, 59. Or as Jaegwon Kim, a rigorous materialist, characterized the view: "[A]ny physical event that has a cause at time t has a physical cause at time t." Jaegwon Kim, "The Myth of Nonreductive Materialism", in Jaegwon Kim, *Supervenience and Mind: Selected Philosophical Essays* (New York: Cambridge University Press, 1993), 280.

We would do what we do—drive cars, build cities, defend theories—even if we were completely unconscious automata.[5] This is why we said that materialists are committed to the view that no one ever ate because of the feeling of hunger or defended a theory because he thought it was a true theory. The set of mental events we call "feeling hungry" or "making a decision" are at best simply the subjective side effects of the physical brain processes, but it is precisely these physical brain processes that drive human behavior.

Thus, the real dividing line between materialism and dualism is not whether one grants that thoughts, desires, and other mental states exist in some degraded sense, but whether one believes that our actions are produced by the choosing self or by physical brain processes. This is the great metaphysical fork in the road that will determine our positions on a host of issues concerning the freedom and responsibility of human beings. Either we are immaterial souls who make free decisions, or we are purely physical beings whose every thought action is physically determined in a cause-and-effect manner.

The Classical Theory of Freedom, Responsibility, and Punishment

There are four recognized approaches to the free will–determinism problem today. Thinkers such as Aristotle, Aquinas, and Descartes, who defended the classical idea that we possess freedom of the will, are known as metaphysical libertarians. The other three approaches

---

[5] In other words, consciousness has no adaptive evolutionary function. This makes it impossible for committed materialists today to explain the presence of consciousness in terms of their own Darwinian commitments. As William Hasker elegantly put it:

> What this means is that, given the physicalist assumption, *the occurrence and content of conscious mental states such as beliefs and desires are irrelevant* to behavior and are not subject to selective pressures. On this assumption, natural selection gives us no reason to assume that the experiential content of mental states corresponds in any way whatever to objective reality. And since on the physicalist scenario Darwinian epistemology is the only available explanation for the reliability of our epistemic faculties, the conclusion to be drawn is that physicalism not only has not given any explanation for such reliability, but it is in principle unable to give any such explanation. And that, it seems to me, is about as devastating an objection to physicalism as anyone could hope to find.

Hasker, *The Emergent Self*, 79 (emphasis in original).

to the problem are called "hard determinism", "soft determinism" (or compatibilism), and "indeterminism". In contrast to metaphysical libertarianism, each of these denies the reality of free will, though for different reasons.

Only when what we do is within the power of our freedom of choice can we be said to be responsible for our actions. It was (again) Aristotle who made the first connection between free will and responsibility in Western philosophy. In chapter 3 of his *Ethics*, he elucidated the two necessary conditions for moral and legal responsibility—conditions to which we still adhere today. For an actor to be responsible for his act, the act must be performed knowingly and freely.[6] These are now sometimes described as the "cognitive" and "volitional" prongs of responsibility. The cognitive condition of responsibility requires that we know and understand our situation and have the capacity to reason about it. This condition can be defeated either by systematic failures of rationality, as with infancy, insanity, or other defects of reason,[7] or when the actor, through no fault of his own, is mistaken about some essential fact concerning his action or the circumstances of the act.[8]

The other way in which the conditions for responsibility can fail is if the actor does not act freely, in other words, if the volitional prong is not satisfied. One way in which a person's act can be "unfree" is if he has been coerced to do something he does not want to do. The criminal law, for example, excuses most acts when they are

[6] Aristotle, *Nicomachean Ethics* 3.5.1113b20–25.

[7] Insanity is the classic case of a systematic failure of rationality. Under the original M'Naghten test for insanity, an offender is excused only if, at the time of the act, he was so deranged that he did not understand the nature or quality of his action (e.g., he strikes his victim in the head with a concrete block, believing that it is a pillow) or did not understand that the act was wrong (e.g., because of mental disease, the individual literally does not understand that murder is wrong). See Thomas Maeder, *Crime and Madness: The Origins and Evolution of the Insanity Defense* (New York: Harper and Row, 1985). Excuses for "mistake of fact" are more strictly limited because they are easily abused. Nevertheless, under the right conditions, lack of information can provide an exculpating defense under the cognitive prong of responsibility.

[8] Generally, the defendant must be *reasonably* mistaken about some fact for this to apply as a defense. Additionally, the mistaken fact must negate an element of the crime. Thus, if larceny requires the willful taking of another's property, a defendant will be excused where he reasonably thought the item was his own. Model Penal Code, sec. 2.04. There are several well-recognized exceptions to this, including cases of statutory rape.

committed under conditions of duress. A man who drives a getaway car after a bank robbery because his family is being held hostage is not held responsible for his act because he acts under conditions of coercion or duress.[9] As Aquinas put it, the agent is not responsible when the act proceeds from an external principle rather than from the agent's will.[10] A second way in which an act can fail to be free is when the actor, though not coerced by another agent, has no real external alternatives (in other words, there is only one unattractive option open to the actor). The legal defense of "necessity" applies, for example, when a man throws cargo overboard in a storm to save a ship from sinking.[11]

Duress and necessity are relatively uncontroversial defenses, though people sometimes disagree about when they should apply. But there is a third issue—one that raises much broader metaphysical issues. This is the problem of determinism, which, as we have seen, is a consequence of holding a materialistic worldview. Whereas the concepts of duress and necessity affect the volitional prong of responsibility even where the will is otherwise free, determinism may entail that *no act is free* in the sense that seems to be required for persons to be responsible. We will take up the responses of hard determinists, soft determinists, and indeterminists in succeeding sections to see what consequences these positions hold for human responsibility. Since metaphysical libertarians reject determinism, the remainder of this section will pass by the problem of determinism and will sketch instead the classical understanding of the relationship between freedom, responsibility, and punishment.

[9] In American criminal law, the Model Penal Code provides that a person may be excused for duress when "a person of reasonable firmness in his situation would have been unable to resist". Model Penal Code, sec. 2.09. The essence of the defense is involuntariness. As one English case put it, duress will apply "if the will of the accused was overborne by threats of death or serious bodily injury so [that] the commission of the offense was no longer the voluntary act of the accused." *Regina v. Hudson*, 2 All E.R. 244, 246 (Crim. App. 1971).

[10] Thomas Aquinas, *Disputed Questions on Truth*, 22, 5, ad 3; Eleonore Stump, *Aquinas* (New York: Routledge, 2003), 298.

[11] *Nicomachean Ethics* 3.1.1110a. See, for example, *Surocco v. Geary*, 3 Cal. 69 (1853) (a tort case denying liability to a homeowner whose home was blown up to prevent the spread of a wildfire). Aristotle noted that acts performed under duress and by necessity are, in one sense, voluntary since the actor decides to perform these acts, though under conditions of exigency or duress. In the end he simply said they are voluntary "but in the abstract perhaps involuntary". *Nicomachean Ethics* 3.1.1110a15–20.

Even for the metaphysical libertarian, however, freedom and responsibility sometimes require practical judgments about the effect of certain conditions on the decision-making processes of the actor. As Aristotle said of ethical judgments generally, we should not expect the precision that we find in the physical sciences. Judgment calls are sometimes necessary. Thus, Aristotle, Aquinas, and other classical thinkers demonstrated great nuance of judgment in advocating the use of equity in determining questions of responsibility while simultaneously limiting the ways in which exculpating conditions can be exploited.

For example, on the cognitive side, Aristotle did not excuse acts that flow from temporary ignorance caused by voluntary intoxication or from ignorance of law since, in each case, it is within the actor's power not to get drunk and to learn the requirements of the law.[12] Modern American law tracks Aristotle's conclusions fairly closely in this respect. On the volitional side, he held people responsible for actions that flow from character traits that they have voluntarily cultivated over time. A person who has pursued a life of debauchery or cultivated the character of a vicious gangster, for example, will not be excused for acts that flow from these voluntarily cultivated dispositions. Aristotle concluded that the individual is responsible for the character he develops because it is the result of choices he has made along the way that inevitably shape his character.[13]

Similarly, Aquinas argued that though an individual is morally responsible for an act committed under sudden passion, such acts are less blameworthy than a fully premeditated act.[14] This comports with our commonsense responses to difficult situations and is also consistent with the criminal law's use of different degrees of mens rea for acts committed with knowledge and forethought, acts committed intentionally but without forethought (e.g., the instantaneous decision to swipe an unguarded purse), and acts committed under the influence of the passions (e.g., an assault committed after the victim made a racist slur against the offender). And notwithstanding Aristotle's position on those who have developed in themselves a character

---

[12] Aristotle, *Nicomachean Ethics* 3.5.1113b30–1114a.

[13] Ibid., 3.5.1114a10–15.

[14] Thomas Aquinas, *Disputed Questions on Truth* 24, 12; Stump, *Aquinas*, 298.

that is unjust or incontinent, his paradigm is easily adapted to cases involving very young people who have grown up in social conditions that have made it difficult to choose a morally responsible lifestyle, as in situations where otherwise good children are coerced into joining street gangs, for example. Finally, we can also appeal to Aristotle's conception of equity to soften the hard lines of draconian legal rules by mitigating punishment in appropriate cases.[15] In sum, the traditional understanding of freedom and responsibility can be sensitively applied in a range of circumstances in modern society.

The traditionalist's theory of punishment follows from this understanding of responsibility. There are three questions that must be answered by any theory of punishment: *When* do we punish, *why* do we punish, and *how much* should we punish for a particular crime? The traditional understanding of punishment is essentially retributive. By its very nature it is backward looking. This means that the *when*, *why*, and *how much* of punishment require that we look back to the nature of the offense to determine the appropriateness of punishment. The traditionalist's answer to these questions is straightforward: When do we punish? When the actor is responsible for committing a wrongful act. Why do we punish? To repay the moral debt brought about by the offense.[16] How much do we punish? The punishment must fit or match the moral wrongfulness of the act—no more and no less than that.

A fully refined theory of punishment would require that we consider each of these questions in much greater detail. For example, in determining how much punishment is justified: Is the quantum to be repaid the harm caused by the act or the moral wrongfulness of the

---

[15] Though all law is universal, Aristotle wrote, it is not possible to make universal statements about some things. Equity is a corrective to this. Aristotle even concluded that whereas justice and equity are both good, equity is the superior. Aristotle, *Nicomachean Ethics* 5.10.1137b. For an excellent overview of Aristotle's idea of equity, see Roger A. Shiner, "Aristotle's Theory of Equity", *Loyola Law Review* 27 (1994): 1245–64.

[16] John Finnis has argued that retributive theories of punishment are forward looking in one respect after all. Punishment has a formative function, i.e., to shape the character of the individual. John Finnis, "Retribution: Punishment's Formative Aim", in *Human Rights and the Common Good: Collected Essays*, vol. 3 (Oxford: Oxford University Press, 2011), 173. Even this function, however, is limited by the backward-looking nature of the other two questions. For example, it would still be inappropriate to punish excessively even if this would successfully reform an offender's character. So the moral wrongfulness of the act is still the touchstone for justifying punishment.

intention behind it? Depending on the answer we give to this question, attempted crimes will be punished quite differently, as will acts of great harm caused by accident. I do not propose to go into these matters in any detail here. But to answer each of the three questions, we must assess the moral responsibility of the actor and the moral wrongfulness of the act, and this requires that we look back to the nature of the action.

As we will see next, modern conceptions of punishment reject the backward-looking theory in favor of a forward-looking or utilitarian conception of punishment that places more emphasis on punishment as a tool of social engineering than on its primary retributive function. This more modern and utilitarian approach to punishment has, in turn, undermined the traditional conception of responsibility. Modern thinkers, in other words, have redefined our ideas of responsibility and punishment to fit not only their social objectives but also their deeper metaphysical commitments—commitments that are, at bottom, rooted in materialism.

The Decline of Free Will in Modern Thought

The modern "problem of free will" emerged with Descartes' rejection of the hylomorphic idea of the person and his abandonment of formal and final causes. Descartes wanted to hold on to free will, of course. In fact, it was precisely our capacity to choose freely—a capacity he could not doubt—that led him to believe that man must be made in the image of God: "My will or freedom of choice is the only thing I find to be so great in me that I can't conceive of anything greater. In fact, it is largely for this reason that I regard myself as an image or likeness of God."[17] He rightly saw that our very capacity to act outside the normal laws of physical necessity evinces the most tangible proof of our spiritual nature.

Yet because Descartes rejected teleology, he had to think of intentions and purposes not as final causes, as classical thinkers had, but as purely efficient causes of human action. This had the effect of

[17] René Descartes, *Meditations on First Philosophy* 4, in René Descartes, *Discourse on Method and Meditations*, trans. Laurence J. LaFleur (Upper Saddle River, N.J.: Prentice-Hall, 1952), 113.

collapsing the *why* and the *how* of human actions. Whereas Aquinas thought of intentions as the final causes of our actions, Descartes had to think of them in terms of efficient causation. Thoughts and desires became the mental billiard balls that bring about physical movements in the body. But this, in turn, led to the problem of interaction discussed in the last chapter: How can an immaterial thought cause a physical movement in the body? After Aquinas' finely tuned multi-step introspective analysis of the mechanism of human choice, Descartes' theory was a huge step backward.

But things only grew worse from there. At least Descartes believed that we possess the capacity for free will. The materialism that sprang from the dust of Cartesian dualism had no place for free will *tout court*. Hobbes dismissed Descartes' idea that the will was an unmoved mover, declaring that "nothing taketh a beginning from itself."[18] All human acts are caused by prior causes—in this case, by our desires, which he conceived as physical entities. Hobbes simply banished the will from his psychology altogether, reducing it to the strongest desire that wins out in the contest of competing desires that emanate in some action.[19] Gone was the Scholastic understanding of the deliberative process with its fine-tuned distinctions between volition and intention, *electio*, and the actual execution of the act. Freedom for Hobbes was not about an internal act of will at all.[20] It was simply the unobstructed movement of a physical body. A man is free to act in the same sense that an undammed river is free to flow. Since freedom is simply unobstructed movement, moreover, there is no contradiction between liberty and necessity. A river may be caused to flow in a certain direction by the physical terrain, but it flows "freely" if it is not obstructed. Similarly, the "liberty of the man ... consisteth in this: that he has no stop, in doing what he has the will, desire or

[18] Thomas Hobbes, "Of Liberty and Necessity", in *The English Works of Thomas Hobbes*, ed. Sir William Molesworth (London: J. Bohn, 1839), 4:274.

[19] The "last Appetite, or Aversion, immediately adhering to the action, or to the omission thereof, is that we call the 'Will'". Thomas Hobbes, *Leviathan*, ed. C.B. Macpherson (New York: Penguin Books, 1968), 127. For a sophisticated version of this thesis, see Donald Davidson, "Actions, Reason and Causes", in *Essays on Actions and Events* (New York: Oxford University Press, 1980), 3.

[20] Hobbes wrote that "from the use of the word Freewill, no Liberty can be inferred to the will." All other uses of the word *free*—as in a "free gift" or "free speech"—are misleading metaphors pleonastic on this more basic physical sense of freedom. Hobbes, *Leviathan*, 262–63.

inclination to do".[21] Thus, Hobbes invented the soft-determinist or compatibilist position, so named because its defenders believe that it shows that freedom and determinism are compatible.

Hobbes' conception of human choice and action dramatically reconceived the nature and the significance of human freedom. All that remained of deliberation according to his account were the billiard balls of impulse and desire banging away at the mechanisms of movement. Deliberation was not the very fount of our freedom, as it was for Aquinas, but was instead its termination in action: to "deliberate", for Hobbes, was literally to *de-liberate*—to end our freedom by choosing one course of action, thereby "putting to an end the Liberty we had of doing, or omitting".[22] Hobbes' attitude toward deliberation is telling: he apparently thought that freedom was not the successful consummation of goal-driven activity, as it was for Aristotle and Aquinas, but the mere keeping open of alternate possibilities for the unobstructed movement of physical bodies. In other words, freedom had more to do with keeping our options open than with successfully choosing one course of action and performing it.

Yet it was poor Locke who waffled most on the question of freedom, torn as usual between his Christianity and his empiricism. At points Locke seems to have wanted to follow Hobbes' compatibilist account of human freedom.[23] It is crucial to see how far Locke went to avoid any lingering ring of teleology in this explanation. The will is not drawn forward by the desire for future pleasure or satisfaction but is pushed from behind by our desire to escape our present feeling of uneasiness, want, or lack.[24] The hungry man does not seek a meal as a final end of his act; he is driven by his present hunger, which

[21] Ibid., 262.

[22] Ibid., 127.

[23] "*Liberty* ... is the power a man has to do or forbear doing any particular action, according as its doing or forbearance has the actual preference in the mind, which is the same thing as to say, according as he himself *wills* it." Later, Locke indicates in other ways that freedom and necessity are compatible: "[E]very man is put under a necessity by his constitution ... to be determined in willing." Even the angels "are more steadily determined in their choice of good than we ... and yet we have no reason to think they are less happy, or less free, than we are". Locke, *An Essay concerning Human Understanding*, ed. Kenneth Winkler (Indianapolis: Hackett, 1996), 2.21.15, 48, 49 (emphasis in original).

[24] "[W]hat is it that determines the will in regard to our actions?" It is "the uneasiness a man is at present under. This is that which successively determines the will.... This uneasiness we may call ... desire, which is uneasiness of the mind for want of some absent good." Ibid., 2.21.31–32 (emphasis omitted).

functions as the efficient cause of his act. We see in these passages the tendency of the moderns to conflate final causes with efficient causes, to reduce goals and intentions to needs and desire states.

At another point, however, Locke offered a slightly more promising interpretation of freedom: freedom consists in being able to reconsider and revalue our desires through an act of conscious reflection. We are "free" to the extent that we can increase our desire for some beneficial thing—an education or a good diet—by coming to understand just how valuable it is for us. Through this act of conscious reflection, we can reorder our desires and, in this way, indirectly influence our will.[25] Freedom in this sense flows from our ability to reprioritize our values.

The problem with this interpretation of freedom, as every freshman philosophy student sees, however, is that if every act of will is motivated by some feeling of uneasiness, then even our acts of conscious reflection must be motivated initially by feelings that arise from sources beyond our control. For example, if we do not first have a sense of uneasiness that drives us to seek to achieve a better physical condition, we will not engage in the conscious reflection necessary to reevaluate our diet. Locke has not escaped the dilemma: either our decision to reflect is not entirely dependent on our feelings of uneasiness, in which case there is something left of the older idea of a self with free will, or it is not really within the power of the will to step outside the web of feelings and desires in order to reprioritize our goals at all, in which case we are driven back to Hobbes' position.

By the time Locke ended his long and vacillating discourse on the subject of free will, he was back to the libertarian conception of freedom. He declared that "liberty is the power to act or not according as the mind directs"—and, crucially, this power to direct action "is the power of the will".[26] He distinguished behavior that is the product of external causes—"a mere passive capacity in the subject"—from

---

[25] Locke allowed that "it is in our power to raise our desires, in a due proportion of the value of that good, whereby in its turn, and place, it may come to work upon the will, and be pursued." Through this process we can change the pleasantness or unpleasantness of certain courses of action. Ibid., 2.21.46, 69.

[26] Ibid., 2.21.71. "The will", moreover, "is perfectly distinguished from desire." Locke noted that there are clearly times when we desire one thing but will something different. The problem, however, is that will is determined not by desire, but by uneasiness—which takes us back in a deterministic direction. Ibid., 2.21:30, 31.

the situations in which an agent "puts itself into *action* by its own power, and this is properly *active* power".[27] It is in these latter passages, incidentally, that Locke reverts to the language of the Scholastics, referring to the person as a "substance". This active power of the substantial person requires, moreover, what no determinist can admit—the libertarian capacity to have chosen otherwise, to act in a way other than the way in which he has, in fact, acted. Revealingly, it is this third interpretation that Locke relies on later in his *Essay* when he discusses the justness of God's punishment. Man can rightfully be punished, he asserts there, only for those sins that he had within his power to avoid.[28]

At the end of the day, Locke tried to resist Hobbes' purely deterministic account of human action but was uncertain how to harmonize the libertarian conception of freedom with his empiricist and mechanistic leanings.[29] To his credit, he recognized his conflict and wrote to a friend to lament that "if it be possible for God to make a free agent, then man is free, though I see not the way of it."[30]

Descartes' inability to explain the relation of matter and mind and Locke's fumblings with freedom led most thinkers, by the eighteenth century, to recognize that the modern forms of dualism were inadequate to the task of explaining the soul and its freedom. It is striking how quickly the indubitable truths of the seventeenth century became objects of ridicule by the eighteenth. Voltaire, among others, mocked free will, declaring, "It would be very comic if one part of the world ... had to happen [while] another part ... did not have to happen."[31] By 1747 the physician and materialist philosopher Julien

[27] Ibid., 2.21.72 (emphasis in original).

[28] Ibid., 4.17.4. Edward Feser noted that Locke might have been adverting to the compatibilist sense of "could have chosen otherwise" but that this clearly would have undercut Locke's point here, which is that it is just to punish only if the actor could have made a different choice from the one he made. Edward Feser, *Locke* (London: Oneworld, 2007), 77.

[29] If I am right about this, Locke was not a compatibilist, as some, including Feser, have thought. Still, the charge is understandable given Locke's wavering between a libertarian and a compatibilist approach to freedom. A charitable interpretation of Locke must take into account his genuine Christianity, however. This would have left him adamantly opposed to determinism.

[30] *Some Familiar Letters between Mr. Locke and Several of His Friends* (1708), 27, cited in Richard Ashcraft, *Locke's Two Treatises of Government* (London: Allen and Unwin, 1987), 50.

[31] Paul Edwards, "Hard and Soft Determinism", in *Determinism and Freedom in the Age of Modern Science*, ed. Sidney Hook (New York: Collier-Macmillan, 1961), 120.

Offray de La Mettrie simply eliminated the inner side of Cartesian dualism, declaring that man is nothing but a machine. And by 1814 the French physicist and mathematician Pierre-Simon Laplace pushed deterministic assumptions to their most dizzying heights, claiming that anyone who knew the laws of science and the position of every particle in the universe at one particular instant could predict the future and flawlessly reconstruct the entire history of the cosmos.[32]

While a few thinkers have continued to struggle to rehabilitate the Cartesian-Lockean idea of the soul, most others have abandoned dualism for materialism and freedom for determinism. It is, of course, deeply ironic that the scientistic hope that men will one day be able to explain, predict, and control everything in the world rests ultimately on the assumption that we cannot control our own choices.[33]

Indeterminism

If materialism entails determinism, as even most materialists have thought, then it poses formidable challenges to the traditional understanding of ourselves as free and responsible agents. But some—including a few materialists—have suggested that perhaps determinism does not apply in reality at all. Indeterminists believe (what may be true) that nature operates with a degree of randomness, that the iron law of cause and effect is not an accurate picture of reality. Quantum physicists tell us that indeterminism is a fact at the subatomic level, though we are less certain about whether indeterminism reigns at the macro level. At any rate, this cosmic randomness in nature is supposed to leave open a space for free choice: since events are not

---

[32] Laplace wrote:

We may regard the present state of the universe as the effect of its past and the cause of its future. An intellect which at a certain moment would know all forces that set nature in motion, and all positions of all items of which nature is composed, if this intellect were also vast enough to submit these data to analysis, it would embrace in a single formula the movements of the greatest bodies of the universe and those of the tiniest atom; for such an intellect nothing would be uncertain and the future just like the past would be present before its eyes.

Pierre-Simon Laplace, *A Philosophical Essay on Probabilities* (New York: J. Wiley, 1902), 4.

[33] One is reminded of the question Jesus posed to His listeners: "For what does it profit a man, to gain the whole world and forfeit his life?" (Mk 8:36).

causally determined, there is an "openness" in the web of cause and effect that makes free choice possible.

Or so the argument runs. Anticipating the quantum physicists by two thousand years, Epicurus argued in antiquity that "it would be better to accept the myths about the gods than to be a slave to the 'destiny' of the physical philosophers."[34] He found a loophole in the web of determinism by claiming that, as the atoms fall through space, some "swerve" inexplicably, producing a randomness in the movement of the atoms. This randomness, he argued, supports freedom.[35] Long before quantum indeterminacy, Epicurus made largely the same argument in an attempt to salvage free will.

Whether or not quantum indeterminism is true, it provides no more of a refuge for the defender of free will than does the swerve of Epicurus' atoms. The indeterminist makes the mistake of confusing a *random* or *uncaused* act with a *free* act. For an act to be free, as the metaphysical libertarian uses the word, it cannot simply occur out of thin air. It cannot happen for no reason at all, as indeterminism entails. Undetermined events have no cause at all. They are completely uncaused. Free acts, on the other hand, are caused, after all. They are caused by the choosing self.[36] Only metaphysical libertarians believe in free choice in this robust sense. Nor can we be held responsible for uncaused events. Indeterminism does not manage to

---

[34] Epicurus, *The Essential Epicurus: Letters, Principal Doctrines, Vatican Sayings, and Fragments*, trans. Eugene O'Connor (Amherst, N.Y.: Prometheus Books, 1993), 67.

[35] In his poem *On the Nature of Things*, Lucretius faithfully captured Epicurus' idea:

> Though atoms fall straight downward through the void
> By their own weight, yet at uncertain times
> And at uncertain points, they swerve a bit.
> Only through this random swerve is the will torn free from fate.

Lucretius, *On the Nature of Things*, trans. Alicia Stallings (New York: Penguin Books, 1977), 2.217–19, 257.

[36] Alfred Lande, "The Case for Indeterminism", in Hook, *Determinism and Freedom in the Age of Modern Science*, 83–89. William James defended an indeterministic conception of freedom as well, but what he says about indeterminism is instructive, for, at the end of the day, his indeterminism seems a species of libertarianism. He says that human behavior possesses a "chance-character", which is irreducible to deterministic laws, but goes on to say that all "this chance-character asserts about it is that there is something in it really of its own, something not the unconditional property of the whole". William James, "The Dilemma of Determinism", in *The Writings of William James*, ed. John J. McDermott (Chicago: University of Chicago Press, 1977), 593. Now, this comes close to saying what the libertarian says, viz., that free human acts flow from the self, that they are not caused by external influences.

save free will and responsibility but, rather, completely undermines these ideas.

Scrapping Freedom and Responsibility: Hard Determinism

In contrast to indeterminists, hard and soft determinists both accept the truth of determinism but disagree about what it means for our conceptions of freedom and responsibility. William James coined the terms *hard* and *soft determinism,* and, though he rejected hard determinism, he found it more consistent than soft determinism.[37] Hard determinists are willing to bite the bullet on the question of free will: no one acts freely, they believe, since determinism entails that every action is bound to happen exactly as it has by necessity. And since no act is free, it is absurd to hold anyone responsible for his actions, as Darrow argued in his defense of Leopold and Loeb. Since people are not really responsible for what they do, finally, we must radically rethink our ideas of responsibility and our institutions of punishment. Retributive ideas of punishment must be scrapped since they rest on the (false) assumption that people act freely.

Hard determinism is the most radical, if consistently extreme, of deterministic conceptions. From the eighteenth century on, it has attracted a small contingent of hearty followers.[38]

---

[37] Hard determinists, James wrote, "did not shrink from such words as fatality, bondage of the will, necessitation, and the like. Nowadays we have a *soft* determinism which abhors harsh words and ... says that its real name is freedom, for freedom is only necessity understood, and bondage to the highest is only identical with true freedom." James, "The Dilemma of Determinism", 590.

[38] These include Baron d'Holbach, Arthur Schopenhauer, and John Hospers, among others. Hard determinists have sometimes attempted to salvage a sliver of freedom after all. The Stoics, for example, whose determinism rested uneasily with Stoic ethical doctrines that prized duty before happiness, taught that the goal of life was to attain apatheia, an imperturbable state of passionless self-control. They claimed that while we possess no real freedom of choice, we do have a limited freedom of assent: we can decide to resist or to accept the necessity that drives all things and, in this way at least, achieve a kind of intellectual liberation from the bondage of physical necessity. It is not clear, of course, how one can freely assent to one's condition when everything else is causally determined, nor is it clear how assenting to our determined condition can suddenly make us free.

Something close to the doctrine of assent was rehabilitated by Spinoza in the seventeenth century, when materialism again became popular. "In so far as the mind understands all things as governed by necessity, to that extent it has more power over emotions, i.e., it is less passive in respect to them." Baruch Spinoza, *The Ethics and Selected Letters*, trans. Samuel Shirley

A legal system premised on hard determinism would tend to treat all offending behavior as unalterable personal conditions that should be treated rather than punished. In some ways we see the tendency toward a universal theory of excuse already. Studies now purport to show that genes and environment powerfully predispose us to everything from gossiping to adultery, from risk taking to bullying. Every traditional vice now has an entry in the psychiatrist's *Diagnostic and Statistical Manual of Mental Disorders*—from compulsive overeating to antisocial disorder to an ever-metastasizing plethora of sexual dysfunctions, including exhibitionism, pedophilia, transvestic fetishism, and sexual sadism disorder. Each of these conditions is believed to operate outside the direct control of the acting person. In the last half century at least forty new defenses have crept into the annals of criminal law, including battered woman syndrome, battered child syndrome, adopted child syndrome, the black rage defense, computer addiction syndrome, distant father syndrome, the mob-mentality defense, parental alienation syndrome, patient-therapist sex syndrome, the "pornography made me do it" defense, postpartum and premenstrual stress syndromes, ritual abuse syndrome (used by members of satanic cults), the steroid defense, the Twinkie defense, and urban survivor syndrome. These are just a representative sample.[39] This breathtaking expansion of criminal defenses constitutes the slow working out of the deterministic hypothesis in modern criminal law.

If this becomes the accepted view, how will we think about punishment? Radical thinkers have occasionally argued that all incarceration and punishment should simply be abolished.[40] Others have suggested more pragmatically that though incarceration will sometimes be the

---

(Indianapolis: Hackett, 1982), 207 (pt. 5, prop. 6). Spinoza's argument is that understanding leads to acceptance: once we understand that each event has a necessary place in the chain of events that make up Nature in its totality—which he calls God—we naturally accept that each event has to occur exactly as it does. It is only when things could have been otherwise that we are led to lament unwanted eventualities, since these did not have to occur. One devastating objection to this view, as the compatibilist A.J. Ayer observed, is that one does not become free by becoming conscious that he is not free. A.J. Ayer, "Freedom and Necessity" in *Philosophical Essays* (New York: Macmillan, 1959).

[39] Alan M. Dershowitz, *The Abuse Excuse: And Other Cop-Outs, Sob Stories, and Evasions of Responsibility* (New York: Little, Brown, 2001).

[40] Michel Foucault, for example, sometimes wrote as if he thought the entire system should be scrapped. Michel Foucault, *Discipline and Punish: The Birth of the Prison* (New York: Vintage Books, 1995).

only appropriate response, particularly in the case of habitual offenders, detention should not involve a punitive, or retributive, element but should be motivated by restorative, empathetic, and therapeutic ends. Preventive detention would protect the public from the still-dangerous offender, and therapeutic rehabilitation would cleanse the offender of the conditions that have made him a criminal.

Calls for a deterministic-therapeutic approach to crime reached their zenith of influence in the West in the late 1960s and early 1970s, when criminologists such as Karl Menninger in the United States and Barbara Wootton in Britain made proposals for radical reform. Menninger and Wootton dismissed the individual moral dimension of crime in favor of a view of criminal behavior as driven by heredity and environment. In *The Crime of Punishment* Menninger argued that criminal behavior is a symptom of a social illness and that society punishes the offender twice—first by imposing the offender's social condition on him and secondly by punishing him for the resultant act. Punishment itself, Menninger argued, is rooted in the human lust for vengeance, part of "an endless cycle of evil for evil".[41] Wootton, too, thought that a good deal of criminal behavior could be treated as a kind of social-psychological illness and that preventive detention was the last resort for habitual offenders who could not be cured.

When we take seriously the idea that the offender is himself a victim and that he is made to pay twice, as Menninger says, we must see that he should be entitled to live a life of maximum happiness and freedom consistent with the preventive and rehabilitative goals of incarceration. A recent proposal claims that the goal of such a system will be "funishment"—the inmate will be entitled to all the pleasures and amenities of those living on the outside with the exception of his freedom.[42] One immediate problem is that a system like this would undermine the deterrent value of punishment, since incarceration would lose much of its unpleasantness. Indeed, to some, this kind of imprisonment might be far more attractive than life on

---

[41] Menninger suspected "that all the crimes committed by all the jailed criminals do not equal in total social damage the crimes committed against them". Karl A. Menninger, *The Crime of Punishment* (New York: Viking Press, 1968), 28.

[42] Saul Smilansky, "Hard Determinism and Punishment: A Practical Reductio", *Law and Philosophy* 30 (2011): 353.

the outside. Worse, as critics have long pointed out, a therapeutic system of justice could have far crueler consequences than a system based on retributive principles. Since the goal of incarceration is to cure rather than to punish, periods of detention could be potentially much longer—indeed, potentially endless—in the therapeutic system.[43]

A deeper problem still is that instilling this determinist self-understanding would undermine the very wellsprings of self-control. If everyone comes to believe that he is merely a product of his environment and that every offense is an understandable response to one's social condition, punishment would lose its deepest source of internal efficacy. Indeed, even if determinism were true, there would be obvious social benefits in reinforcing the idea that people are responsible for their acts and that they will be punished if they break the rules—even if this social message simply operates as another causal determinant on our behavior.[44]

Other paradoxes abound. How can the hard determinist deny that the offender is free to change his behavior toward society while insisting that society must change its behavior toward the offender (by rethinking its conceptions of responsibility and punishment)? The assumption that we are free (even if "we" means society as a whole) keeps creeping back into our deepest moral intuitions. But perhaps the most bizarre consequence of the hard determinist's conception of criminal responsibility is that it makes the offender more than a victim: he is now, rather, a kind of martyr who is to be sacrificed for the good of his country. As Justice Oliver Wendell Holmes, who was drawn to materialism and utilitarianism once ominously wrote:

---

[43] C. S. Lewis, "The Humanitarian Theory of Punishment," *Res Judicatae* (1953), 224–30, reprinted in *Morality in Practice*, ed. James P. Sterba (Belmont, Cal.: Belmont, 1984), 262–66.

[44] In other words, perhaps even *believing* that we are in control of our own behavior will have a causal influence on how we behave. Yet this raises many questions of its own. If the belief in self-control is false, as determinists claim, how can that influence our behavior? Yet determinists have a plausible response here: even false beliefs can change our attitudes and responses to a situation. A person who believes that he can win a race, if only he practices hard, might well work harder than someone who does not have this belief—even if the race were "fixed". Thus, a determinist could argue that the illusion of self-control is a "noble myth" that should be maintained. Of course, this raises other questions of a moral nature: e.g., is it just to punish someone who lacked self-control in order to influence the beliefs and responses of others for whom the illusion might produce an effect?

If I were having a philosophical argument with a man I was going to have hanged (or electrocuted) I should say, I don't doubt that your act was inevitable for you but to make it more avoidable by others we propose to sacrifice you to the common good. You may regard yourself as a soldier dying for your country if you like. But the law must keep its promises.[45]

Here we see the final consequence of misunderstanding human nature and the metaphysical basis of freedom of the will—the total inversion of the moral order itself. In the hard determinist's world, the good man is looked upon merely as lucky, much like the child of a millionaire who was born to good circumstances through no effort of his own. The bad man, on the other hand, must be applauded as a soldier dying for his country.

Redefining Freedom and Responsibility: Soft Determinism

Though hard-deterministic ideas have crept into our conceptions of criminal punishment, most thinkers still find hard determinism and the rejection of freedom and responsibility unacceptable. Sophisticated materialists from Bentham's time on have instead opted to redefine freedom and responsibility, thereby appearing to preserve these two ideas as foundations of the criminal law. Soft determinists (or compatibilists) offer a new conception of freedom and responsibility that is consistent, they argue, with determinism. I will describe the position in very general terms here, but there are many variations among contemporary thinkers.

Let us begin with the redefinition of freedom. The compatibilist argument goes something like this: yes, everything in the world is causally determined, but why should this be thought inconsistent with freedom? To be free is simply to do what one wants, to act in accordance with one's desires and motives. Thus, we are free even though our desires and motives are inevitably causally determined. A man who opts for Thai food over a hamburger is free when he eats what he desires, even if he has been causally predisposed to spicy

---

[45] Oliver Wendell Holmes and Harold Laski, *The Holmes-Laski Letters*, ed. David Howe (Cambridge, Mass.: Harvard University Press, 1953), 1:806.

food by some combination of his genetic and environmental background conditions.

Compatibilists claim that freedom is opposed not to causation but to compulsion or constraint. We are only unfree when we are forced to act against our will or desires, not when we act from our own motives. The man who robs a bank because his background and disposition have inclined him to criminal behavior is free and responsible, even though we can trace his behavior to these background causes. But the man who robs the bank because criminals are holding his family hostage is not free: he has been compelled to act against his will and should not be held responsible.

Compatibilism has been a powerfully attractive position among modern thinkers, including Hobbes, Locke (at some points), Hume, Bentham, Mill, G. E. Moore, A. J. Ayer, and Donald Davidson. The position is appealing because it appears to permit its defenders to hold a materialistic picture of the world while superficially appearing to retain intact the ordinary man's moral and legal beliefs about freedom, responsibility, and punishment. Yet compatibilism is another example of the modern penchant for putting new wine into old bottles—using traditional labels such as "freedom" and "responsibility" in new ways to camouflage the consequences of materialism.

The two standard objections to compatibilism are probably obvious. The first is that it is hard to see how persons can be "free" if they can never do anything other than what they are determined to do—even if what they are determined to do comports with their desires. Imagine a scenario in which an actor acts in accordance with his desires, but where these desires have been carefully manipulated: a mad scientist, let us suppose, has implanted electrodes in the brain of an unsuspecting man and then manipulates his desires to make him want to rob a bank.[46] The actor meets the compatibilist's requirements for freedom since he is acting in accordance with his desires, but he is no freer than a puppet. Indeed, we would say that he has simply become an instrument of the mad scientist. Simply

---

[46] Thus, both libertarians and hard determinists will argue that compatibilism falters on this point. For a hard-determinist response to compatibilism and libertarianism, see, e.g., John Hospers, "What Means This Freedom?", in Hook, *Determinism and Freedom in the Age of Modern Science*.

doing what one desires is not a sufficient condition for an act to be considered free.[47]

Second, whether one wants to call a determined act "free", it makes no sense to hold someone responsible for performing an act that he was causally determined to perform from the beginning of time. "Ought" implies "can". We should be held responsible for performing an act only if it was possible for us *not* to have performed it. To be responsible, a person must have a genuine choice, in other words, he must have been able to have chosen differently than he has. We hold the criminal offender responsible not simply because he does what he wants *but because he did not forbear from doing what he wanted when he could have.*

Compatibilists have responded to this second objection in two ways. Some have produced examples of situations in which we hold a person responsible even though he could not have chosen otherwise. Back to the electrodes in the head: imagine a case in which a mad scientist has implanted his electrodes in the head of a known bank robber to ensure that, on a particular day, the robber will rob a bank. But the electrodes are activated only if the robber chooses *not* to rob the bank. When the robber proceeds on his own (without the electrodes being activated) to rob the bank, we rightfully hold him responsible. This shows, they claim, that we do hold people responsible even in cases where there was no other possibility open to them. In other words, though the robber chose to rob the bank, had he chosen otherwise, the electrodes would have been activated and would have caused him to rob the bank. Thus, the requirement that a person "could have chosen otherwise" is too strong a condition for responsibility.[48]

---

[47] Minimally, our first-order desires must be brought into some kind of general integration with our various second-order desires. We must affirm our desires before the acts that flow from them can be called "free". For example, the drug addict may be able to procure his drug of choice, but if he does not *want* to want drugs—if his first-order desire for the drug conflicts with his second-order desire to be drug-free, he cannot be said to be free when he obtains a drug for use. As philosopher Harry Frankfurt put it, an actor who merely acts from first-order desires is a "wanton", a being that falls short of having the capacity for full agency. Harry G. Frankfurt, "Freedom of the Will and the Concept of a Person", *Journal of Philosophy* 68 (1971): 5.

[48] Harry G. Frankfurt, "Alternate Possibilities and Moral Responsibility", *Journal of Philosophy* 66 (1969): 829.

But examples like this are easily dealt with: we hold the robber responsible here because he chose to rob the bank and because it was open to him to choose otherwise before the electrodes kicked in. Again, he did not forbear from doing as he wanted when, at the moment of his choice, he could have. If, on the other hand, the man had decided not to rob the bank, thereby triggering the electrodes to override his normal desires, he should not be held responsible since his act did not flow from his own choice.[49]

The second way compatibilists try to save their position is to concede that holding someone responsible does require the ability to choose otherwise while reformulating what we mean by "could have chosen otherwise". They argue that a person who acts from his desires and whose act is not coerced meets the condition for responsibility since he "could have chosen otherwise" in the sense that nothing external prevented him from making another choice. The man who picked cherry pie rather than chocolate ice cream at the dessert counter could have chosen otherwise in the sense that no external impediment prevented him from choosing the chocolate ice cream—even though the choice of the cherry pie was inevitable, given the particular constellation of causes that make him choose the cherry pie.[50]

The problem with this response is that it subtly shifts the meaning of "could have chosen otherwise". When the metaphysical libertarian insists that a person normally has the choice to act other than he has, he means something considerably more than that the person

---

[49] Incidentally, Aquinas himself agreed that agents can be held responsible for free acts they commit in situations where the only external possibility open to the actor is precisely the alternative he would have pursued even if there had been other options open. A man who wants to remain in his room is acting perfectly freely even though it should turn out that, unbeknownst to him, his door has been locked from the outside. Similarly, the will is free even when it wills the only good course of action open to it. This is how Aquinas accounts for the freedom of will of the redeemed in heaven, who are free even though it is impossible for them to will evil. Stump, *Aquinas*, 298–99. What distinguishes these examples from the man with the electrodes implanted in his brain is that, in the case of these free acts, the actor is moved by an internal principle—by his own preferences or judgments of the Good—rather than by an external principle that countermands his own judgments and preferences.

[50] For a heroic attempt to salvage compatibilism on this point, see C. L. Stevenson, "Ethical Judgments and Avoidability", in *Facts and Values: Studies in Ethical Analysis* (New York: Praeger, 1975), 138–52. See also Ayer, "Freedom and Necessity".

was not externally foreclosed from the other choice. The libertarian means that the actor *really* could have chosen otherwise—that it was physically possible for him to have chosen otherwise given the actual conditions as the agent made his choice. But this is precisely what determinists deny: if determinism is true, it is always *physically* impossible for a person to act other than he actually has acted under the circumstances.[51] In fact, what the compatibilist response really boils down to is the claim that the actor could have chosen otherwise if, at the moment of his choice, a different set of causes and conditions had existed from those that had precipitated the actual choice. But this is itself a physical impossibility on the determinist's own terms (since nothing can be different from the way it is at any given moment). Only by sneaking in some exception to the iron law of cause and effect—if not at the moment of choice, then in the prior conditions and causes that actually bring about a particular choice—can we make any real sense of this reformulation of the condition that the actor could have chosen otherwise.

This is where modern materialists make a second move, redefining our conception of responsibility to mean something very different from the traditional, backward-looking idea. This reconceptualization of responsibility appeals to utilitarian ideas. As we said earlier in the chapter, the classical ideas of responsibility and punishment are backward looking (i.e., we hold a person responsible and punish him when, looking back to the act, we see that it was performed freely and with full information). The utilitarian approach to responsibility, in contrast, is forward looking: the utilitarian holds an actor responsible if punishing him produces some benefits. In determining responsibility, the utilitarian looks *forward* to the consequences of punishment. The utilitarian would punish the offender when doing so would deter other would-be offenders (general deterrence), when it would deter the offender himself after his period of incarceration

[51] As philosopher Antony Flew, who became a theist late in life, put it, "[C]ompatibilism does not work. A law of nature is not a statement of a mere brute fact that one particular sort of happening will, as it happens, succeed or accompany some other sort of happening. It is, rather, a claim that an occurrence of one particular sort physically necessitates the occurrence of another sort such that *it makes its non-occurrence physically impossible*. This is clearly not the case with a free choice." Antony Flew, *There Is a God* (New York: HarperOne, 2008), 60 (my emphasis).

(specific deterrence), when punishment would make him a better person (rehabilitation), or, minimally, when it would keep him from committing crimes during his incarceration (prevention). These are the four main utilitarian justifications for punishment.

Notice that utilitarianism inverts the relationship between responsibility and punishment and, in doing so, changes the very concept of responsibility. Whereas the traditionalist holds that if the actor is responsible he can be punished, the utilitarian holds that if he should be punished (because doing so is conducive to deterrence and other forms of social utility), he should be "held responsible". Responsibility is no longer the premise of the argument justifying punishment, as it is for traditional theories of responsibility and punishment. Instead, it is the *conclusion* of the argument. The utilitarian conception of responsibility is *prescriptive* rather than *descriptive*. Or, as legal philosopher H. L. A. Hart put it, the traditionalist's conception of responsibility is a "capacity" idea (i.e., a person is responsible only if he had the capacity to understand and control his action), whereas the utilitarian's is a "liability" idea (the actor is responsible if it is conducive to utility to hold him liable).[52]

This was essentially Bentham's and Mill's conception of punishment and responsibility. Bentham tried to preserve the traditional theory of excuse by reinventing its function. He argued that we excuse certain acts not because they fail to satisfy Aristotle's two conditions but when the acts could not be legally deterred.[53] This permits sophisticated utilitarians today to remain agnostic on the metaphysical question of human freedom.[54] It does not matter whether a person is free in some metaphysical sense. All that matters is whether holding him responsible will have some utilitarian benefit on his behavior or the behavior of others.

The utilitarian theory of punishment has been justly criticized for severing the essential link between punishment and the moral

[52] H. L. A Hart, *Punishment and Responsibility: Essays in the Philosophy of Law* (Oxford: Oxford University Press, 1968), 212–30.

[53] Jeremy Bentham, *The Principles of Morals and Legislation* (Amherst, N.Y.: Prometheus Books, 1988), 180–81 (ch. 13, par. 9).

[54] As Hart wrote, "we should neither assert nor deny that the accused could have done otherwise than he did. Instead we should look upon his act as a symptom of the need for either punishment or treatment". Hart, *Punishment and Responsibility*, 179.

blameworthiness of the act. Punishment is no longer about desert but about social expediency. Since the severity of punishment depends not on the wrongfulness of the act but on the deterrence value of the criminal sanction, horrible acts will be underpunished in cases where some lesser punishment achieves all that can be achieved in a particular case.

Worse still, overpunishment is justified whenever this serves social utility: if it were possible to deter 99 percent of petty theft by cutting off the hands of the convicted thief, utilitarianism not only justifies but *requires* this gruesome penalty just so long as what is gained by deterring 99 percent of theft more than offsets the price paid by the occasional offender. Indeed, as critics have recognized, factual guilt is not even required in cases where punishing the blameless will avert some greater social calamity (as in the case of the man scapegoated to assuage the anger of a rioting mob). Though utilitarians have responses to some of these criticisms, they usually turn on some questionable appeal to states of affairs in the world—for example, that cutting off hands is not an effective deterrent or that scapegoating the blameless will place everyone in fear for his life, thus causing even greater negative utility. These kinds of appeals are not convincing both because they depend on empirical claims that may turn out to be false and, more importantly, because the justness of a particular punishment should not turn on these factual claims at all. Punishing the blameless is unjust irrespective of its social consequences. Any theory that might require this (if the facts permit) is wrong.

At the end of the day, the compatibilist idea of freedom and the utilitarian idea of responsibility are misnomers. They are attractive only because they appear to preserve, though in name only, the notions of freedom and responsibility that are indispensable to any meaningful conception of moral and criminal justice. They represent, moreover, significant concessions to a very unhumanitarian conception of responsibility. To call a wrongdoer "free" when his act was causally determined strikes most of us as a wholesale degradation of our intuitive understanding of freedom, and to say that this same wrongdoer is "responsible" when he could not have done other than he did is about as draconian a conception of responsibility as one can imagine. It was for these reasons that William James called compatibilism a "quagmire of evasion".[55]

Conclusion

A worldview is an intricate mosaic of coherent beliefs and assumptions that fit together, each a precious stone in a pattern that forms a holistic image of our understanding of reality. One cannot substitute a stone of a radically different color without affecting the entire mosaic, without having to replace the others as well. The compatibilist-utilitarian reinterpretation of freedom and responsibility attempts to mask the gradual transformation of our moral self-understanding by passing off newer meanings under older labels. This reconceptualization of freedom and responsibility is insidious and dangerous—insidious because it cloaks its changes in the older moral lexicon and dangerous because the newer meanings inevitably alter the entire mosaic. And as we will see shortly, changing the meaning of freedom and responsibility in turn subverts the meanings of other concepts, including liberty, human rights, equality, and human dignity.

The next two chapters explore the effects of these changes on modern moral theory and on Western civilization's highest political ideals.

[55] James, *The Dilemma of Determinism*, 590.

8

The Disintegration of Moral Truth
and the Unraveling of Law

A moral code "freely adopted" that ignores the built-in teleologies of human nature can only lead to disaster.

—Peter Geach

And because lawlessness will abound, the love of many will grow cold.

—Matthew 24:12

In the wake of World War II, Allied prosecutors sought to bring the leading officials of the Nazi party and the Third Reich to justice for atrocities committed during the war. Some, including Winston Churchill, preferred that the worst of the Nazis and their collaborators be summarily executed. But others insisted that the prosecutions must have the force of real law: they must take place under established legal precedents and according to just legal procedures. It was vitally important that these punishments not be perceived as unprincipled retaliation, a form of "victor's justice". This would make the Allies' methods no better in principle than the Nazis'.

The Nuremberg prosecutions were heralded as the greatest trial in history—but there was a problem. There was no validly enacted law under which to prosecute the Nazis. The defendants argued that the events that occurred in Germany, in particular, were governed by German law and that their actions were fully protected under the law of the Third Reich. Allied laws could not be applied to the Germans in some extraterritorial way: the laws of the Allies were not *their* laws.

P. T. Geach, *The Virtues* (Cambridge: Cambridge University Press, 1977), vii.
New King James Version (Nashville: Nelson, 1982).

Some of the proposed "laws" under which the defendants were to be prosecuted, moreover, were passed after the prohibited acts had occurred. The roughly two dozen defendants and seven organizations were being prosecuted under what were essentially ex post facto laws. And perhaps most damning as a practical matter was that the Allies themselves had committed some of the same acts the Germans had. Even the lead American prosecutor, United States Supreme Court Justice Robert Jackson, wrote privately to President Truman:

> Some of the allies have done or are doing some of the very things we are prosecuting the Germans for. The French are so violating the Geneva Convention in the treatment of prisoners of war that our command is taking back prisoners sent to them. We are prosecuting plunder and our Allies are practicing it. We say aggressive war is a crime and one of our allies asserts sovereignty over the Baltic States based on no title except conquest.[1]

As Joachim von Ribbentrop, the Nazi minister of foreign affairs and the first to be hanged after the conclusion of the trial, warned, "You'll see. In a few years the lawyers of the world will condemn this trial. You can't have a trial without law."

The Germans, of course, were correct that no *positive* law could be applied to them within the accepted bounds of established legal procedure. Only if there was a law above the positive law—a natural law binding on all men's consciences—could the prosecutions be anything more than retaliation in the guise of legal formality. But by the twentieth century, the natural law had become an object of ridicule among many of the most influential legal minds. Justice Oliver Wendell Holmes laughed the natural law out of court a few decades earlier, calling it "a brooding omnipresence in the sky".[2] He wrote in the *Harvard Law Review*:

> It is not enough for the knight of romance that you agree that his lady is a very nice girl. If you do not admit that she is the best that God ever made or will make, you must fight. There is in all men a demand for the superlative, so much so that the poor devil who has no other

---

[1] Robert E. Conot, *Justice at Nuremberg* (New York: Harper and Row, 1983), 68.
[2] *Southern Pacific v. Jensen*, 244 U.S. 205, 222 (1917) (Holmes, J., dissenting).

way of reaching it attains it by getting drunk. It seems to me that this demand is at the bottom of the philosopher's effort to prove that truth is absolute and of the jurist's search for criteria of universal validity, which he collects under the head of natural law.[3]

By 1945, Holmes' skepticism had become a platitude. Even Justice Jackson's colleague Chief Justice Harlan Fiske Stone wrote privately to a friend: "Jackson is away conducting his high-grade lynching party in Nuremberg. I don't mind what he does to the Nazis, but I hate to see the pretense that he is running a court and prosecuting according to common law. This is a little too sanctimonious a fraud to meet my old-fashioned ideas."[4]

Modern lawyers sometimes describe natural law theory as the conjunction of two basic principles—what we might call the "moral-objectivity" thesis and the "overlap" thesis. The moral-objectivity thesis holds that moral truths are objective, real—they are not mere products of human whim or convention. They exist as truths in the world independently of what we may wish or believe. They are practical truths that we discover rather than invent. Aquinas and other natural lawyers had argued that the objectivity of morality is grounded in truths about Nature, particularly facts about human nature. The moral good is that which is conducive to the realization of our human telos, individually and collectively.[5]

Where the moral-objectivity thesis connects morality to human nature, the overlap thesis connects law to morality. To qualify as a law in the fullest sense, a rule or statute must be grounded in the objective moral order. A rule that conflicts with, contradicts, or runs

---

[3] Oliver Wendell Holmes, "Natural Law", *Harvard Law Review* 32 (1918): 40.

[4] Stone to Sterling Carr, December 4, 1945, cited in A. T. Mason, *Harlan Fiske Stone: Pillar of the Law* (New York: Viking Press, 1956), 716.

[5] A caveat is necessary here. To speak of moral principles as "truths" is to invite the misconception that there is always some right answer to every moral question. Yet Aristotle and Aquinas and others in the natural law tradition always emphasized the practical and variegated nature of moral reasoning. See chapter 2 for a discussion of this. To say that morality is objective is not to say that we can draw moral conclusions with deductive precision from moral and factual premises. Owing to certain peculiarities of modern moral thought, we tend today to confound the objectivity of our moral conclusions with their logical determinacy. We tend to think that a moral principle is not "objective" unless it follows with absolute deductive precision from our premises. This is one of the reasons so many people today doubt the objective nature of moral principles.

afoul of the moral order is not truly a law. As St. Augustine famously put it, "An unjust law is no law at all."

By the mid-twentieth century, both tenets of natural law theory seemed an impossible illusion to most philosophers and lawyers. This chapter explores how this came about. Most of the chapter is devoted to the progressive collapse of the idea of moral objectivity in modern thought. The last section traces the abandonment of the overlap thesis.

Natural Law without Teleology

With the abandonment of essences and universals, the natural law tradition splintered into two strands by the seventeenth century. Each borrowed and distorted what had once been complementary halves of Aquinas' eternal law, which encompassed both God's moral law and the empirical laws of science.

Theorists of the "moralized" strand continued to think of natural law in primarily moral terms but dramatically altered the source and content of this law. Among the first of these thinkers was the Dutch legal theorist Hugo Grotius (1583–1645), often considered today the father of international law theory. Grotius conceived of natural law as a body of God-given moral truths, as the Scholastics had, and is most remembered for his attempt to apply these truths to moral rights and duties in time of war. He thought of Holy Scripture as a guide and support for human reason in determining the content of the law, just as Aquinas had conceived the divine law. In these respects, Grotius was a close descendant of Aquinas and the Scholastics.

In two other ways, however, his thought was a departure from the classical natural law tradition. First, as a rationalist (he probably had met Descartes, in fact), he was considerably more optimistic than the Scholastics about the prospect of deriving a whole system of moral truths from a system of basic axioms. Whereas Aquinas often drew particular moral conclusions with nuance and caution, ever mindful of the contingency of moral reasoning, Grotius offered a comprehensive system of conclusions on such particular issues as the rights of prisoners of war, the treatment of ambassadors, the right of burial, and the use of civilians' property. We see here the rationalist's penchant for deductive certitude. Where equity filled the moral gap between premises and conclusions for Aristotle, and love for Aquinas, pure logic now had to suffice for Grotius.

We also find in Grotius' writings a discernible shift away from the idea that moral truths are grounded in Being and expressed in Nature. Whereas Aquinas had taught that men participate *through reason* in the rational order that pervades the universe—an order that reflects the divine essence itself—Grotius saw reason purely as a human faculty and natural law as something external to human nature, a body of truths to be discovered "out there". The validity of these truths did not depend—in any direct way, at least—on the truths of metaphysics. In fact, Grotius wrote that the principles of the moral law would be exactly the same "even if we should concede that which cannot be conceded without the utmost wickedness, that there is no God, or that the affairs of men are of no concern to Him".[6] Morality depends on reason alone, in other words. This was a return to the more extreme rationalism of Plato in the *Euthyphro*.

The most influential of all thinkers of the moralized strain, John Locke, drifted even further from the classical understanding of the natural law. Like Grotius, he conceived natural law as a body of binding divine commands. But, with Ockham, he viewed the principles of natural law as commands of God, dictates of the divine will, rather than expressions of divine reason. What made natural law obligatory for Grotius was, at least in part, its reasonableness. What made it obligatory for Locke was that God had *willed* it and that He could punish those who flouted the law. Moral truth was not only outside human nature, it was binding upon us by compulsion, rather than because of its reasonableness. Locke's voluntarism also left the content of the moral law potentially arbitrary since it made the rightness of an action depend not on the intrinsic nature of the act but on whether God had commanded or forbidden it. In later and less subtle thinkers after Locke, particularly among Protestant thinkers, the rejection of reason as the foundation for moral truth led to a correspondingly greater emphasis on revelation and on literalist readings of the Bible.

---

[6] Hugo Grotius, *On the Law of War and Peace* (New York: Cambridge University Press, 2012), Prolegomena 11. For a discussion of Grotius' place in the history of the natural law, see Heinrich A. Rommen, *The Natural Law* (Indianapolis: Liberty Fund, 1998), 62–66.

Bereft of its foundation in reason, the moralized strand of natural law was bound to become increasingly authoritarian.

The second, more empirical strand of the newer natural law tradition includes Hobbes, Rousseau, and Samuel von Pufendorf. These thinkers conceived of natural law not primarily as a body of moral truths to guide human conduct but as a theory of the unvarnished natural man—man as he is in the state of nature. Without teleology, "nature" came to mean not the unfolding of the human essence but a static and abstracted notion of man untouched by civilization. For these more radical thinkers, the "natural" was not how men *should* act but how they do in fact act in the state of nature. "Law" became for them not the organic expression of men's innate sociability but a system of conventional rules built up defensively out of self-interest.

The content of their theories of human nature are radically different. For Hobbes, natural man was driven by two overriding instincts—simple human selfishness and an overriding fear of death. Man enters the social contract to escape the ravages of life in the state of nature, a life "solitary, poor, nasty, brutish and short". Society is born of an agreement in which the individual trades the entirety of his natural freedom for security. Rousseau, by contrast, thought that the precivilized state is the happiest for men and that natural man became civilized by "some fatal accident". The social contract was, for Rousseau, a bad bargain in which the masses were hoodwinked by those who hoped to exploit their labor. They traded away their natural freedom, "for they had just wit enough to perceive the advantages of political institutions, without experience enough to enable them to foresee the dangers".[7] For Hobbes, civilization was the lesser of two evils; for Rousseau, the greater.[8]

Both Hobbes and Rousseau profoundly influenced the liberal and socialist traditions of the nineteenth and twentieth centuries in making the social state the antithesis of nature rather than its fullest

---

[7] Jean-Jacques Rousseau, *Discourse on the Origin of Inequality: The Social Contract and the Discourses*, trans. G. D. H. Cole (London: J. M. Dent and Sons, 1973), 91, 98.

[8] Rousseau's conception of society was the antithesis of Aristotle's. Whereas Aristotle taught that society humanizes us, gives us our "second nature", our true humanity, Rousseau thought society corrupts human nature. He found in modern civilization a condition of "honour without virtue, reason without wisdom, pleasure without happiness". Rousseau, *Discourse on the Origin of Inequality*, 116.

expression. The newer conception of nature was a direct consequence of the abandonment of essences, especially of the idea of the human telos. Thinkers of the empirical strand of the newer natural law opposed Nature to civilization because they conceived Nature in purely static, immanent, and material (physical and psychological) terms, rather than in dynamic and formative terms, as Aquinas had. Nature was now *what men are before they are socialized*, rather than *what men can be at their best with the aid of civilization*.

This was nothing short of a complete inversion of the classical idea of the natural. In classical thought, *natural* was a synonym for reason and order. Society itself was the natural outworking of the human telos to form families and then broader communities that serve to humanize the individual. The process that modern thinkers call "socialization" is, in fact, as classical thinkers recognized, our *humanization*. Only in the social condition does a human being achieve his second nature. Only in society does he become an *individual*. This is why Aristotle said that a man outside society must be either a beast or a god—either he is less than human or divine.[9] The civilized state is our proper and natural condition, a condition intermediate of brutes and angels. To "follow nature" was not "to do what comes naturally" but, as Aristotle said, to strain every nerve to live in accord with the best thing in us.[10]

This ennobling, dynamic, and inherently moralized idea of Nature changed with the empirical conception of the natural law. As Hobbes and Rousseau conceived it, Nature was left behind in the precivilized state. Society was not an organic expression of our innate human sociability but a utilitarian development motivated by self-interest and grounded on contract. The family, the church, and the secondary social and economic associations were no longer expressions of the communitarian instinct but conventional, superadded, revisable. Rousseau went even further, completely inverting the Aristotelian understanding of our relationship to society: rather than perfecting us, he taught, civilization inevitably corrupts us. The task of reforming the individual now became the work of the State. Rousseau went so far as to suggest that a fully democratic society should abandon these

[9] Aristotle, *Politics* 1.2.1253a29.
[10] Aristotle, *Nicomachean Ethics* 10.7.1177b31–1178a2.

secondary associations: no social institution should be permitted to mediate between the individual and the State.[11] Subsequent liberal and socialist thinkers further exaggerated the cleavage between natural man and society. John Stuart Mill, the father of modern progressive liberalism, viewed society as a constant threat to our freedom, a thwarter, rather than a nurturer, of our individuality. For Marx and Engels, the family, the church, and economic associations were all the oppressive vestiges of feudalism, to be submerged and obliterated in the overawing power of the State.

It is no coincidence that Hobbes and Rousseau also defended the view that the State is the source of all standards of right and wrong. Without any sense of irony, Hobbes called the State the "Mortall God"—both because it is the source of all morality and because its power must be unlimited. Like Ockham and Locke, Hobbes was a voluntarist, but his brand of voluntarism was radically secularized: he insisted that it was not God's will but the will of the sovereign that determined not only the standards of right and wrong but even the proper interpretation of Scripture.[12] Rousseau, too, thought that the power of the State must be unlimited. He argued in *The Social Contract* that no constitutional rights could limit the power of the State and that the general will of the people was necessarily right and good.[13] In these two thinkers we find the germinal expressions of modern right-wing and left-wing totalitarianism.[14]

---

[11] Citizens must always make up their minds for themselves. "But if groups, sectional associations are formed at the expense of the [state], the will of each of these groups will become general in relation to its own members and private in relation to the state.... Thus, if the general will is to be expressed, it is imperative that there should be no sectional associations in the state." Jean-Jacques Rousseau, *The Social Contract*, ed. Maurice Cranston (New York: Penguin Classics, 1972), 73.

[12] "It belongeth therefore to him that hath the sovereign power to be judge, or constitute all judges of opinions and doctrines, as a thing necessary to peace." Thomas Hobbes, *Leviathan*, 233 (2.18). This includes determining the appropriate interpretation of Scripture and all religious authority. Hobbes, *Leviathan*, 370–72 (2.29).

[13] "[T]he general will is always rightful and always tends to the public good." Rousseau, *The Social Contract* 2.3. The sovereign power is absolute, inviolable, and without any theoretical limit. Rousseau, *The Social Contract* 2.4.

[14] Isaiah Berlin accounted Hobbes and Rousseau two of the most influential architects of modern totalitarianism. Isaiah Berlin, *Freedom and Its Betrayal: Six Enemies of Human Liberty*, ed. Henry Harty (Princeton, N.J.: Princeton University Press, 2002), chaps. 1 (on Hobbes) and 2 (on Rousseau).

These moralized and empirical strands of postclassical natural law continue on today, though in progressively more diluted forms. We find a remnant of the moralized strand in Lon Fuller's "procedural natural law"[15] and the empirical strand in the theories of Adam Smith and classical economists and those of modern liberal and libertarian thinkers.[16]

Gradually, as the organic element in law was dissipated, older synonyms became antonyms: Nature was now opposed to reason, to order, and to society itself. Indeed, Nature was now entirely the contrary of "law" in the civil or moral sense. The very idea of "natural law" was on its way to becoming an oxymoron.

Moral Objectivity without Natural Law: Utilitarianism

When Enlightenment thinkers began to abandon the natural law tradition in the eighteenth century, they did not leap straightaway into the abyss of modern moral skepticism. Even as they jettisoned much of the earlier worldview, they sought to hold on to the one thing that no moral theory worth the name can do without—the moral-objectivity thesis. Because they rejected the teleological conception of the world, however, they had to find another foundation for morality.

It was in the 1780s that two contrasting schools of thought emerged, both of which have dramatically and irrevocably influenced modern moral philosophy. Though they are different in many crucial ways, these two systems of moral thought—utilitarianism

[15] Fuller argues that there are eight rational and normative elements necessary for any rule to be considered a binding legal rule, i.e., a law. These include that laws must be promulgated, that they cannot operate retroactively, that they cannot be changed too frequently, and that they cannot conflict with each other. As Fuller notes, however, this conception of natural law has nothing to do with God's higher law or even with morality in any substantive sense. These elements are, rather, the rational requirements of legal rule making. Lon Fuller, *The Morality of Law* (New Haven, Conn.: Yale University Press, 1964).

[16] Among the most influential liberal thinkers of the last century was H. L. A. Hart. Hart conceded that there exists a core of good sense in the natural law doctrine—but it amounts to five "truisms" about human nature: that men are vulnerable, that we are more or less equal in talents and abilities, and that we have limited altruism, limited resources, and limited understanding and strength of will. H. L. A. Hart, *The Concept of Law*, 2nd ed. (Oxford: Clarendon Press, 1994), 190–95. For a recent libertarian version, see Randy E. Barnett, *The Structure of Liberty* (New York: Oxford University Press, 1998).

and Kantian deontology—represent the two last gasps of the moral-objectivity thesis in modern philosophy. That two such philosophically epochal systems of moral theory appeared within just a few years of one another is a testament to the significance of the problem faced by moral thinkers at that moment in history.

In 1781 Jeremy Bentham (1748–1832) published his *Introduction to the Principles of Morals and Legislation*, a work that defended and applied utilitarianism as a guide to moral and legal judgments. Bentham neither invented utilitarianism nor created the name. It was the chemist and Unitarian minister Joseph Priestly who in 1768 argued that the only appropriate measure of the goodness of an act was its tendency to maximize "the good and happiness of ... the majority of the members of any state".[17] This became Bentham's "greatest-happiness principle". And it was Bentham's disciple John Stuart Mill who claimed to be the first to use the term *utilitarian* in its ethical sense.[18] Yet Bentham did more than any other thinker to develop and apply utilitarian ideas in a wide variety of contexts. He was a philosopher and lawyer who spent eight to twelve hours most days writing on utilitarian themes and was for many years a member of Parliament who used his influence to change the structure of the English law to comport with utilitarian principles. No other single thinker in history has had as great—and as baleful—an influence on English and American law.

It is crucial to see that the movement from natural law to utilitarianism was more than a change in moral outlook; it reflected a deeper metaphysical shift, from theism to a de facto materialism, among eighteenth-century intellectuals. Bentham's life and thought makes this clear. Though he occasionally pretended to deism, he was a thoroughgoing atheist and materialist. He declared the soul a "corporeal substance", said that God was a "nonentity", and characterized death as a process of "altering the modification of matter".[19] His invectives

---

[17]Joseph Priestly, *An Essay on the First Principles of Government* (New York: Gale ECCO: 2010), 17.

[18]John Stuart Mill, *Utilitarianism*, ed. George Sher (Indianapolis: Hackett, 1979), 7, n. 1.

[19]Jeremy Bentham, "A Fragment on Ontology," *The Works of Jeremy Bentham* 8.196, cited in James E. Crimmins, "Bentham on Religion: Atheism and the Secular Society", *Journal of the History of Ideas* 47, no. 1 (January–March 1986): 97n13, 98. For a general review of Bentham's conception of philosophy and politics, and the influence on, and of, his thought, the locus classicus is still Elie Halevy, *The Growth of Philosophical Radicalism*, trans. Mary Morris (Boston: Beacon Press, 1955), especially 5–34, 435–54.

against Christianity, often published under pseudonyms during his life and some only posthumously, were some of the most radical for his time (though they are tepid by contemporary standards). His earlier writings attack Christianity on utilitarian grounds,[20] but his hatred of Christianity seems to have grown with age, and some of his later work (published posthumously) attacked Jesus and St. Paul. Notwithstanding his utter contempt for religion, however, he described himself as "a founder of a sect", "the Luther of jurisprudence", and hoped he would be remembered as a "person of great sanctity". His sense of messianic self-importance was notorious. When Lord Shelburne asked him what must be done to "save the nation", Bentham replied, "[T]ake my book and follow me."[21]

Bentham's utilitarianism is built on three premises. The first is psychological hedonism, the empirical claim that men are inherently motivated to act by the desire for happiness, which Bentham equated with pleasure. In the opening line of his *Introduction to the Principles of Morals and Legislation* he wrote, "Nature has placed mankind under the government of two sovereign masters: *pain* and *pleasure.*"[22] This is not yet saying that the pursuit of pleasure is good, only that we are biologically driven by the quest for pleasure and the avoidance of pain. The second premise, ethical hedonism, provides the moral element, that happiness (pleasure) is indeed the measure of the goodness of an act or a state of affairs. Ethical hedonism is hardly a new idea. Epicurus and some of the Sophists had defended ethical hedonism two thousand years before Bentham. But Bentham's greatest-happiness principle introduced a third element, the pleasure-maximization idea. It builds on the second principle by requiring that the goodness of an act is measured by the *overall*

---

[20] Bentham summed up many of these arguments in a later work, *Of the Influence of Natural Religion on the Temporal Happiness of Mankind*, coauthored with George Grote under the pseudonym Philip Beauchamp and published in 1822. Religious doctrine and practice, he argued, "inflicts unprofitable suffering", "imposes useless privations", "presses undefined terrors" upon the believer, and "taxes pleasure" by "the infusion of preliminary scruples and subsequent remorse". Beyond this, religion creates unwarranted antipathies between those of different faiths, "perverts popular opinion and corrupts moral sentiment". But he went on as well to attack, from an empiricist standpoint, belief in God, the soul, and the afterlife. Beauchamp (Bentham) quoted in Crimmins, "Bentham on Religion", 103.

[21] Ibid.

[22] Jeremy Bentham, *The Principles of Morals and Legislation* (Amherst, N.Y.: Prometheus Book, 1988), 1 (emphasis in original).

happiness of all human beings or, according to some modern versions, by the happiness of all sentient beings. The pleasure-maximization principle establishes a practical tension between the first and third elements of utilitarianism, since utilitarianism requires the sacrifice of the individual's happiness for the sake of generating a greater sum of happiness for the many.

Utilitarianism was attractive to Enlightenment thinkers because it appeared to provide an objective, quantitative standard for morality. Among alternative courses of action, the standard of what we *ought* to do is measured by an objective state of affairs that represents the greatest happiness for everyone. Collective happiness states are facts. The goodness and badness of actions are objective in the sense that they are measured by these psychological facts reflecting the totality of happiness in the world. Thus, utilitarianism seemed to promise that ethics could become a branch of science. In theory at least, the utilitarian-minded legislator could send his social scientists to investigate and to calculate the consequences of any particular set of alternative actions. Given any legal or political question—whether to raise or to lower a tax, to prohibit or to decriminalize an activity, to regulate or to deregulate an area of industry—the proper answer would depend on the overall sum of net happiness that could be achieved by a course of action, reduced by any unhappiness caused by it. In contrast to Aristotle's observation that ethics is a matter of practical reasoning and that frequently the right answer could only be approximated, utilitarianism offered the panacea of scientific precision in ethical thought—an intoxicating idea within the milieu of eighteenth-century rationalism.

In two respects, utilitarianism bore superficial similarities to natural law theory. Both theories connected morality to human nature, though in very different ways. Psychological hedonism was an analogue to the Aristotelian principle that Nature has implanted in us an inborn propensity to seek the Good. For Aristotle, we naturally seek a kind of self-realization in the fulfillment of our telos. For Bentham, we are naturally driven to achieve pleasure and to avoid pain. Though Bentham's conception of happiness was obviously very different from Aristotle's—Aristotle specifically denied that happiness is pleasure—and though Bentham thought the natural prods of pain and pleasure operate mechanistically, rather than teleologically, there is at least a vestige of the older idea that Nature has provided us with a guide to right action.

Second, both Aristotle's teleology and Bentham's utilitarianism are forms of ethical naturalism in that moral truth is grounded in natural facts about the world. Bentham grounded these truths not in the achievement of our natural essence or telos but in the maximal realization of happiness states. Aristotle would have been dubious of any attempts to think about ethical judgments in quasi-mathematical terms, and Aquinas was clear that consequences alone are not the quantum of the Good. Still, both natural law theory and utilitarianism measured the goodness or badness of an act in reference to the natural states they produce. In this respect, Bentham was as much in violation of Hume's injunction against drawing an "ought" from an "is" as was Aristotle.[23]

There the similarities end, however. For one thing, utilitarianism degraded the nature of the object of human action. There was a world of difference between Aristotle's eudaimonia, the pursuit of human perfection, and Bentham's principle of pleasure maximization. In Bentham's hands, our human ends lost their inherent moral character: they embody what we *do* want rather than what we *should* want in order to realize our human potential. In this Bentham was just following the Hobbesian line that Nature is not what leads us forward to our greater perfection—as Aristotle put it, "what each thing is, when fully developed"[24]—but simply the strongest force or desire in us.

This forced a second fundamental alteration in moral thought—one that continues to reverberate in contemporary politics. Aristotle and the classical thinkers reconciled virtue and happiness by insisting that the pursuit of the former leads to the latter.[25] Social order was

[23] G. E. Moore called this the "naturalistic fallacy". He pointed out this problem with utilitarianism in his "open question" argument, that is, it is always an open question whether the maximization of pleasure really is the Good. G. E. Moore, *Principia Ethica* (Cambridge: Cambridge University Press, 1903; Mineola, N.Y.: Dover, 2004), 38–60. See Anthony J. Lisska, *Aquinas's Theory of Natural Law: An Analytic Reconstruction* (New York: Clarendon Press, 1993), 57–62, describing the "open question" argument and its consequences for ethical theory.

[24] Aristotle, *Politics* 1.2.1252b32–33.

[25] According to Aristotle, the happiness of all depends upon the virture of each. See Henry B. Veatch, "Telos and Teleology in Aristotelian Ethics", in *Studies in Aristotle*, ed. Dominic J. O'Meara (Washington, D.C.: Catholic University of America Press, 1981), 279, 281.

a natural outgrowth of individual order in Aristotle's view. In Bentham's view, on the other hand, the well-ordered society does not flow from each individual following his innate human nature. Bentham was able to reconcile duty with happiness only by making it our duty to make *everyone* happy, or at least as many as possible. Here an irreducible collectivism enters moral theory. Where the oughtness of moral obligation was built into our *individual* ends in Aristotle's thought, it became a *social* end for the utilitarians. It was "social" at first only in the sense that everyone's happiness counts, and later in the larger sense that we must *respond collectively* to the utilitarian imperative by maximizing utility through the mechanism of the State. It is largely because of the influence of utilitarian thinking that modern political morality became a thoroughly collectivistic affair.[26]

Some Problems with Utilitarianism

The difficulties with utilitarianism are both philosophical and practical. Though we do not have the space here to explore the many problems and objections to utilitarianism, the theory suffers from at least three central difficulties—what we will call the problem of quantification, the problem of ethical hedonism, and the problem of justice.

The problem of quantification is methodological and practical. The problem is that it is impossible to calculate the sum total of relative states of happiness and unhappiness to be achieved by different courses of action. The problem has several facets. Starting most basically, how are we actually to measure different amounts of happiness generated by alternative courses of action—even within

---

[26] Veatch made the point more broadly about all modern forms of consequentialism:

> The moral life is no longer thought of as consisting principally in the individual's pursuing his rightful goal or end or *telos* just as a human being and trying not to be deflected therefrom by the myriads of chance impulses and drives and inclinations and likings and preferences that never cease to manifest themselves in the life of any one of us. No, morality will be largely an affair, if we might so put it, of the individual's having to try to bring himself to be other-regarding rather than exclusively self-regarding. His duties, that is to say, are not toward himself at all, but only towards others.

Veatch, "Telos and Teleology in Aristotelian Ethics", 287.

the context of one person's activities? Consider the most everyday choice—whether to attend a concert tonight or to visit friends or to stay at home to write. It is difficult enough to decide which of these is preferable, much less to assign each, as the utilitarian must, a certain number of units of happiness, for example, ten to the concert and twelve to visiting friends. In fact, it is much more complicated even than this, since Bentham suggested that there were several distinct dimensions of a happiness state: intensity, duration, certainty or uncertainty, and propinquity or remoteness.[27]

Yet the quantification of happiness states only gets worse when we must also calculate the long-term consequences of each activity. Though I might have less happiness tonight by staying home to write, the time spent advancing this book must be worth something in terms of happiness over the long haul—but how much? It is impossible to say. Even these, however, are minor difficulties in comparison with the problems that arise when we attempt to implement the theory over the whole population. How will a certain change of law affect everyone? How are we to assess the value to each group to be affected, subtracting from that the disutility to those negatively impacted? These population-wide calculations become purely intuitive at this point.

Consider, finally, one last aspect of this problem, which looms large in the litany of issues that bedevil utilitarian thought. Even if these other shortcomings could be surmounted, we are never able to anticipate fully all the unintended consequences of particular changes. Liberalizing divorce laws might seem to make utilitarian sense from the perspective of married couples who wish to have a divorce (while those who are happily married are not affected at all). But how will this affect the children of the increased number of broken homes? And how will the effects play out in the long-term psychological health of these children or their educational achievement? How will this, in turn, influence their ability to obtain professional skills, to hold a job, to raise their own families, to be good citizens? And these are consequences that can be anticipated. What about the completely unforeseen aspects of any legal change? How will liberalizing divorce laws change (and possibly undermine) the institution

---

[27] Bentham, *The Principles of Morals and Legislation*, 29.

of marriage itself over the long term? And how are the effects of *this* change to be calculated?

We could develop these problems at great length, but there is no point in gilding the lily here. Even a brief recitation of the kinds of problems that beset the utilitarian's claim to be able to calculate long-term happiness states over the entire population makes abundantly evident the methodological problems with utilitarian theory. But the problem of quantification is the least of the difficulties with utilitarianism.

The second problem arises from the ethical-hedonist principle. Happiness defined as pleasure is simply not the measure of the Good. Pleasure (whether or not it is maximized) is neither necessary nor sufficient for the goodness of an action. Nor is pleasure a lowest common denominator to which all other values can be reduced, as utilitarianism seems to require.

For instance, even if we could calculate alternative states of happiness, it seems clear to most people that doing the right thing is not always a matter of maximizing happiness or pleasure. Imagine a state in which we could all hook ourselves up to machines that would sustain us all while providing us with enduring and fully maximized states of pleasure throughout our lives. Suppose we could even propagate ourselves, thereby assuring that we continue to maximize pleasure by ensuring that the next generation is born. If this could be achieved only by giving up all external activities so that we merely sat in a comfortable chair and experienced this maximum pleasure for the rest of our lives, fully nourished and cared for by some cadre of machines, would this really be the exalted pinnacle of ethical achievement? It hardly seems to be a life worth living at all, yet it would be preferable, on utilitarian principles, to the lives most of us actually live.[28]

There is, moreover, a second aspect to this problem. Values such as trust, altruism, fidelity, civic-mindedness, courage, compassion, and so forth do not seem to translate directly into pleasure, and vice versa. They may sometimes lead to pleasure and sometimes to its opposite, but they cannot be reduced to, or measured by, pleasure

---

[28] Robert Nozick raised a version of this problem with his "experience machine" example. Robert Nozick, *Anarchy, State, and Utopia* (New York: Basic Books, 1974), 42–45.

states. Philosophers refer to this as the *incommensurability* of ethical values. In other words, there is no lowest common denominator (pleasure or anything else) by which all values and all states of affairs can be measured. Diverse values are apples and oranges with one another. The world is simply more complex than the ethical hedonist assumes. This is why ethics is a matter of practical, not theoretical, reasoning.

But the third difficulty, the problem of justice, is the most damning of all. In its simplest form, the problem consists of the ever present potential conflict between maximizing utility and protecting rights. We recognize that there are many situations in which overall net utility of the population as a whole can be achieved only by violating the rights of a few. Suppose we could elevate the overall happiness of everyone by enslaving 5 percent of the population. If what the 5 percent lose in terms of their utility could be more than compensated for by the rest of us, utilitarianism seems to require this. Basic rights cannot be cashed out in utilitarian terms. We can imagine many situations in which the protection of rights conflicts with utilitarian principles.

Consider the well-discussed situation in which convicting an innocent man will prevent a crowd from rioting and killing several others. Are we justified in railroading one innocent life in order to save others? Or consider the possibility that seven dying children could be saved by sacrificing an eighth child, by donating the needed body parts of the eighth to the other seven. To be sure, utilitarians have responses to hypotheticals like these, but they often depend on empirical claims about how permitting rights violations of this sort will have long-term disutility for everyone. But these empirical responses may or may not be true. If utilitarianism sanctions these kinds of basic abuses *even in principle*, it seems to be wrong (or at least to conflict with most people's strongest moral intuitions to the contrary).

The problem of justice, as philosopher John Rawls pointed out, stems from the fact that utilitarianism does not take the boundaries between persons seriously.[29] It treats pleasure or happiness as one

[29] John Rawls, *A Theory of Justice* (Cambridge, Mass.: Harvard University Press, 1971), 26–27; see also Nozick, *Anarchy, State, and Utopia*, 28–29.

omnibus commodity that must be maximized over the entire population, even at the expense of violating the rights of a few. The penchant for maximization reflected by the problem of justice has much broader moral and political consequences as well. Utilitarianism abstracts from the individual to focus our moral attention on the system as a whole, rather than recognizing that morality is a function of individual character and action. Second, its inherent thrust toward maximizing states of happiness engenders an interminable activism, a political ethic in which we are always seeking to achieve something more—something better. Together these two tendencies toward a collectivistic and maximizing ethic have deeply influenced the progressive conception of the State as a machine for happiness maximization. Yet they often have only the opposite effect over time.

Kantian Morality

In 1785, just four years after the publication of the first edition of Bentham's *Theory of Morals and Legislation*, Immanuel Kant published his *Groundwork of the Metaphysics of Morals*, which represents the antithesis of utilitarianism in ethical thought. Kant was born in the German city of Königsberg (then part of Prussia, now a part of Russia). He never married and never traveled more than ten miles from his hometown, though he is reputed to have been a man of lively wit, debonair charm, and preternatural regularity. A common story relates that he was so consistent in his daily habits that his neighbors could set their clocks by his four o'clock stroll through the town.

To understand Kant is to read the metaphysical assumptions of the traditionalist through the skeptical lens of modern epistemology. It is sometimes said that Kant's thought is the culmination and synthesis of the rationalist and empiricist traditions. Reading Hume, he said, had "awakened him from his dogmatic slumber". But unlike Hume and most of the later empiricists, Kant did not doubt the existence of God, the soul, or human freedom. He thought that we could not know these in the way that we know the phenomenal things of the world. Like Descartes, he was enthralled with physics, and he was a great admirer of Newton's mechanistic theory of the universe. He seems to have been the first to conjecture that the frictional resistance of the tides on the earth's surface must cause a reduction in the earth's speed of rotation—a hypothesis later confirmed by scientists. But how could he harmonize his religious worldview with a mechanistic and materialistic outlook of eighteenth-century physics? Descartes' attempt to cordon off from the physical world an entirely separate realm for the soul simply would not do.

Kant's response, in a nutshell, was to accept the empiricist critique of reality and the scientific outlook as descriptions of *physical phenomena*. All those things that Hume and other empiricists had banished from the realm of possible knowledge—substance, space, time, causation, and the self—became for Kant unprovable but necessary assumptions for any coherent worldview. God, freedom, and immortality become "regulative ideas"—postulates that help us to make sense of our moral experience, though we cannot prove they exist. Space, time, causation, and other fundamental physical notions, which Aristotle and Aquinas taught were real, but which the empiricists attacked as unprovable, Kant claimed were projections of the mind—categories of thought by which the mind organizes its experience of the world. This he called his "Copernican revolution in reverse". Whereas classical theorists insisted that the mind must conform to reality, Kant took the audacious step of arguing that reality must conform to the mind.[30] If this left objective knowledge in a precarious position, Kant wrote in the preface to the second edition of the *Critique of Pure Reason*, "I have had to deny knowledge to make room for faith."[31]

---

[30] Kant was not an idealist in Berkeley's sense: he believed that there was a real world "out there". But he insisted that the mind structures and organizes the "noumenal" reality, giving us our phenomenal experience of the world. This was, in one sense, a development of Descartes' own premise that we begin not from the things we know of the world (since we can be mistaken about these) but from inner experience, the *cogito*: all warrantable knowledge begins with knowledge of the self. Since all we can be certain of initially is the existence of the self (I think, therefore I am), all knowledge begins from within, with what is not doubtable. From the foundation of the self, Descartes built up our knowledge of the rest of the world. Kant magnified this insight a thousand times. All "phenomenal" knowledge—i.e., knowledge of the world that comes through the senses—is a product of the mind itself. Space and time, cause and effect, selves and substances—these are ideas caused by the way the mind organizes our experience of the world.

[31] Immanuel Kant, *Critique of Pure Reason*, trans. J. M. D. Meiklejohn (New York: Barnes and Noble, 2004), xxxviii.

Kant's moral thought is grounded not in happiness, as it was for Bentham and the utilitarians, but in reason and freedom. Kant's ethic is one of duties and rights, not costs and benefits. "Morality is not the doctrine of how we make ourselves happy," he said, "but of how we make ourselves worthy of happiness."[32] The rightness or wrongness of an action does not depend on its consequences—on the happiness or pleasure produced by the act—but on each act's intrinsic nature. Taking innocent life is wrong in and of itself, not because of the unhappiness it may produce. Whereas utilitarians make the good prior to the right, Kant's deontology (from the Greek *deon*, "duty"), makes the right prior to the Good: we must seek to do right and avoid wrong as a matter of duty. The goodness or badness (pleasurableness or unpleasantness) that follows from the act is at best a secondary consideration.

Kant's moral theory is deep and yet gossamer; it is subtle and complex but leaves the details unresolved. He began the *Groundwork of the Metaphysics of Morals* by asking: What thing is good in itself? Not riches, or intelligence, or good health—not even happiness. Each of these can be squandered or, worse, misused. The only thing that is good in and of itself is the "good will". And what is a good will? It is the will that acts "in accordance with duty *and for the sake of duty*".[33] The good will does what is right precisely because it is right. And what does this duty require? It requires (negatively) that the rational person not act from impulse, desire, or feeling and (positively) that he act purely for rational reasons. To act from impulse or desire is to act heteronomously, from sources outside the self that we do not control. To act from reason alone is to act autonomously. Duty leads us to follow reason, and to follow reason is to be free.

Kant formulated his most basic principle of morality in several versions of his "categorical imperative". The first version was: "I am never to act otherwise than that I can also will that my maxim can become a universal law."[34] Another version of his categorical imperative is a bit more substantive: "So act as to treat humanity, whether

[32] Immanuel Kant, *Critique of Practical Reason*, trans. Werner S. Pluhar (Indianapolis: Hackett, 2002), 164–65.

[33] Immanuel Kant, *Groundwork of the Metaphysics of Morals* (Cambridge: Cambridge University Press, 2012), 9 (emphasis mine).

[34] Ibid., 18.

in your own person or that of any another, always at the same time as an end, and never merely as a means."[35] We must accord others the same autonomy and dignity as rational human beings that we insist upon for ourselves.

In sum, for Kant, the goal of human life is not happiness, not even virtue. It is autonomy. The autonomy of the will is "the supreme principle of morality." In fact, autonomy is the capacity of the will to give a law to itself—to determine our own ends in life.[36] This is the true core of freedom: autonomy, perhaps paradoxically, is the capacity to give ourselves a law to live by. This "law", however, must comport with the categorical imperative. No moral deed, moreover, is truly and fully right unless it is done autonomously. (Even Aristotle's virtuous man, who acts from well-formed habits, is not fully autonomous for Kant.) In fact, even our obedience to God must be grounded not in our love of God but in our own autonomy: before we can obey God, we must give ourselves the principle—and do so from duty to reason alone—that God is to be obeyed. To base our obligation to obey on fear of punishment or even on the desire to please God is heteronomy.

Superficially, Kant's ethical system appears in some ways to be a development of the natural law tradition and a culmination, in particular, of the moral strand of newer versions of the natural law. To act from duty is to act from binding reason, a reason that is lawlike.[37] Kant accepted the basic dignity and equality of all human beings and taught that, though we cannot prove the existence of freedom, it is a necessary postulate of practical (moral) reasoning. And like Aristotle and Aquinas, he accepted the distinction between theoretical and practical reason and concluded with them that moral knowledge is knowledge not of what is but of what ought to be.[38]

In another way, however, Kant's ethical thought is the antithesis of the classical natural law tradition. Whereas classical thinkers insisted

---

[35] Ibid., 47.

[36] Ibid., 59.

[37] "Duty is the necessity of acting out of reverence for the law." Kant, *Groundwork of the Metaphysics of Morals*, 16.

[38] Kant taught that there is only one general capacity for reason but where theoretical reason applies itself to a datum of experience, practical reason determines the will. Kant, *Critique of Practical Reason* 1.1.

that the Good cannot be divorced from Being—that metaphysics must be the foundation for ethics—Kant thought they *had to be* separated in order to give morality a more certain foundation.[39] That surer foundation was none other than *human reason alone*. Moreover, whereas Aquinas thought that reason and Nature were coextensive, Kant made them contraries. Reason was, he thought, opposed to Nature (again, because he held the modern, purely static and descriptive conception of Nature). Only the person who acts from reason alone is truly free—autonomous. The person who follows impulse or desire—who acts from Nature—acts heteronomously: he is a slave to the "phenomenal" impulses of human nature. Reason and autonomy lead the free person to act not from desire, happiness, self-interest, or even well-formed habit—but from duty alone. To live autonomously and to treat all other persons as autonomous (as ends in themselves) is to do our duty—to be free and to recognize the autonomy of every other person.[40]

The most important single critique of Kant's ethical system is that it is virtually substanceless. His categorical imperative was a purely formal principle without any material content. It was not so much a

[39] Kant had three reasons for wishing to divorce morality from metaphysics and Nature. First, he was skeptical that we can have any metaphysical knowledge. To ground our morality on so shaky a foundation would be to make it vulnerable to attack. Second, Kant had read Hume and was concerned to avoid the fallacy of going from an "is" (i.e., a factual statement, such as a statement about Nature or reality) to an "ought" (i.e., a moral conclusion). In the twentieth century, philosopher G. E. Moore called this the "naturalistic fallacy". If this is indeed a fallacy (see chapter 3), utilitarians and natural law theorists are equally in violation of it—utilitarians because they draw their moral conclusions from factual claims about human happiness, and natural law theorists because the Good is a function of the unfolding of our natural essence. As a careful reader of Hume, Kant wanted to avoid drawing his moral conclusions from any naturalistic (factual) premises. But Kant had another reason for divorcing morality from metaphysics. He wanted to make human autonomy, rather than God or nature, the basis for all moral truth. Moral truth would come from the deepest sources within ourselves rather than from any "given" natural order.

[40] Kant's ethical theory resembles in some way that of the Stoics—that we must act from duty, not in pursuit of happiness, that acting from duty requires that we overcome our desires in favor a state of disinterested justice that gives each person his due, etc. But Kant's theory adds something crucially modern: the centrality of freedom. The Stoics taught that to be free is simply to understand and accept the conditions of our nature. The condition of apatheia was largely negative: we escape the bondage of our condition by understanding it. Kant, on the other hand, argued that the autonomous person creates his own ends, charts his own course, decides what kind of life to live, and that this is part of what autonomy permits.

first substantive principle of ethics (like Aquinas' first principle that good is to be done and evil avoided) as it is a *criterion* for moral judgment, a procedure for judging the validity of ethical principles. By sundering reason from nature, and morality from Being, Kant left ethics with little to guide it other than the negative injunction against violating the rights of others. Worse, Kant's theory of autonomy was seductively amenable to distortion by later thinkers who adopted only half of Kant's philosophy: radical thinkers of the nineteenth and twentieth centuries accepted Kant's teaching that each person must choose his own ends but abandoned Kant's admonition against acting from desire. Without Nature to guide the individual's selection of ends, the concept of autonomy was set adrift on the hedonic seas of contemporary culture. Autonomy has come to mean, for many liberal thinkers today, a right—not a capacity—to do whatever one wishes consistent with the same right of all others.

The Slide into Moral Subjectivism

Though it is not surprising that Enlightenment thinkers tried to hold on to objectivity in moral thought, what is surprising is how quickly their efforts ended in futility. One problem was that both Kantianism and utilitarianism shifted morality's emphasis away from the virtues and the centrality of human character, in other words, away from the *actor* and onto the *act*. Utilitarianism did this by emphasizing external outcomes, the consequences of acts irrespective of the motives that brought these consequences about. Kantianism did it by severing the link between the rightness of an action and the natural sources of human motivation. Kant suggested that actions performed out of love or benevolence—or even from virtuous *habits*—were not fully autonomous and thus did not meet the strictures of his categorical imperative. In both cases, post–natural law moral theory devolved into the search for the right *action*, and this led, in practice, to an overreliance on rules, commandments, and prohibitions.

The emphasis on the moral act, rather than on the actor, had two further consequences. On one hand, it could (and perhaps often did) lead to moral pharisaism. The emphasis shifted, especially with utilitarianism, to the outward performance of the action—the observance of external rules or the achievement of certain consequences—at the expense of the moral health of the inner person. But an overemphasis on the act also led to skepticism. Since the good was now parceled out in particular acts, there was an increasingly greater emphasis on achieving the "right answer" in every situation. Aristotle's old idea that moral knowledge was *practical* knowledge and that we should not expect to be able to achieve the same degree of truth in moral reasoning as in speculative reasoning was lost to modernity. Precision became the touchstone of objectivity itself as "moral science" (as it was increasingly called in the eighteenth and nineteenth centuries) became a theoretical matter. The burden was too heavy for the concept of moral objectivity to bear. The inherent impossibility of drawing precise answers with deductive certainty in every case increasingly led modern moral thinkers toward moral relativism.

Philosophical developments in the nineteenth and twentieth centuries accelerated these more general developments. The foundations of the utilitarian and Kantian systems began to crumble under the weight of their own assumptions. Within a generation of Bentham's death, his greatest disciple, John Stuart Mill, abruptly rejected Bentham's notion that happiness could be measured in purely quantitative terms. To Bentham's assertion that "[q]uantity of pleasure being equal, pushpin is as good as poetry", Mill responded that "some kinds of pleasure are more desirable than others."[41] Happiness or pleasure, he insisted, possesses a *qualitative* dimension: there were "higher" and "lower" forms of pleasure. "Few human creatures would consent to be changed into any of the lower animals for the promise of the fullest allowance of a beast's pleasures", he wrote in his essay *Utilitarianism*. "It is ... better to be Socrates dissatisfied than a fool satisfied."[42]

The qualitative dimension undercut the mechanistic (and egalitarian) appeal of Bentham's utilitarianism. Mill was claiming that we could not quantify total happiness over large groups of persons in a quasi-mathematical way. In *On Liberty*, he claimed to base the case for freedom on utility, "but it must be utility in the largest sense, grounded on the permanent interests of man as a progressive being."[43]

---

[41] Mill continues, "It would be absurd that in estimating all other things, quality is considered as well as quantity, the estimation of pleasures should be supposed to depend on quantity alone." Mill, *Utilitarianism*, 8.

[42] Ibid., 9, 10.

[43] John Stuart Mill, *On Liberty*, ed. Gertrude Himmelfarb (New York: Penguin Classics, 1985), 70.

This was no verbal quibble. Mill was importing into the concept of happiness other normative values—values that looked almost Aristotelian. Indeed, talking of man's "permanent interest as a progressive being" has a distinctively teleological flavor to it. All this seemed to show that, even among Bentham's most faithful followers, few thought his univocal concept of happiness could do the normative job of grounding virtue, self-development, liberty, or other values.

Not only did Mill's criticism undercut the social-scientific appeal of utilitarianism, however; it also raised the question about who was to be the judge of which pleasures were "higher" and "lower".[44] Ironically, Mill's insistence that there was a qualitative dimension to happiness suggested to others that perhaps no one can judge another man's concept of happiness—that the very concept of happiness is so contested that we might as well leave it to each individual to decide for himself what makes him happy. By the early twentieth century, a growing number of utilitarians were arguing exactly that: utility should be measured not in terms of happiness states but in terms of particular individual choices. We should maximize *choices*, not happiness. "Preference utilitarianism", as it came to be called, had a triple appeal. It combined the apparent virtues of moral neutrality (let each person decide for himself what he values) with empirical rigor (people's revealed preferences can be quantified by looking at the results in the marketplace). At the same time, this approach appeared to reduce the conflict between freedom and utility. If utility could now be measured in terms of individual choices, the old conflict between liberalism and utilitarianism could be overcome.

The philosophy was consistent with the classical liberalism of the period since it entailed that markets should be as free as possible and government should "get out of the way" and let people arrange their own lives as they wish. The Austrian economist Ludwig von Mises wrote in 1949, "There is no standard of greater or lesser satisfaction than individual judgments of value, different in various people, and for the same people at various times."[45] The notion of objective worth had vanished. All things have their value only through human choice:

---

[44] Mill answered that this is decided by a majority vote of the preference of those who have experienced both forms of pleasure. Mill, *On Liberty*, 8–9.

[45] Ludwig von Mises, *Human Action: A Treatise on Economics* (Chicago: Contemporary Books, 1966), 14.

> Choosing determines all human decisions. In making his choice, man chooses between not only various material things and services. All human values are offered for option. All ends and all means, both material and ideal issues, the sublime and the base, the noble and the ignoble, are ranged in a single row and subjected to a decision which picks out one thing and sets aside another. Nothing that men aim at or want to avoid remains outside of this arrangement into a unique scale of gradation and preference.[46]

Let one man pursue pushpin, and the other poetry. The overall goal should be not to judge the value of individual choices but simply to maximize them.

Kant's conception of autonomy was soon reduced to essentially the same idea. Without the concept of human nature to ground and guide our choice of ends, Kant's sober conception of autonomy quickly devolved into the idea of unfettered, spontaneous choice. To be "autonomous" was, at most, to have an internally consistent network of subjective desires and beliefs that "fit together". Libertarian law professor David A.J. Richards, for example, proposed as a foundation for our legal system "an autonomy-based concept of treating persons as equals". A scheme of life is autonomous, in his view, if it makes consistent or internally coherent a person's subjective beliefs, experiences, and desires. Every "autonomous" lifestyle is as good as any other. There exist no legitimate reasons for choosing one over another. We have no more right to criticize the heroin addict, for example, than we do to criticize the man who doggedly pursues love or wealth. The drug addict's life is autonomous, Richards argues, since "the psychological centrality of drug use for many young addicts in the United States may, from the perspective of their own circumstances, not unreasonably organize their lives and ends."[47]

In this way, the two great modern moral systems, utilitarianism and Kantianism, had largely converged on the idea that the individual preference was the ultimate unit of moral measurement. No decision or action or lifestyle is irrational when to be "rational" simply means to seek to satisfy one's preferences. Von Mises, the "right-wing"

---

[46] Ibid., 3.

[47] David A.J. Richards, *Sex, Drugs, Death and the Law* (Lanham, Md.: Rowman and Littlefield, 1986), 172, 176–77.

classical economist, was in fundamental agreement with Richards, the "left-wing" pseudo-Kantian. "Human action is necessarily always rational," von Mises concluded, because the "ultimate end of action is always the satisfaction of some desires of the acting man. Since nobody is in a position to subordinate his own value judgments for those of the acting individual, it is in vain to pass judgment on other people's aims and volitions."[48]

The Triumph of Nihilism

At a still more abstract level, the slide into subjectivism was reflected in the metaethical theories of the twentieth century. Cambridge philosopher G. E. Moore (1873–1958) was neither a typical utilitarian nor a deontologist, but he, too, wanted to hold on to moral objectivity. He criticized utilitarians for committing what he called the "naturalistic fallacy"—basically the same "fallacy" Hume had discovered of going from an "is" to an "ought". Utilitarians were as much in violation of the naturalistic fallacy, Moore argued, as natural law theorists since they attempted to move from factual premises about states of happiness to moral conclusions about what should be done.[49] But Moore did not see much hope in the Kantian project either. Reason alone had proved too unstable a foundation for moral objectivity. Still, he believed that "good" and "bad" had an objective foundation in the world. But since it could not be Nature or reason, he had to find a third realm.

Moore argued that the concept of the Good is a simple, indefinable, and nonnatural property of certain actions and things. Like the color red, the Good cannot be defined or reduced to another property. But unlike colors, goodness was, he argued, a nonnatural property. It does not exist in the natural realm, it does not track any state of affairs in the world (happiness, the realization of the human telos, etc.), nor is it known by reason. Rather, we simply know the Good when we see it by a direct act of intuition.[50] The Good exists but as a mysterious quality in a mysterious realm (a nonnatural but

[48] Von Mises, *Human Action*, 19.

[49] Moore argued that the fact that anyone can meaningfully ask, "Yes, but is maximizing happiness really good?" means that it will always be an "open question" whether or not some natural value really is equivalent to the Good. Thus, natural properties are not surrogates for ethical properties. G. E. Moore, *Principia Ethica*, 18–21.

nevertheless "objective" realm) that we come to appreciate through an equally enigmatic capacity for direct intuition.

Moore's ethical intuitionism was temporarily seductive. It gave moral principles a foundation while avoiding the naturalistic fallacy of the utilitarians, on the one hand, and the recourse to ungrounded Kantian reason, on the other. In fact, Moore's nonnaturalistic ethic shared many of the same features as Descartes' dualism. It divided the world between two realms, natural and nonnatural (moral) properties, and argued that we rationally derive our moral principles from self-evident truths that we apprehend by a direct act of intuition. A few thinkers built on Moore's intuitionist theory of ethics in the 1920s and 1930s,[51] but ultimately Moore's theory was more out of touch with the tenor of twentieth-century philosophy than anything a natural law theorist might offer. For one thing, Moore's realm of "nonnatural" properties was a scandal in the face of modern philosophy's materialism: In what sense do these properties exist if they are not "natural"? And what is this "moral sense", this act of intuition by which we are directly acquainted with the Good? Moore's intuitionism flouted the empiricist dogma that all knowledge comes through the senses and can be verified by some appeal to quantifiable commodities. If this was the only morally objectivist alternative to natural law theory in the twentieth century, only two ways seemed open to moral philosophy: to return to natural law or to proceed in the direction of total moral skepticism.

It was precisely at this point—by about the 1950s—that the two paths diverged. A small but far-from-inconsequential group of philosophers began to see their way back to natural law.[52] The majority,

---

[50] For a discussion of Moore's place in the history of ethical theory, see Lisska, *Aquinas's Theory of Natural Law*, 58–62.

[51] W.D. Ross developed a kind of deontological intuitionism—a duty-based conception of ethics in which various prima facie duties are known directly by an act of intuition. W.D. Ross, *The Right and the Good* (Oxford: Oxford University Press, 1930).

[52] Some of the most important of these are the following: G.E.M. Anscombe, "Modern Moral Philosophy", in *Human Life, Action and Ethics* (Charlottesville, Va.: Imprint Academic, 2005); Henry Veatch, *Rational Man: A Modern Interpretation of Aristotelian Ethics* (Bloomington, Ind.: Indiana University Press, 1962); Germain Grisez, "The First Principle of Practical Reason", *Natural Law Forum* 10 (1965); 168–201; Alasdair C. MacIntyre, *After Virtue: A Study in Moral Theory* (Notre Dame, Ind.: University of Notre Dame Press, 1981); John Finnis, *Natural Law and Natural Rights* (Oxford: Oxford University Press, 1980); Russell Hittinger, *A Critique of the New Natural Law Theory* (Notre Dame, Ind.: Notre Dame Press, 1987).

however, pushed along further in the direction of skepticism and relativism.[53] A fountain of newer and progressively more refined versions of moral subjectivism, relativism, and skepticism flowed from the pens of professional philosophers. One group, influenced by the findings of anthropologists, claimed that "good" and "bad" are simply culturally relative conventions. To say that murder is wrong is to say that murder is not accepted in a particular society. The cultural relativist maintains that there are no real moral truths beyond particular social institutions that embody or represent certain moral positions.[54]

The chief advantage of cultural relativism is also its greatest difficulty. If there are no values that transcend particular cultures, then those of one culture can never legitimately criticize those of another. There can be no moral measuring stick by which any society can rightfully be criticized, since "right" and "wrong" are themselves cultural artifacts. But this entails that the rest of the world had no legitimate ground to criticize Nazi culture or South African apartheid or the slave culture of the antebellum South since, in each case, the culture in question accepted the norms that we criticize. If the cultural relativist were right, all we could do about the Nazis was say that we disagree with them and then punish them for the actions we found abhorrent once we had the power to do so. But the consistent cultural relativist must admit that we had no rational ground for our disapproval and no moral ground for finding the Nazis guilty of "crimes against humanity".

Cultural relativism also entails that the idea of moral progress is an illusion. There must be some objective moral standard by which to judge whether things are better today than they were yesterday. If the cultural relativist were correct, what was considered right in the past, for example, slavery, was right because most people believed it was, and what is considered right now is right for the same reason, regardless of how it might be judged in the future. Indeed, one of the real

---

[53] In 1957, philosopher Brian Medlin summed up the feeling: "[I]t is now pretty generally accepted by professional philosophers that ultimate ethical principles must be arbitrary." Brian Medlin, "Ultimate Principles and Ethical Egoism", *Australian Journal of Philosophy* 35 (1957): 111.

[54] Melville J. Herskovits, "Cultural Relativism and Cultural Values", in *Ethical Relativism*, ed. J. Ladd (Lanham, Md.: University Press of America, 1985). For one of the classic anthropological views of morality as a cultural integrating force, see Ruth Benedict, *Patterns of Culture* (Boston: Houghton Mifflin, 1934).

problems with cultural relativism for progressives is that it entails that the reformers, the activists—the Gandhis and Martin Luther Kings of the world—are always wrong *in principle* when they begin to agitate for a change in the culturally accepted values of the time. In fact, as with all forms of relativism, the cultural relativist can have no transcultural conception of human rights, since he denies any moral standard independent of the positive morality of a particular culture.

Another form of moral nonobjectivism, ethical subjectivism (sometimes called individual relativism), holds that moral claims are nothing but first-person reports of the speaker's beliefs. To say that murder is wrong is to say nothing more than "I believe murder to be wrong." Moral subjectivism of this sort is so incoherent that even most moral skeptics reject it out of hand. Not only are many subjectivists radically inconsistent—insisting that social injustices be righted even as they deny that there can be a standard for justice outside their own particular set of beliefs—but the position cannot even be formulated coherently.[55]

A third and still more subtle form of moral nonobjectivism, ethical emotivism, avoids some of these difficulties of pure subjectivism. Emotivists such as A.J. Ayer and C.L. Stevenson proposed that ethical statements have no descriptive or objective content whatsoever.[56] Moral statements do not describe even our own individual beliefs. Rather, they are *expressions of feelings*. To say that murder is wrong is nothing more, according to these thinkers, than to express disapproval of the act of murder or to prescribe to others that they should abstain from murder. Whereas the subjectivist claims that moral statements are factual claims, though of a highly impoverished sort (i.e., they reflect facts not about the world but about what the speaker happens to believe), emotivism avoids the problems with subjectivism by claiming that moral statements are not factual claims at all. Moral statements do not function descriptively but only *expressively*

---

[55] As G.E. Moore pointed out, subjectivism leads to an infinite regress: if "x is good" simply means, "I believe x is good", then to say, "I believe x is good" is to say, "I believe that I believe that x is good", etc., etc. The point is, again, that without an object for the moral belief, moral statements become not simply subjective but meaningless gibberish. G.E. Moore, *Ethics* (New York: Oxford University Press, 1912), 51–52.

[56] A.J. Ayer, *Language, Truth and Logic* (New York: Dover, 1952); Charles L. Stevenson, *Ethics and Language* (New Haven, Conn.: Yale University Press, 1944).

or *prescriptively*. Their semantic function is similar to a jilted lover declaring, "How could you!" or a general yelling, "Charge!" They are mere expressions of feeling or, at best, exhortations to act in a certain way.[57]

Some twenty-five hundred years after Protagoras and the Sophists, it seems we have come full circle. In the wake of the loss of the natural law, twentieth-century philosophy has apparently completed the task of demolishing the moral foundations of all moral knowledge. There is nothing left to justify even the preferences of the utilitarian or the autonomous choices of the libertarian—other than that they *are our preferences*. The only position left today seems to be moral nihilism. As John Barth summed up the modern philosophy, "The reasons that people have for attributing value to things are always ultimately arbitrary, irrational. In short, there is no ultimate reason for calling anything important or valuable; no ultimate reason for preferring one thing to another."[58]

The Divorce of Law and Morality

Moral relativism obviously compromises the second constitutive thesis of natural law theory, the overlap thesis. If there is no objective moral order, there can hardly be a moral order with which the law must somehow overlap. Yet even before modern philosophy had resigned itself to the collapse of morality, the leading legal theorists had, by the nineteenth century, come to reject any intrinsic connection between law and morality. In contrast to St. Augustine's old insistence that an unjust law is no law at all,[59] the most influential legal theorist of the nineteenth century, John Austin

---

[57] Under the influence of more recent philosophical trends, emotivists claimed that the meaning of any statement is the function it plays, i.e., the job it does, in language. Moral claims such as "Murder is wrong" were, they argued, simply expressive, not descriptive of any condition in the world. They expressed the speaker's attitude toward some state of affairs or prescribed what one should do. "Murder is wrong", in other words, was the equivalent of saying, "I detest murder" or "One should not murder." There was no objective or descriptive content otherwise. J. O. Urmson, *The Emotive Theory of Ethics* (Oxford: Oxford University Press, 1969).

[58] John Barth, *The Floating Opera and the End of the Road* (New York: Anchor, 1988), 216–17.

[59] "Non videtur esse lex quae justa non fuerit." St. Augustine, *De Libero Arbitrio* I, 5.

(1790–1859), proposed that law was a creature of politics, pure and simple. The validity of a legal rule has nothing to do with its goodness or justice. "The existence of law is one thing," Austin wrote, "its merit or demerit is another."[60] With this, Austin rejected the overlap thesis.

Austin was a protégé of Bentham and was part of the circle of younger utilitarian thinkers, including John Stuart Mill, who dominated English intellectual thought in the mid-nineteenth century. Austin is considered the father of modern legal positivism, a movement that sought to reconceive law in more "objective", quantifiable, nonmoral terms. As H. L. A. Hart summed up Austin's position, law is an "order of the sovereign backed by threats".[61] Law, as distinguished from ethics, etiquette, cultural norms, and other forms of social authority, consists of rules promulgated by the political authorities of the community (e.g., the king or the legislature), whose violation carries with it an enforceable penalty. There is nothing more to law than this.

Later legal positivists—most famously, Hart—refined Austin's overly simplistic definition.[62] What is important to see, however, is that utilitarianism and legal positivism were the nineteenth century's one-two punch to natural law theory. Utilitarianism offered a new foundation for moral objectivity, while legal positivism was the response to the overlap thesis, decoupling law from morality. Both

---

[60] John Austin, *The Province of Jurisprudence Determined* (London: John Murray, 1832; Indianapolis: Hackett, 1998), 278.

[61] H. L. A. Hart, *The Concept of Law*, 21.

[62] Twentieth-century legal positivist H. L. A. Hart, for example, argued that the definition is inadequate in several ways. Contracts and wills, for example, are legally binding instruments, but they are not commands of the sovereign; they are made by private parties. There are problems, moreover, with determining who the "sovereign" is: Does it change every time there is a new member of Congress, for example? And how is the model accurate in a democracy, in which the people are supposed to be the sovereign? In what sense is international law "law" (since Austin's "sovereign command" model cannot be applied to nation-states). Finally, Austin's simplistic model may apply to the "primary rules" of law, i.e., criminal and civil law that binds the citizen directly, but it leaves out the essential "secondary rules" of any legal system, e.g., constitutional rules that govern how the sovereign is to make law, how law changes, and how legal disputes are to be adjudicated. In what sense, for example, is the right of equal protection or the principle of separation of powers a command of the sovereign backed by threats? Hart proposed a more sophisticated idea of law as the "union of primary and secondary rules". H. L. A., Hart, *The Concept of Law*, 79–99.

sought a more empirical foundation for morality and law. Both, moreover, tended to emphasize the importance of determinate rules as essential ingredients of any objective moral or legal system.[63]

By the twentieth century, however, legal positivism was to have a fate similar to that of utilitarianism. As the nineteenth century's faith in objective moral and legal rules dissolved under the strain of more recent criticism, and as Bentham's utilitarianism deteriorated into the subjectivity of preference utilitarianism, so, too, legal positivism was largely supplanted by legal realism in the twentieth century.

The legal realists were the radical nominalists of modern legal thought. They argued that law is not embodied in objective legal rules—there are no objective legal rules. Law "happens" when the gavel comes down and one party is made to pay a civil judgment or sent to jail. It is the residue of politics but a particularly mercurial form of politics at that. Law is not found in the statutes or the case reporters. "The Prophecies of what the courts will do", Holmes said, "are what I mean by the law."[64] Or as Judge Jerome Frank, a leading legal realist of the mid-twentieth century put it less reverently, "Law is what the judge had for breakfast."[65] All that remains of the objectivity of the law is the momentary preference of the judge.

---

[63] In order for law to be called "objective", legal positivists emphasized the importance of determinate legal rules that are binding on judges who decide law and on the citizens themselves. Positivists tended to argue that judges are not free to depart from established legal rules in the interest of doing justice. Hard cases had to be decided according to established legal rules, not by seeking to do justice in each case. Most positivists held that departing from these rules not only usurped the prerogatives of the legislature but also made the legal system unpredictable. As a theoretical matter, moreover, determinate rules were necessary to make law "objective". Where was "the law" if it could not be identified and pinned down in determinate legal rules?

Rule utilitarianism sought the same goal in moral theory. In contrast to act utilitarianism, rule utilitarians argued that we should follow a system of moral rules that, over the long haul, maximizes utility. These rules should be followed even when the rule does not maximize utility in a particular case. A system of utility-maximizing rules produces more utility overall, they argued, than deciding each particular case on its own merits without the benefit of stable rules. In both moral and legal thought, it was the adherence to particular rules that grounded and gave substance to law and morality.

[64] Oliver Wendell Holmes, "The Path of the Law", *Harvard Law Review* 10 (1897): 461.

[65] Jerome Frank, *Courts on Trial: Myth and Reality in American Justice* (Princeton, N.J.: Princeton University Press, 1973), 162.

Conclusion

Only in times of deepest distress are men forced to come to terms with realities that they can ignore in more quotidian times. Just a decade after Frank and legal realists had denied the existence of law in any substantive sense, and at the very point in history when philosophers were on the brink of abandoning the very notion that there is an objective moral order, Justice Jackson, chief prosecutor at Nuremberg, invoked the central principles of the natural law in his closing argument. Though he did not call it the natural law, Jackson spoke of the need to follow "reason, instead of outcry". He foreswore any result "that the calm and critical judgment of posterity would pronounce unjust". He found damning, finally, one of the defendants' assertions that "National Socialism and Christian concepts are irreconcilable." The defendants' guilt was as manifest as the higher law by which they must be judged. "If you were to say of these men that they are not guilty," he proclaimed in his closing argument, "it would be as true to say there has been no war, there are no slain, there has been no crime."[66]

[66] Robert H. Jackson, "Closing Arguments for Conviction of Nazi War Criminals", Robert H. Jackson Center website, accessed April 24, 2015, http://www.roberthjackson.org /speech-and-writing/bibliography/closing-argument-for-conviction-of-nazi-war-criminals/.

9

The Lost Foundations of Our Moral
and Political Ideals

*A dogmatic belief in objective value is necessary to the very idea of a rule which
is not tyranny or an obedience which is not slavery.*

— C. S. Lewis

We are now at the point at which we can draw together the basic conclusions traced in the preceding chapters. As the teleological–natural law framework has slowly given way to a broadly secular-materialist worldview, our moral and political ideals have been left in a metaphysical limbo. Our moral heritage is rooted in a view of human nature that is now quietly vanishing. Like a storefront on a western movie set, we continue to cling to ideas such as freedom and human dignity, human rights and objective moral standards as the very ground for these commitments is slowly worn away. Contemporary secular thinkers find themselves in much the same position as Protagoras and other Sophists of the fifth century B.C. Schooled in materialism and relativism, they cannot make sense of their own broadly humanitarian political commitments. The result is that, intellectually, they (and we) live an almost schizophrenic existence with one foot in each of two very different ways of understanding ourselves and our world. Still, we are not fully at home in either.

This chapter examines the three core moral and political ideals of Western civilization: freedom, responsibility, and human dignity. It argues that these values make little sense outside a broadly teleological–natural law worldview and certainly cannot be harmonized with the prevailing relativism and materialism of our age. These three core

C. S. Lewis, *The Abolition of Man* (New York: HarperOne, 2008), 73.

ideals, moreover, are each nested within a broader network of other values with which they are linked. Freedom, in the sense of free will, is linked to political liberty and to our understanding of human rights. Responsibility is connected to our ideas of merit, remorse, forgiveness, and mercy. Human dignity, finally, undergirds our commitments to equality and to the sanctity of human life. Each of these three ideals loses its significance in a materialistic, deterministic world. And when each core ideal goes, the other correlative values must follow. Thus, for the last two or three centuries, we have been witnessing the gradual implosion of an entire moral worldview.

If what we have said so far in part II seems to reject everything modern, this chapter will also set the record straight in that respect. It will argue that, though natural law is a necessary foundation for freedom, responsibility, and human dignity, these values themselves did not assume central significance in the classical tradition. The Greeks had little to say about freedom and human dignity, and even their idea of responsibility was limited. While Christianity provides a powerful corrective to these defects, only in the modern period did these values emerge as the core political ideals of Western civilization. It is as if the entire Western tradition had a telos of its own waiting to be realized in modern liberal thought. Yet no sooner did freedom and dignity emerge as important values than they were debased by the philosophical course of modernity. In sum, though natural law is the only possible foundation for freedom, responsibility, and human dignity, it was the liberal tradition that brought these values to their fruition.

Freedom and the Natural Law

The emergence of freedom as a core animating value of modern political thought has been stymied by two modern philosophical developments: the decline of an objective understanding of morality and the spread of determinism. The first has deformed our understanding of what freedom *is*; the second obscures why we value it. We will discuss the first in this section and the second in the next.

The natural law tradition provides a normative foundation for understanding what freedom is. Freedom is acting in accordance with the moral law, which is, again, acting in accordance with the human good, the unfolding of the human telos. Freedom cannot be properly understood in abstraction from the human good. Because modern thought has divorced freedom from normativity, it is faced with a host of problems and paradoxes that threaten to undermine freedom's very significance.

John Locke was the first true liberal thinker.[1] With the exception of Kant, he was the last to connect freedom to the moral law. Near the beginning of his *Second Treatise of Government*, Locke wrote that "though this [state of nature] be a state of liberty, yet it is not a state of license." There is "a law of nature to govern it, which obliges everyone". This law of nature is none other than God's moral law.[2] Freedom consists, Locke maintained, in the liberty of the individual to live as he desires *consistent with this moral law*.

This moral law that binds the individual is also binding on government. Echoing St. Augustine's comment that an unjust law is no law at all, Locke wrote that the laws of particular countries "are only so far right, as they are founded on the law of nature, by which they are to be regulated and interpreted".[3] In the Anglo-American tradition, this normative conception of freedom as limited government—what

---

[1] Locke's *Second Treatise of Government* has been called liberalism's founding document. What makes it liberal (in the broad sense) is the following. With Hobbes, Locke was the first to attempt to justify the power of government by resort to the consent of the governed. Whereas the classical tradition followed Aristotle in claiming that "the State is, by nature, prior to the individual" (Aristotle, *Politics* 1.2), Hobbes and Locke assumed the opposite: the power of the State derives *from* the individual. Yet Hobbes was not a liberal. Against Hobbes' highly statist idea of government, Locke argued for limited government, the right of revolution, and the trio of classical liberal rights: the rights of life, liberty, and property. The Framers of American government incorporated these rights into the due process clause of the Fifth Amendment of the U.S.Constitution. Hobbes and Locke began from a similar premise and developed their political thought in opposite directions.

[2] He wrote:

There is a law of nature to govern it, which obliges everyone, and reason, which is that law, teaches all mankind, who will but consult it, that being all equal and independent, no one ought to harm another in his life, health, liberty, or possessions, for men, being the workmanship of one omnipotent, and infinitely wise maker; all the servants of one sovereign master, sent into the world by his order, and about his business, they are his property, whose workmanship they are.

John Locke, *Second Treatise of Government* 6.

[3] Ibid., 12.

would later be called "negative liberty"[4]—began to emerge in the twelfth or thirteenth century and continued to unfold with its full normative force with the American Revolution.[5]

The same moral law that prevents the government from infringing the basic rights of the individual also prevents the individual from infringing the rights of others. In both cases, freedom consists of being able to live free of the unwarranted infringements of government and of private parties. Aquinas and the Scholastics would have recognized this idea, but they tended to think of (what we now call) individual rights as *derivative* of the general moral order. Aquinas used the word *ius*, which we translate as "right", to mean that an individual is free to act within the limits of the moral law. Of course, Aquinas also thought that law could not, and should not try to, prevent every vice or perfect every virtue. So in a sense he recognized a residual sphere of freedom beyond what was, strictly speaking, "right", a realm where enforcing the moral law would be counterproductive.[6]

Locke would not have disagreed with this way of conceiving rights in principle, but he viewed rights from the side of the individual rather than from the perspective of the general moral order. His theory of property rights, for example, focused on the efforts of the individual in creating a thing of value: a man mixes his labor with the bounty of nature, cutting down a tree and building a boat out of it, for example.[7] While the individual's right flowed from the general moral order, the individual (we might say) actualized his own ius by cutting down the tree and building the boat. In sum, Locke's

---

[4] For the classic discussion of the distinction between negative and positive freedom, see Isaiah Berlin, "Two Concepts of Liberty", in *Four Essays on Liberty* (Oxford: Oxford University Press, 1969).

[5] For the classic treatment of the development of this negative idea of freedom, see Edward S. Corwin, "The 'Higher Law' Background of American Constitutional Law", *Harvard Law Review* 42, no. 2 (1928). The concept of law as a normative idea is the subject of an excellent book by Reid. John Phillip Reid, *The Concept of Liberty in the Age of the American Revolution* (Chicago: University of Chicago Press, 1988).

[6] Thomas Aquinas, *Summa Theologiae* I-II, 96, 2–3. Human laws should not attempt to prohibit all vices or to enjoin all virtues. Aquinas gives two reasons for this. First, some men are capable of a higher degree of virtue than others, but the law should prohibit only the more destructive kinds of activities. Second, requiring too high a level of virtue is likely to be counterproductive, as some will rebel against too heavy a yoke. Better to require only what is reasonably attainable for most men.

[7] Locke, *Second Treatise of Government* 27.

interpretation of individual rights can be read as supplementing the Scholastic understanding of ius.

Viewed from this individualistic perspective, however, it was easy for later liberal thinkers to forget that individual rights flowed from the moral order itself. This led later liberals to invert the relationship between the moral order and individual rights—in other words, to think of rights not as *derivative* of the general moral order but as *prior* to it. After Locke, rights were increasingly understood as reservations of natural liberty against government (which, in part, they were) rather than as emanations of the natural moral order (which they were more generally). Rather than viewing rights as a mirror image (from the individual's side) of the collective good, as Aquinas would have recognized them, liberal thinkers increasingly saw them purely as checks or *limits* on government.

With time, liberal rights assumed an increasingly anticollectivistic and antimoralist cast. By the mid-twentieth century, liberal thinkers began to view rights not merely as *prior* to the moral claims of collective society but as *opposed* to them. As the traditional sources of morality lost their power over men's minds, morality increasingly became a creature of the secular power of the State. The stage was set for the fateful tryst of liberalism and secularism. When Locke's idea that rights were reservations of liberty against the State met Hobbes' idea that morality was a creation of the secular State, rights became individual trumps against collective morality.[8] In other words, they came to have exactly the opposite function they had in classical thought. From here it took only a short while for liberal thinkers to begin to suggest that there is a "right to do wrong"[9]—an idea as oxymoronic as it is a total inversion of the classical conception of ius.

These developments have had baleful consequences for our modern conceptions of freedom. They have led to our thinking of freedom as opposed to morality, as opposed to the collective good, and even as opposed to the individual's own good. Kant gave all of this a sublime foundation by maintaining that *the right is prior to the*

---

[8] This is the way Ronald Dworkin famously described the function of rights. Ronald M. Dworkin, *Taking Rights Seriously* (Cambridge, Mass.: Harvard University Press, 1978).

[9] Jeremy Waldron, "A Right to Do Wrong", *Ethics* 92, no. 1 (1981): 21–39.

good. Mill argued that the only legitimate function of the State is to prevent harm to third parties—that law should have no authority to reinforce the moral order, even when this is done to protect the individual from his own patently self-destructive behaviors. Following from these premises, contemporary liberal thinkers have argued that there is a right to pornography,[10] to euthanasia,[11] to use dangerous drugs,[12] to hire a prostitute,[13] to have an abortion,[14] and even to kill a child before he has attained the age of reason.[15] In sum, freedom knows no bounds today. It is nothing more and nothing less than the unfettered demand that the individual be allowed to do anything he wishes, so long as this does not interfere with another adult's similar demand.

Disregarding the normativity of freedom has even deeper consequences, however. It means that we cannot make sense of freedom *even in its contemporary nonnormative sense*. To say that I have a right to do anything that does not violate the rights of another requires me to know what rights the other has. If all that limits my freedom is his freedom, where is the line to be drawn between his sphere of freedom and mine? This is inevitably a moral question that requires an objective moral standard.

Secular liberals have recognized the problem and have sought nonnormative ways of drawing the boundaries of freedom. One

[10] Ronald M. Dworkin, "Do We Have a Right to Pornography?", in *A Matter of Principle* (Cambridge, Mass.: Harvard University Press, 1985).

[11] Two federal appellate courts held not only that persons have a constitutional right to refuse unwanted medical treatment in the face of death, a right previously recognized by courts, but that there is an affirmative right to have physician-assisted suicide. These arguments were rejected in *Washington v. Glucksberg*, 521 U.S. 702 (1997), but even this case left it open to the states to permit physician-assisted suicide (PAS). At least two states, Washington and Oregon, have legalized PAS.

[12] Arguments to legalize drugs have been made on the liberal Left and the libertarian Right. For a penetrating philosophical defense of the right to use drugs, see Douglas N. Husak, *Drugs and Rights* (Cambridge: Cambridge University Press, 1992).

[13] Lars O. Ericcson, "Charges against Prostitution: An Attempt at a Philosophical Assessment", *Ethics* 90, no. 3 (1980): 335.

[14] The arguments for this have been legion, even before *Roe v. Wade*. For one of the more outlandish arguments, see Andrew Koppelman, "Forced Labor: A Thirteenth Amendment Defense of Abortion", *Northwestern Law Review* 84 (1990): 480 (prohibiting abortion is equivalent to permitting slavery).

[15] For the classic argument, see Michael Tooley, *Abortion and Infanticide* (Oxford: Clarendon Press, 1983).

route is simply to define freedom in terms of utility, to argue that our freedom is limited by the greatest-happiness principle. But the utilitarian approach to freedom has always been deeply hostile to the idea of unconditional rights. Bentham called natural rights "nonsense on stilts", insisted that natural rights talk is "terrorist language", and wrote that "there is no right which, when the abolition of it is advantageous to society, should not be abolished." Nor should rights be propped up "under any such vague general terms as property, liberty, and the like".[16] When freedom is bounded by utility, it is utility, not freedom, that drives the moral syllogism.

John Stuart Mill tried another route. He attempted to define the boundaries of freedom by appealing to the concept of "harm" as the limit. Each person can act within a self-regarding sphere of liberty, he argued, just so long as he does not harm anyone else. As he put the principle in On Liberty, "The only purpose for which power can be rightfully exercised over any member of a civilized community, against his will, is to prevent harm to others. His own good, either physical or moral, is not a sufficient warrant."[17] Since the concept of harm has an empirical cast measured by some objective injury to the person or his property, it appears to avoid any appeal to normative ideas. In applying his principle, Mill argued that laws prohibiting prostitution, private sexual acts of a noncommercial nature, and drug use (opium in his time), among other activities, were illegitimate, though he thought the State could curtail the public effects of these activities in certain ways.[18]

Yet even the concept of harm is not purely empirical, as later liberals have recognized.[19] Harm is a normative idea through and through. Indeed, Mill's "harm principle" is brigaded with normative assumptions. Punching someone in the nose is harmful unless the puncher is rightfully defending himself or the other party has consented to a

[16] Jeremy Bentham, "Critique of the Doctrine of Inalienable, Natural Rights", in *The Works of Jeremy Bentham*, ed. John Bowring (New York, Adamant Media, 2001), 2:501, 503.

[17] John Stuart Mill, *On Liberty*, ed. Gertrude Himmelfarb (New York: Penguin Classics, 1985), 68.

[18] Mill discussed these in chapters 4 and 5 of *On Liberty*. For example, he thought that laws could limit public solicitation by prostitutes and similarly argued that the public consequences of private drug use could be reached by the power of the State.

[19] See Joel Feinberg, *Harmless Wrongdoing*, vol. 4 of *The Moral Limits of the Criminal Law* (New York: Oxford University Press, 1988).

boxing match. Putting a competitor out of business by threatening his customers is harmful, but putting him out of business by providing a better service is not—even though the consequences are exactly the same in both cases. In sum, it is impossible to separate fully the concept of *harmfulness* from the concept of *wrongfulness*. Mill himself, moreover, recognized the need for restrictions on many kinds of acts that he would describe as nonharmful. He argued that government could limit offensive behaviors and nuisances of a social nature, for example, public displays of sexual activity. In sum, no purely nonnormative limit on freedom (that nevertheless preserves a real sphere of freedom) has ever been successfully defended.

But perhaps the most troubling consequence of a nonnormative conception of freedom is that it makes it impossible to explain human rights. To say that a member of a religious minority in Iran has a human right to freedom of religion or that a Chinese dissident has a basic human right to freedom of speech is to say that there must exist a standard by which the laws of these countries can be measured and found wanting. One of the greatest ironies of our age is that liberal humanitarians make a shibboleth of human rights even as they deny the existence of any objective moral standard on which to ground them.

In sum, normativity does not simply provide the limit to the sphere of individual freedom; it *grounds* our freedom: the moral law, which is expressed in the concept of the human good, is the very fount of human freedom. We protect freedom because it is bound up with the human good, because it helps to unfold the human good. The next section explores how freedom does this and shows how determinism threatens our understanding of the ultimate *value* of freedom.

Free Will and Liberty

It is no coincidence that we use the same word, *freedom*, to describe both our civil rights and liberties (freedom in its external sense) and our capacity to make free choices (the inner freedom of the will). Freedom in the external sense is philosophically dependent on the existence of freedom in the inner sense. Political rights and liberties have traditionally been understood to be protections for activities that express or manifest our free or autonomous choices. Deny the reality of inner freedom, and we can make little sense of political liberty.[20]

Freedom (in its outward sense) has frequently been distilled into negative and positive freedom.[21] Negative freedom is freedom *from* government interference, what Justice Louis Brandeis once called "the right to be let alone".[22] It includes the right of the individual to live as he wishes; to develop his tastes, opinions, and thoughts; and to pursue his life's interests and professional goals. These are protected because, in normal cases, the individual knows his best interests, because his choices are presumed to be autonomous (a reflection of his considered beliefs and values), and because the act of choosing is necessary to the development of one's moral character. Freedom is thus bound up with the human good. Our free choices have instrumental, expressive, and self-constituting significance. Negative rights and liberties create a sphere of protection for these three essential human activities. They permit us (instrumentally) to choose the best means to our chosen ends. They permit us (expressively) to reflect who we are in the world—to express our thoughts and beliefs and, more generally, to manifest who we are as persons internally.

Most important of all, rights protect our choices in a way that has *constitutive* significance. They give us the social space, free of coercion, to become the best person each of us can become as an individual. As Mill recognized, making a choice is itself morally and personally significant in our self-development.[23] Each of these three functions is necessary to achieving our human telos. Positive freedom, too—the

[20] There have always been thinkers who have tried to reduce one pole of the dichotomy of freedom to the other. The Stoics thought that social and political freedoms were irrelevant to human happiness so long as one has attained true inner freedom. They thought that even the man on the rack could be happy. Buddhists advanced a similar one-sided conception of freedom, the inner freedom of escape from all desires. These purely internalized ideas of freedom usually become popular, as Hannah Arendt once suggested, in times of tyranny, when the possibility for genuine political freedom has been lost. Hannah Arendt, "What Is Freedom?", in *The Portable Hannah Arendt*, ed. Peter Baehr (New York: Penguin Books, 2000), 441–42.

[21] Berlin, "Two Concepts of Liberty".

[22] *Olmstead v. United States*, 277 U.S. 438 (1928) (Brandeis, J., dissenting).

[23] "He who lets the world, or his own portion of it, choose his plan of life for him, has no need of any other faculty than the ape-like one of imitation. He who chooses his plan for himself employs all his faculties.... It really is of importance, not only what men do, but also what manner of men they are that do it." Mill, *On Liberty*, 123.

right to choose our leaders, to take part in self-government, and to shape our society—depends on our capacity as autonomous citizens.

Contemporary political thinkers frequently forget this internal dimension of freedom. Some do this to sidestep the philosophical puzzle of freedom and determinism—to get on with the important business of politics without becoming entwined in metaphysical muddles.[24] Others worry that overemphasizing inner freedom can lead to a dangerous withdrawal from politics.[25] But a purely external conception of freedom has problems of its own. For one thing, a regime of rights divorced from inner freedom always threatens to ossify into a pure entitlement theory of freedom. Freedom and rights come to mean little more than access to goods and services provided for by the State. It is no coincidence that contemporary progressives sometimes confuse access to goods with freedom, conflating both under the general rubric of "rights". When freedom is conceived merely as access to *things*, it has become purely an entitlement concept, the only concept that makes sense to a materialist.

True freedom derives its value from its instrumental, expressive, and constitutive functions. Yet each of these three functions becomes questionable in a deterministic world. Determinism threatens freedom at its very source—by denying the reality of our free choices. In a determinist world, we do not protect the life choices of the individual, for they are not really choices in any significant sense. If everything we feel, think, and believe is a mere function of external

[24] The Austrian classical economist von Mises wrote, "Monism teaches that there is but one ultimate substance, dualism that there are two, pluralism that there are many. There is no point in quarreling about these problems. Such metaphysical disputes are interminable. The present state of our knowledge does not provide the means to solve them with an answer which every reasonable man must consider satisfactory." Ludwig von Mises, *Human Action: A Treatise on Economics* (Chicago: Contemporary Books, 1966), 17. Still, von Mises concluded that our economic system, like our political system, depends on our worldview. He stated that "we have to face an insurmountable methodological dualism.... Reason and experience show us two separate realms, the external world of physical, chemical and physiological phenomena, and the internal world of thoughts, desires, valuation and purposeful action." Von Mises, *Human Action*, 18.

[25] Isaiah Berlin called this the "retreat to the inner citadel". Berlin, "Two Concepts of Liberty", 235–41. Friedrich von Hayek insisted that the idea of inner freedom could become a conceptual dead end that leads political thinkers in a totalitarian direction. Friedrich A. von Hayek, *The Constitution of Liberty*, ed. Ronald Hamowy (Chicago: University of Chicago Press, 2011), 15–19.

factors—if there is nothing original to the self, in all its mystical, inexplicable beauty—it makes little sense to protect our decisions and choices (and we cannot even use these words quite accurately, if determinism is true).

The movement toward a purely externalist conception of freedom has been evident throughout the nineteenth and twentieth centuries. It is a function of modern political thought's turn away from metaphysics. Political liberalism has advanced hand in hand with metaphysical determinism only because liberals have decided that (what they accept as the truth of) determinism is irrelevant to their conceptions of liberty. Modern liberalism advances the case for the liberality of government—the need to redistribute wealth, to make restitution for past wrongs, and to equalize opportunities—while denying the liberality of the human soul. This is what Chesterton meant when he observed that secular liberals try to show their liberality by denying our liberty, for to be liberal in the modern sense, we have to treat everyone as puppets of Fate.

The tacit acceptance of determinism also explains why our sense of individual responsibility is dramatically on the wane at precisely the point in history when the demand for more "freedom" is heard from every television talk show and lecture hall. It is why liberals who deny that the individual has any real control over his life simultaneously demand that this same individual be given wider and wider latitude to do whatever he wants, to makes his choices, to engage in his "experiments in living" in the personal sphere. The modern liberal's worldview is a potent, dynamic, and radically inconsistent blend of paternalism and libertarianism—the kind of inconsistency that permits the same mind to demand an absolute right to an abortion while denying a woman should be able to decide for herself whether to buy health insurance.

Determinists have a possible response to all of this: they can try to harmonize political liberty with determinism by arguing that choices that accord with a person's desires are still "free" in the only sense that we can make of "freedom"—even if these desires have been causally determined. In other words, they can assert that, to be free is simply to be able to do or to get what one desires. Protecting political rights and liberties is simply a way of clearing the field of obstacles, letting the individual live as he wishes since living as one desires has value in itself. This was Hobbes' idea—the compatibilist idea that freedom is opposed to coercion but not to the causation of one's desires. A compatibilist could argue that political rights have nothing to do with free will and that we protect the individual's right to pursue his interests, to live as he wishes, to say what he thinks, et cetera—even if his acts are causally determined—simply because *they are his desires*, which have value as such.

There are at least two problems with this position. First, even most determinists recognize that not all desires seem equally free or autonomous. We may protect the artist's right to paint and the philosopher's right to plumb the depths of metaphysics because we assume that these are the expression of authentic desires. But most would agree that the drug addict's desire to continue to shoot heroin is not free in any genuine sense of the word.[26] The fact that he strongly desires to use the drug, if anything, seems to *undercut* (and certainly not enhance) the freedom of this choice. In sum, action in accordance with desire is not always free and, paradoxically for the compatibilist, the stronger the desire, the less free the action might be. Similarly, persons who act in accordance with desires that have been caused or manipulated may not be free in any recognizable sense.

Consider Aldous Huxley's novel *Brave New World*. Huxley envisioned a utopia in which individuals are artificially reproduced in laboratories and conditioned to love the function they will serve in society. The Alphas are the tall, intelligent class, the leaders of society. The Deltas, at the other end of the social scale, are short and ugly and bred to love their lot in life—which is essentially to sweep the streets and do the dirty jobs. The Deltas even feel pity for the Alphas, whose lot in life seems so overwhelming. Better to be a simple Delta, with his simple pleasures and no real responsibility.

The desires of both the Alphas and the Deltas are "rational" in the modern instrumental sense of the term: indeed, they have been designed to be rational. The Brave New World has been engineered to permit them to have what they want and to want what they have.

---

[26] Nor is the problem necessarily that the addict's desires are irrational. They are not, according to some definitions of rationality. According to one prevailing conception of rationality, "human action is always necessarily rational" since it is always rational to want to get whatever one desires. Von Mises, *Human Action*, 19. This, of course, makes rationality a purely instrumental value.

The social planners have spared no expense to ensure that their subjects' preferences are maximized. If the compatibilist is right, the Brave New World is the freest of all societies in history. Why, then, are we so horrified by Huxley's utopia? Why does it seem like such an affront to human liberty and dignity? The problem is not simply that we find the Deltas' existence trivial and unappealing. We feel the same aversion, after all, for the life of the Alphas. Being bred and conditioned to want even the "higher pursuits" still violates our considered intuitions about human freedom.

There seems to be something deeper at work in our love of freedom. The reason even the Alphas' existence seems so dwarfed and dreadful to us is that they are not really making their own choices for themselves. Put simply, there is no place for the constitutive aspect of freedom in the Brave New World. The men and women of that society are not self-made. They are simply *made*. As Aquinas would have it, freedom involves our *participation* in God's eternal order. The denizens of the Brave New World do not participate in their world. They do not thrive; they merely abide.

There is a second problem with the compatibilist approach to liberty. If we now ask not *how to define* freedom but *what makes freedom valuable*, the compatibilist is likely to answer in utilitarian terms.[27] Freedom will be valuable to the extent (and only to the extent) that it maximizes happiness or individual preferences. If political liberty itself is defined and measured by its utilitarian value, it can be *limited* by this value as well, as we have already seen. But the problem is not simply that utility will swallow up freedom. More likely, it will swallow up freedom by disguising itself as freedom.

If we define liberty as preference satisfaction, what should prevent the social engineers from tinkering with the preferences themselves? If freedom is more or less equivalent to the satisfaction of desires, what makes any particular desire any better than another? Are not desires themselves fungible—important only insofar as they are *desired*? This brings us back to the same problem of the Brave New World.

---

[27] As we saw in chapter 7, those drawn to compatibilism—thinkers such as Hobbes, Hume, Mill, and others—are usually utilitarians of one sort or another. Utilitarianism and compatibilism are complementary philosophies: both tend to be expressions of philosophical materialism; both value desire satisfaction as the ultimate end (utilitarians value this as a proxy for happiness; compatibilists value it as a proxy for freedom). Compatibilism, moreover, typically relies on a utilitarian conception of responsibility.

Even the most benevolent of those who view the human condition through the prism of philosophical materialism cannot help but be drawn to a more or less totalitarian conception of government according to which it is a proper function of the State to "perfect" individual preferences in the name of achieving greater happiness. We have seen these proposals from psychologists and social thinkers for several decades.[28] Totalitarianism is always the most likely political consequence of determinism, even when that determinism couches itself in the temporarily fashionable cant of progressive liberalism.

There is simply no principled reason for protecting a sphere of political freedom if our actions are the product of a random cacophony of external social and biological influences. Unless we rekindle the traditional understanding of freedom as a normative ideal grounded in the human good and valued as an expression of our inner self, it will be only a matter of time before the very concept of freedom becomes not simply meaningless but inconceivable.

Responsibility

It was once a commonplace of political thought that freedom and responsibility were indissolubly linked, serving as moral and practical counterweights to one another. The bounds of one could not extend beyond the bounds of the other. To say that a person freely acted was to say that he is responsible for his act, and to say he is responsible was to say that he acted freely. To hold a person responsible for an act that was not within his free agency is the epitome of injustice. To make him free to do things for which he will not be responsible is the epitome of improvidence.

The traditional understanding of responsibility depends on the traditional understanding of freedom. Because it denies the latter, modern thought has had to reconceptualize the former. When the traditionalist says that a person is responsible for his act, he means

---

[28] B. F. Skinner, for example, wrote that the object of all social regulation "is not to free man from control but to change the kinds of control to which they are exposed". B. F. Skinner, *Beyond Freedom and Dignity* (Indianapolis: Hackett, 2002), 221. Political theorist Cass Sunstein, who became the Obama administration's regulatory czar, argued thirty years ago that it was government's role to "perfect" individual preferences. Cass R. Sunstein, "Legal Interference with Private Preferences", *University of Chicago Law Review* 53 (1985): 1129.

that the person freely acted and that he will be made to answer for its consequences. On more recent accounts, however, it means *only* that the person will be made to answer. Contemporary thinkers knit together strands of Bentham's utilitarianism and Hobbes' compatibilism to redefine responsibility as a *prescriptive* term. A person is now held responsible if punishing him will have some utilitarian benefit to society—by deterring similar acts on the part of the actor (lawyers call this "specific deterrence") or by others ("general deterrence"). Modern thinkers have thus redefined responsibility from the traditionalist's backward-looking idea (i.e., looking back to the action to see whether the actor performed it freely) to a forward-looking idea (looking ahead to the consequences of punishment to determine whether we should hold the actor responsible). This redefinition of responsibility is yet another way in which modern thinkers attempt to put new wine into old wineskins, retaining words that resonate powerfully with us morally while gutting their inner meanings.

Those who have found attractive this utilitarian rethinking of responsibility (Bentham, Mill, Hayek, and Hart, among others) sometimes try to hold on to a vestige of the traditional idea of freedom by suggesting that we hold the actor responsible only when the threat of punishment *might have made a difference* in his action. As Hayek put it:

> We assign responsibility to a man, not in order to say that as he was he might have acted differently, but in order to make him different.... The only question that can be legitimately raised, therefore, is whether the person on whom we place responsibility for a particular action or its consequences, is the kind of person who is accessible to normal motives (that is, whether he is what we call a "responsible person") and whether in the given circumstances such a person can be expected to be influenced by the considerations and beliefs we want to impress upon him.[29]

It is the threat of being held responsible that causes the actor to alter his course and to "become responsible".

But this account of responsibility is manifestly incoherent. If (as he was) the actor could not have acted differently (as determinism entails), what sense does it make to hold him responsible "in order

[29] F. A. Hayek, *The Constitution of Liberty*, 75.

to make him different"? How can our intention of wanting to make him act differently possibly matter to his responsibility if he did not act differently *even with the influence of the motives provided by the law*? In other words, in the case of the man who has broken the law, the law has *not* changed his behavior. It has *not* made him different. It has had no apparent influence on the outcome of his act. Indeed, what can it even mean to say that we assign responsibility when "a person can be expected to be influenced" by the law if, by definition, he has *not* been influenced? This threat of being held responsible may have deterred others (though we will never know whether or how many since they have been deterred from acting), but the utilitarian approach to responsibility means, paradoxically, that we will assign responsibility only in those cases where our expectations were *destined to be disappointed*.

More generally, the only possible basis for expecting legal sanctions to alter an actor's course of action is if the actor can consider the threats and change his behavior to avoid them. But isn't this exactly what we mean by freedom of choice—the freedom to alter our actions in accordance with what we know about their likely consequences? Indeed, the determinist's position is stranger still since it seems to entail that it is the inducements and restrictions of the law that *make us free* in a functional sense. For it is only when the actor is confronted with the prod of punishment or the invitation to some reward that he makes the necessary effort to change his behavior from his previous course. But if this is all there is to freedom, it is precisely the threat of punishment that makes us free—rather than restraining us.

The modern conception of responsibility does its gravest injury, however, not to our institutions but to our inner, moral being. The determinist can make no sense whatsoever of those two capacities of the soul most expressive of our moral responsibility and most necessary for our moral healing: remorse and forgiveness. Genuine remorse requires the wrongdoer to recognize not simply that he was *wrong* but that things might have been otherwise—that his act was not inevitable. Remorse is an inherently *counterfactual* emotion. It is piqued by the wrongdoer's acute knowledge *of what might have been* (the saddest words of tongue and pen). Remorse has no place in a deterministic world since, in that world, "what might have been" is a figment of the imagination. Everything is exactly as it *must be* in the determinist's world.[30]

As modern philosophy and psychology have demolished the internal structures of the morally reflective self, what was once rightly regarded as a moral *capacity* is now a simple *feeling*. All that remains of remorse in modern psychology is guilt, a fundamentally reactive emotion rooted in the internalized threat of punishment. Where the traditionalist understands remorse as a salvific *capacity*, a power of the reflective conscience that draws us forward, fixing our painful gaze on the chasm between the ought and the is of some past action, modern thinkers find in guilt only the pathological (if socially necessary) residue of the internalized threat of punishment.

Not just remorse but forgiveness and mercy, too, lose all significance in a causally determined world. Forgiveness is an intentional state of a victim directed toward his wrongdoer. It is an act of self-transcendence grounded in the overcoming not of the harm but of the *wrong* done to the victim. In forgiving, the victim absolves the wrongdoer of his wrong, cleansing the moral slate and, in the process, liberating himself from the hatred or resentment he feels toward the wrongdoer.[31] But there can be no true forgiveness in the determinist's world. One can forgive only a morally responsible agent. The offender who was fated from the beginning of time to commit his act *cannot* be forgiven any more than the victim of a shark attack can forgive the shark.

---

[30] As William James put it, "The judgment of regret calls the murder bad. Calling a thing bad means, if it means anything at all, that the thing ought not to be, that something else ought to be in its stead. Determinism, in denying that anything else can be in its stead, virtually defines the universe as a place in which what ought to be is impossible—in other words, as an organism whose constitution is afflicted with an incurable taint, an irremediable flaw." William James, "The Dilemma of Determinism", in *The Writings of William James*, ed. John J. McDermott (Chicago: University of Chicago Press, 1977), 597.

[31] In Jeffrie Murphy and Jean Hampton's famous exchange on the concepts of resentment, forgiveness, and mercy, Murphy defined *forgiveness* in largely psychological terms as an overcoming of resentment. Hampton pointed out in response that the Hebrew terms used in the Old Testament for *forgiveness* include *kipper* (to cover), *nasa* (to lift up), and *salach* (to let go). Forgiveness is ultimately a moral act, not simply a psychological change, which covers the wrongdoer and frees the victim of anger. The act of forgiveness, wrote Hampton, "puts the two parties on an equal footing once more, and makes possible renewed relationships". Jeffrie G. Murphy and Jean Hampton, *Forgiveness and Mercy* (New York: Cambridge University Press, 1998), 37, 38.

Mercy, too, is out of place in the determinist's world. Mercy is the *lenient treatment* of someone who is not entitled to such leniency. It need not be dispensed by the victim—indeed, usually it is dispensed by an official or a functionary—and it need not even be a response to wrongdoing, though usually it is.[32] Mercy is an expression of *agape*, not of justice. It is given to the undeserving, not to the nonresponsible. The man who could not help but do what he did is not shown mercy; he is simply excused and rehabilitated.

The modern redefinition of *responsibility* rends this spiritual fabric of remorse, forgiveness, and mercy. It means that this entire constellation of moral concepts associated with our taking responsibility for our trespasses, along with our responsibility, grounded in love, to forgive those who have trespassed against us, must be jettisoned.

Not even the determinist, however, can ever really banish responsibility. Like nature, responsibility abhors a vacuum. It must rest somewhere—if not with the individual in restraining his own behavior, then with society at large for creating (or failing to create) the conditions that produce (or fail to produce) the necessary self-restraint. Crime and social ills thus become a matter of collective responsibility. But does the compatibilist ever wonder why the same determinism that infects the individual's capacity for proper judgment and self-restraint should not also infect collective society's capacities for the same? How is the (collective) freedom to make the right judgments and instill the proper incentives possible when it inevitably eludes the individual? If determinism is true, there is no reason to believe that the collective is any better at stepping outside the deterministic web than is the individual.

There is an anecdote from antiquity about an educated slave brought into his Roman master's household to school his master in philosophy. One day the slave accidentally toppled and smashed his master's most treasured vase. As the master was about to box his ears, the learned slave said, "Remember, master, all things are determined to happen exactly as they must. That vase was condemned to destruction from the first moment of time." The master, however, having learned the

---

[32] Murphy gives the example of a knight who shows mercy to an opponent whom he has the right to kill. Forgiveness can motivate an act of mercy, but since mercy is usually dispensed by someone other than the victim, it is usually motivated by other reasons. Murphy and Hampton, *Forgiveness and Mercy*, 20.

lessons of determinism even better than his teacher, replied, "Indeed, and so, too, were your ears condemned to be boxed." Like the slave in this story, the modern humanitarian determinist seems to assume a capacity for freedom in society's response to offending behavior that he will not admit for the behavior itself.

Determinism entails not only that we should take no responsibility for our bad acts and failures, however, but that we have no right to accept credit for our good deeds and successes either. Our ideas of merit and praiseworthiness are just as dependent on the assumption of freedom and responsibility as our ideas of moral culpability are. It is, after all, no fairer, in a deterministic world, to reward a person for his accomplishments than it is to punish him for his crimes. The genius, the artist, the athlete, and the saint are no more responsible for what they do and for who they are than the murderer, the molester, and the street-corner panhandler.

Determinism is the great cosmic equalizer, explaining away every achievement and canceling every debt. This explains the peculiar constellation of social attitudes, particularly on the Left—the skepticism directed toward meritocratic ideals, the tendency (to one degree or another) to see the criminal as a victim of failed social institutions, and the desire to reduce all differences in wealth and success to social causes. Schemes for radical economic redistribution are usually driven as much by deterministic assumptions as by compassion for the poor—as we find in Marx and Engels and, in more muted form, in contemporary American progressivism and European social democratic thought.

Whereas the Left discounts meritocratic ideals, however, the Right misunderstands them—and in two ways. Some—often those of a libertarian bent—are as much the children of late modernity as progressives are. They are every bit as skeptical of merit as those on the Left and have traded in the older idea of the *worth* of a thing for its market value. Since there are (they assume) no objective standards of moral worth beyond the preferences of individuals, the only thing we have to measure value is what another person will exchange for something. "The operative function of payment in accordance with product in a market society," Milton Friedman wrote, "is not primarily distributive, but allocative."[33] In other

[33] Milton Friedman, *Capitalism and Freedom* (Chicago: University of Chicago Press, 2002), 166.

words, wages serve to allocate labor efficiently but not in accordance with any objective standard of merit. Or, as Hayek put it, in a free market, a person's remuneration must necessarily "correspond to [his] usefulness to the other members of society, even if this should stand in no relation to subjective merit".[34]

Conservatives sometimes misunderstand merit in yet another way: they overvalorize it, misconceiving merit's nature and significance by drawing the wrong conclusion from the fact that we are essentially free. They forget that we are not self-creations ex nihilo. They conflate what we have inherited with what we have merited, pretending that a person's worldly fortunes are all the products of his own energies and efforts. J. Budziszewski called this one of eight errors (from the Christian perspective) made by contemporary conservatives.[35]

What conservatives sometimes fail to see is that, though our *choices* are real, they are always made within a set of given options. And though our *efforts* are real, the talents and energies with which we pursue our ends emanate from sources that far transcend the farthest reaches of the active self. Each person starts from his own starting line, with a different course set before him to run, and with those inherent gifts and limits that make him who he is, a quintessentially unique human being. Each of us realizes his potential only provisionally, only partially, and in part by chance (grace). Every step of the race is made with a dedication and effort conditioned by factors beyond our control, and under better or worse circumstances far from our own making. Even the passion with which we develop our raw capacities into polished talents is a gift of grace that cannot be fully reduced to the authentic strivings of the original self. In sum, we are free, but we are not self-creations. Every thoughtful Christian understands that the very sources of our merit are themselves unmerited. Only in a world where freedom and grace comingle as the joint blessings of our Creator can it be true that "every one to whom much is given, of him will much be required."[36]

---

[34] Friedrich A. von Hayek, *The Road to Serfdom*, ed. Bruce Caldwell (Chicago: University of Chicago Press, 2007), 122.

[35] J. Budziszewski, "The Problem with Conservatism", *First Things* (April 1996): 38–44.

[36] Lk 12:48.

Human Dignity

Freedom and responsibility are values that derive from the active nature of the self. Our third value, human dignity, derives from a deeper source still. It is rooted in the very nature of the human person as a substance composed of body and soul and bearing a moral status reflective of this reality. Let us begin with the concept of dignity—of what it is and how it evolved in Western intellectual thought—and then work our way back to its foundation.

There are two complementary components of our concept of dignity—an "inclusivist" and an "exclusivist" aspect. The inclusivist sense entails that all men are morally equal, that each person has the same moral worth as every other person irrespective of his particular abilities, talents, or social value to others. In its exclusivist sense, on the other hand, human dignity is connected to what makes the human species special as compared with other animals. Dignity unites all men and distinguishes us from the rest of the natural world.[37]

The concept of human dignity made its appearance nowhere in Aristotle or even in the Old or the New Testament. The Hebrew word translated as "dignity", *gedula*, occurs infrequently in the Old Testament and means something akin to one's stature or standing in the community. But there is no single term that fully approximates the modern idea of human dignity. The Greek term that comes closest to the modern cognate for dignity, *aksioprepeia*, is absent in Plato, Aristotle, and the New Testament, though occasionally each used the term *semnotes*, connoting seriousness or gravity of character.[38] If a predecessor to dignity in its egalitarian sense can be found anywhere in premodern thought, it was in the Stoic idea of *oikeiosis*, which is linked to Stoic humanitarianism and cosmopolitanism. *Oikeiosis* refers to the family-like resemblance of all humanity. Even this, however, falls short of its modern moral connotation.

---

[37] As George Kateb succinctly put it, "All individuals are equal; no other species is equal to humanity. These are the two basic propositions that make up the concept of human dignity." George Kateb, *Human Dignity* (Cambridge, Mass.: Harvard University Press, 2011), 6.

[38] In Aristotle, *semnotes* refers to a state of character consisting of the mean between servility and unaccommodating rigidity. It is not a moral value inherent in all men, and the word is used only three times in the *Eudemian Ethics* and never in the *Nicomachean Ethics*. Daniel P. Sulmasy, "Human Dignity and Human Worth", in *Perspectives on Human Dignity: A Conversation*, eds. Jeff Malpas and Norelle Lickiss (New York: Springer, 2007), 10–11.

It was Aquinas who, afresh with Aristotle's theory of essences and universals, began to use the term *dignitas* in its exclusivist sense, in other words, to refer to the relative status of men in the hierarchy of Being.[39] Two centuries later, the Renaissance humanist Giovanni Pico della Mirandola encapsulated the idea of human dignity in his *Oration on the Dignity of Man* in 1486. Every niche on God's Great Chain of Being, from the worm to the angel, he wrote, was occupied. There was no place left except for the creature who had no specific place on the Chain of Being—one who could, through the exercise of the gift of free will and his quest for knowledge, ascend to the angelic heights or descend to the purely vegetative depths of Being.[40] Mirandola was the first to link dignity with man's freedom and sentience. This was dignity in its exclusivist sense.

The inclusivist aspect, according to which all men are equal, was certainly implicit in the Christian understanding of the brotherhood of all mankind, but it was Immanuel Kant who did the most to develop the inclusivist idea of dignity as an intrinsic value that unites all human beings: "The respect I bear others or which others can claim from me (*conservantia aliis praestanda*) is the acknowledgement of the dignity (*dignitas*) of another man, i.e., a worth which has no price, no equivalent for which the object of valuation (*aestimii*) could be exchanged."[41]

The intrinsic nature of human dignity makes little sense from the materialist's perspective. Hobbes, for one, was entirely unable to conceive of dignity as anything other than a person's price or social value. "The value or worth of a man, is as of all other things, his price, that is to say, so much as he would be given for the use of his power." Thus, "the publique worth of a man, which is the value set on him by the Commonwealth, is that which men commonly call DIGNITY."[42] There are vestiges of Hobbes' reductionism in

---

[39] Aquinas used the term *dignitas* and its cognates roughly 185 times in the *Summa*, but its meaning does not seem to extend to the modern notions of the equality or autonomy of all persons. Sulmasy, "Human Dignity and Human Worth", 11.

[40] Giovanni Pico della Mirandola, "Oration on the Dignity of Man", in *The Renaissance Philosophy of Man*, ed. Ernst Cassier, trans. Elizabeth L. Forbes (Chicago: University of Chicago Press, 1948), 224–25.

[41] Immanuel Kant, *The Metaphysical Principles of Virtue*, pt. 2 of *The Metaphysics of Morals*, in *Ethical Philosophy*, trans. James W. Ellington (Indianapolis: Hackett, 1983), 127.

[42] Thomas Hobbes, *Leviathan*, ed. C.B. Macpherson (New York: Penguin Books, 1968), 151–52.

modern economic thought. The economist may pay lip service to the value of human dignity, but in the end, it is a person's *productivity* that measures his prospects for a good life.

The final step was to unite the two aspects of human dignity: there is a value in human life that unites all human beings, even as it distinguishes human beings from other species. The search for the *natural foundation* for human dignity leads us right back to Aristotle and to Christianity. For we can only understand the source of human dignity by recognizing that our shared dignity cannot be based on individual talents and capacities, which vary from person to person and which are sometimes absent. Only with an understanding that each human being is a *substance*, an ontologically unified center of gravity whose essence precedes his existence and whose formal properties reflect the *imago Dei*, God's reflection in our own nature, will dignity ever make sense. These strands of our philosophical and theological traditions were fully integrated only a little more than a century ago.[43]

But all Creation groans in futility. No sooner did we arrive at a fully integrated ideal than we began to pull the strands apart again. The modern Left and Right are drawn to the opposite poles of dignity. Right-wing thought sometimes finds it difficult to accept the egalitarian consequences of dignity, while left-wing thought embraces the inclusive, egalitarian aspect but balks at the exclusivist, species aspect of dignity. Authoritarian thought has frequently denied the moral equality of all human beings even as progressive thought finds dignity's exclusivist aspect unserviceable to progressive commitments to abortion rights and animal rights. Both sides have, in different ways and for different reasons, reverted to the view that nothing lies beneath the socially serviceable properties of the person.

In modern ethical thought, the capacity for rationality, for self-consciousness or sentience, is often the focus of questions about rights. Since animals manifest some of these capacities—they suffer, and higher animals clearly engage in basic reasoning—they must be accorded rights or treated with a certain measure of dignity. And since an unborn human child, or even an infant, can have fewer

---

[43] The writings of Antonio Rosmini, a Kantian Catholic theologian, influenced Pope Leo XIII, who defended the dignity of workers in his social encyclical *Rerum Novarum*. These developments are succinctly recounted in Sulmasy, "Human Dignity and Human Worth", 11–12.

of these capacities than some animals, he can be excluded from the circle of moral worth. Bentham thus said that an adult horse has a greater right to exist than a newborn baby. According to contemporary bioethicist Peter Singer, an ape that hides a banana, thus proving a rudimentary capacity for reasoning and at least an inchoate notion of self, has a greater claim to legal protection than a young child who cannot perform the same task.[44] In this way, the ontology of modernism inverts the hierarchy of Being, deconstructing what is higher and exalting what is lower, likening men to machines, and animals to men.

This modern "property view" of the person[45] makes it difficult to explain the egalitarian (inclusivist) aspect of dignity. The progressive Left cannot consistently take a "property view" on the exclusivist prong of human dignity while hoping to rescue equality by adopting a nonproperty view on the inclusivist prong of dignity. They cannot have it both ways. It is precisely our shared human nature that accounts for our equality. It is our sharing in the same *form*, a form that bears the marks of our likeness with God, that makes us one with all mankind. And if this is what grounds our equality, it must encompass the fetus, the comatose, and all other persons.

A refined and appropriately updated version of the classical conception of the person holds that the line between human beings and lower animals is not one of degree but of absolute distinction. There is an *ontological* distinction—a difference in *kind*, not simply in scale, between man and beast. In the classical worldview, mankind straddles

---

[44] Peter Singer, *Practical Ethics*, 3rd ed. (New York: Cambridge University Press, 2011), 72–78. For Singer's attack on the sanctity of human life, see Helga Kuhse and Peter Singer, *Should the Baby Live?: The Problem of Handicapped Infants* (New York: Oxford University Press, 1988), chap. 6. Singer's *Animal Liberation: A New Ethic for Our Treatment of Animals* (New York: Random House, 1975) argues that even all animals capable of sentience, including lower mammals and nonmammals, such as chicken and fish, have a defensible moral interest not to be killed. For an updated exchange on this subject, see Don Marquis, "Singer on Abortion and Infanticide", in Jeffrey A. Schaler, ed., *Peter Singer Under Fire: The Moral Iconoclast Faces His Critics* (Peru, Ill.: Carus, 2009), 133–52, and Singer's response, 153–62.

[45] This is the term that Moreland and Rae use to describe the modern conception of the person, contrasting it with the substantial conception of the person associated with the natural law tradition. J. P. Moreland and Scott B. Rae, *Body and Soul: Human Nature and the Crisis in Ethics* (Downers Grove, Ill.: InterVarsity Press, 2000); see also Patrick Lee and Robert P. George, *Body-Self Dualism in Contemporary Ethics and Politics* (Cambridge: Cambridge University Press, 2009).

the boundary between the purely material and the spiritual worlds. In Aquinas' philosophy we are on the highest rung of the material world and the lowest rung of the spiritual. The human capacities for rationality, autonomy, and self-consciousness are *marks* of our distinction, but these marks are properties of something deeper—a substantial distinction between men and animals.

Human dignity protects all human beings, including the fetus and the comatose. Contra Singer, our dignity is rooted not in our individual capacity for rationality, and contra Bentham, it is rooted not purely in our capacity to suffer. The treatment of higher animals should matter to us because they have the capacity to suffer, and we should do all that we can to limit this suffering, but we should not confuse the capacity to suffer with what gives us dignity. Even in men, sentience, rationality, and freedom are simply the *marks* of our moral status, not its foundation.

In sum, human dignity is not another right. It is the source and the foundation of all other rights. It is rooted not in our rationality but in our humanness—a humanness that embraces, even as it transcends, our material nature.

CONCLUSION

Why God Matters

It is easy to say there is no God. It is not so easy to believe it and to draw the consequences.

—Iris Murdoch

Like an undiscovered planet that exerts its gravitational force on its closest neighbors, the perturbations of materialism have been observable in liberal thought for nearly two centuries now. It is manifest in liberalism's glib moral relativism, in the deterministic tenor of many of its psychological assumptions, in its conflation of the sacred with the natural, and in the growing conviction that all truth and all value is a projection of the human mind. Now that the foundations have crumbled beneath our feet, when darkness comes, life is no longer tragic; it is simply absurd—for tragedy has no place in an essentially meaningless world.

The noblest values of liberalism—its commitments to human rights, to freedom, and to human dignity—are radically inconsistent with the materialist outlook. This is why our moral, political, and legal concepts hover ambiguously between the classical and the secular materialist paradigms. We continue to use the vocabulary of the classical worldview, with its concepts of freedom, rights, responsibility, and the self, while casting these concepts increasingly in terms that are more consistent with the insidious materialism of our age. We employ this vocabulary even as the metaphysical foundations of the

Iris Murdoch, *Existentialists and Mystics: Writings on Philosophy and Literature* (New York: Penguin Books, 1999), 226.

classical worldview have long been dangerously eroding. As the edifice is worn away, we sometimes cling to the older meanings, though there is an awkward incongruence between what we say and what we believe. The discordance is at times piquant. We make freedom of choice the central animating idea of our modern liberal political system even though most philosophers no longer believe that we make free choices. We use the concepts of natural rights as Locke did when we no longer believe in transcendent moral standards of any kind. We have virtually sanctified the ideal of individuality and self-realization at the moment when the metaphysical presuppositions of the self and the soul are thought by many to be beyond reclamation. We have banished God even as we cling to the tectonic structure of the theological vision of the world. The light is on, as the saying goes, but no one is home.

Modern thinkers have responded to this gap between our moral and our metaphysical assumptions largely by bracketing the question of God's existence. In recounting his rigorous education under his father's stern tutelage as a child, John Stuart Mill, the greatest intellectual architect of modern liberalism, wrote in his autobiography:

> It would have been wholly inconsistent with my father's ideas of duty, to allow me to acquire impressions contrary to his convictions and feelings respecting religion: and he impressed upon me from the first that the manner in which the world came into existence was a subject on which nothing was known: that the question: "Who made me?" cannot be answered because we have no experience or authentic information from which to answer it.... I am thus one of the very few examples, in this country, of one who has, not thrown off religious belief, but never had it.[1]

Yet Mill's agnosticism was camouflage for his own confusion. The liberal political theory he developed in *On Liberty* is wildly at odds with the materialistic tenor of his more academic writings on philosophy.

Perhaps as a result of the growing chasm between our politics and our metaphysics, more recent thinkers refuse even to raise the question of God's existence. It is no longer a matter of being agnostic—or

[1] John Stuart Mill, *Autobiography*, ed. Jack Stillinger (Boston: Houghton Mifflin, 1969), 27.

even atheistic. Rather, it is an embarrassment even to ask whether God exists. As philosopher John Searle recently put it:

> Nowadays ... it is considered in slightly bad taste to even raise the question of God's existence. Matters of religion are like matters of sexual preference: they are not to be discussed in public, and even the abstract questions are discussed only by bores.... For us, the educated members of society, the world has become demystified.... The result of this de-mystification is that we have gone beyond atheism to a point where the issue no longer matters in the way it did to earlier generations.[2]

If this seems a strange thing for a philosopher to say, we should remember that the source of this attitude is rooted in philosophy itself. Indeed, it goes back to Plato. It was Plato who first asked the question in the *Euthyphro* whether moral principles are correct because God has willed them, or whether God has willed them because they are correct (e.g., Is murder wrong because God prohibits it, or does God prohibit it because it is wrong?). If the answer is the latter— if God has willed certain things because they are (intrinsically) right or wrong, as Plato thought—then perhaps God is dispensable. Perhaps we can construct a system of moral principles without recourse to the divine. This has been the upshot of the groundwork assumptions of modernity's most influential moral thinkers—from agnostics such as Bentham to believers like Kant.

The problem with this, however, is that certain things about reality can be true only if certain other things are true. To be plausible, our worldview must be an internally consistent system of beliefs possessing a holistic integrity of its own that supports and binds together

---

[2]John R. Searle, *Mind, Language, and Society: Philosophy in the Real World* (New York: Basic Books, 1998), 34–35, quoted in Edward Feser, *The Last Superstition: A Refutation of the New Atheism* (South Bend, Ind.: St. Augustine's Press, 2008), 18. Sometimes this dismissal of the question takes the form of a dismayed chagrin. Mark Lilla opened his book *The Stillborn God* in this way:

> We find it incomprehensible that theological ideas still inflame the minds of men.... We assumed that this was no longer possible, that human beings had learned to separate religious questions from political ones, that fanaticism was dead. We were wrong.

Mark Lilla, *The Stillborn God* (New York: Vintage Books, 2008), 3.

our beliefs into a coherent whole. We can alter particular beliefs at the periphery without doing serious damage to the integrity of the system as a whole, but certain cardinal assumptions are central; they are literally hinges on which the rest of the structure depends.

God's existence is the cardinal assumption of all philosophy, whether philosophers want to admit this or not. We cannot cabin our ideas about God from our metaphysics, nor our metaphysics from our politics and our morality. The theist's and the materialist's worldviews are each a seamless garment. If the world operates as the theist believes it does, certain ineluctable consequences, moral and political, must follow. The same holds true for the secular materialist. To believe in God's existence is to invest in a comprehensive vision of reality, a metaphysical mosaic of the world with a logical coherence of its own. One cannot excise God while retaining the rest of the metaphysical picture intact.

Thoughtful materialists (if they will permit us to use the adjective) understand this linkage. They recognize that it is but a short hop from the immaterial mind to the noncorporeal soul and from the soul to God. This may explain why only a small minority of contemporary philosophers are theists or mind-body dualists.[3] As Searle (again) remarked, modern materialism is chiefly motivated "not so much by an independent conviction of [its] truth but by a terror of what are apparently the only alternatives".[4] Anything short of a comprehensive commitment to materialism draws the consistent thinker back to God, with all that this entails metaphysically, theologically, and morally.

When the atheist is at his most introspective, he may find that it is not logic or philosophy that motivates his unbelief. It is the fear of what God's existence entails for our lives that leads so many to agnosticism, to atheism, or to the still more recent position that claims to dismiss the relevance of God altogether. But isn't this, after all, exactly St. Augustine's insight that his own resistance to God was more a matter of the will than of the intellect? For those who believe,

[3] According to a recent poll of professional philosophers, about 73 percent of recent philosophers "accept or lean toward" atheism, and less than 15 percent "accept or lean toward" theism. Similarly, 56 percent accept or lean toward mind-brain materialism, and 27 percent accept or lean toward nonmaterialism (with 16 percent choosing "other"). This survey, conducted in 2009, is found at http://philpapers.org/surveys/results.pl.

[4] John R. Searle, *The Rediscovery of the Mind* (Cambridge, Mass.: MIT Press, 1992), 4.

every decision and action possesses an ultimate cosmic significance. The consequences of what we do and what we make of ourselves reverberate not only within our own souls but outwardly beyond the personal sphere—and outwardly not only in the sense that our actions have consequences for others, but in the subtler but more pervasive way in which, with each decision and act, we seem to take sides in a grander Moral Scheme.

There is undoubtedly a weighty burden in all of this, a burden as weighty as the soul itself. And it is from this burden, I believe, that contemporary materialists seek refuge in the tepid anonymity of cosmic insignificance. There is little of Epicurus' resignation and even less of Lucretius' anger in the spiritual sinews of modern materialism. There is only a shrinking from the possibilities, a wearisome sense of dread that eternity has placed too great a weight upon our shoulders. It is in this spirit that as thoughtful a philosopher as Thomas Nagel could write:

> I want atheism to be true and am made uneasy by the fact that some of the most intelligent and well-informed people I know are religious believers. It isn't just that I don't believe in God and, naturally, hope that I'm right in my belief. *It's that I hope that there is no God! I don't want there to be a God; I don't want the universe to be like that.* My guess is that this cosmic authority problem is not a rare condition and is responsible for much of the scientism and reductionism of our time.[5]

God is the touchstone of the classical understanding of the human condition and the foundation for what remains of our most important moral and political ideals even today. Without God, there cannot be an adequate understanding of our own spiritual nature; nor can there be a moral order, a transcendent set of moral standards that teach and guide us and that provide the basis for divine sanction when they are violated. Without God morality is nothing but human convention. And without a transcendent morality that stands above the positive law, even the idea of human rights is an empty sophism. Without God, even the assumptions of modern secular liberalism do not make sense.

[5] Thomas Nagel, *The Last Word* (New York: Oxford University Press, 2001), 130 (my emphasis).

We are now at a crossroads. Over the last four centuries, we have eaten fully of the tree of knowledge, yet we have forgotten. We have probed and prodded Nature until she has yielded a harvest of scientific facts, yet we seem to know less than previous generations. The more *how* questions we answer, the less we seem to be able to answer the *whys*. Since the Enlightenment we have enshrined happiness as our highest human ideal and grown miserable in its pursuit.

We have come full circle—back to Athens of the fifth century B.C. Our moral and political debates echo eerily and revealingly the exchanges between Socrates and Protagoras. Whether there is a moral order, whether we can have objective knowledge, whether the world is an expression of the Divine Mind or simply the ephemeral polyphony of atoms in the void—these questions cannot be bracketed. Our moral and political order will deeply and inevitably reflect the answers we give to them.

ACKNOWLEDGMENTS

This book was written with the generous support of a John S. Grimes Memorial faculty fellowship and with support provided by the Indiana University, Robert H. McKinney School of Law.

I would also like to thank two of my colleagues, Susan DeMaine and Fran Quigley, who have provided helpful comments and revisions of portions of this book. I also want to thank several of my research assistants—Michael Buschbacher, Alexander Carlisle, L. Michael Schlitt, and Vanessa Woolsey—for the great help they provided throughout the writing of this book.

Finally, I am deeply grateful to J. Budziszewski, whose books and personal correspondence have warmed and illuminated my path during my journey from atheism to faith.

BIBLIOGRAPHY

Adams, Robert Merrihew. *Leibniz: Determinist, Theist, Idealist*. New York: Oxford University Press, 1994.

American Humanist Association. *The Humanist Manifesto I and II*. Edited by Paul Kurtz. New York: The American Humanist Association, 1973.

Anscombe, G. E. M. "Modern Moral Philosophy". In *Human Life, Action and Ethics*. Charlottesville, Va.: Imprint Academic, 2005.

Aquinas, Thomas. *On Love and Charity: Readings from the "Commentary on the Sentences of Peter Lombard"*. Translated by Peter A. Kwasniewski, Thomas Bolin, O.S.B., and Joseph Bolin. Washington, D.C.: Catholic University Press, 2008.

———. *Summa Contra Gentiles*. Notre Dame, Ind.: University of Notre Dame Press, 1975.

———. *Summa Theologiae*. Translated by the Fathers of the English Dominican Province. New York: Benziger Bros., 1947–1948.

Arendt, Hannah. "What Is Freedom?" In *The Portable Hannah Arendt Reader*, edited by Peter Baehr, 438–61. New York: Penguin Books, 2000.

Aristotle. *The Basic Works of Aristotle*. Edited by Richard McKeon. New York: Random House, 1941.

Ashcraft, Richard. *Locke's Two Treatises of Government*. London: Allen and Unwin, 1987.

Athanasius. *On the Incarnation*. Christian Classics Ethereal Library. http://www.ccel.org/ccel/athanasius/incarnation.

Aubrey, Thomas. *Brief Lives*. Edited by John Buchanan-Brown. New York: Penguin Classics, 2000.

Augustine. *The City of God*. Translated by Henry Bettenson. New York: Penguin Classics, 2003.

———. *Confessions*. Translated by R. S. Pine-Coffin. New York: Penguin Books, 1961.

————. *On Free Choice of the Will.* Translated by Thomas Williams. Indianapolis: Hackett, 1993.

Austin, John. *The Province of Jurisprudence Determined.* London: John Murray, 1832. Reprint, Indianapolis: Hackett, 1998.

Ayer, A.J. *Language, Truth and Logic.* New York: Dover, 1952.

————. *Philosophical Essays.* New York: Macmillan, 1959.

Bacon, Francis. *The New Organon.* New York: Cambridge University Press, 2000.

Barnett, Randy E. *The Structure of Liberty.* Oxford: Oxford University Press, 1998.

Barron, Robert. *The Priority of Christ: Toward a Postliberal Catholicism.* Grand Rapids, Mich.: Brazos Press, 2007.

————. *Thomas Aquinas: Spiritual Master.* New York: Crossroad, 2008.

Barth, John. *The Floating Opera and the End of the Road.* New York: Anchor, 1988.

Beckwith, Francis. *Defending Life: A Moral and Legal Case against Abortion Choice.* New York: Cambridge University Press, 2007.

Benedict, Ruth. *Patterns of Culture.* Boston: Houghton Mifflin, 1934.

Bentham, Jeremy. *The Principles of Morals and Legislation.* Amherst, N.Y: Prometheus Books, 1988.

————. *The Works of Jeremy Bentham.* Edited by John Bowring. New York: Adamant Media, 2001.

Berkeley, George. *Philosophical Writings.* Cambridge: Cambridge University Press, 2008.

————. *The Principles of Human Knowledge with Other Writings.* Edited by G.J. Warnock. London: Collins, 1975.

Berlin, Isaiah. *Four Essays on Liberty.* Oxford: Oxford University Press, 1969.

————. *Freedom and Its Betrayal: Six Enemies of Human Liberty.* Edited by Henry Harty. Princeton, N.J.: Princeton University Press, 2002.

Budziszewski, J. "The Problem with Conservatism". *First Things* (April 1996): 38–44.

————. *What We Can't Not Know: A Guide.* San Francisco: Ignatius Press, 2007.

Burtt, Edwin A. *The Metaphysical Foundations of Modern Physical Science.* New York: Harcourt Brace, 1927.

Campbell, C. A. *Selfhood and Godhood: The Gifford Lectures Delivered at the University of St. Andrews during Sessions 1953–1954 and 1954–1955*. New York: Macmillan, 1957.

Cessario, Romanus. *The Moral Virtues and Theological Ethics*. 2nd ed. Notre Dame, Ind.: University of Notre Dame Press, 2008.

Chesterton, G. K. *The Everlasting Man*. San Francisco: Ignatius Press, 2008.

Cicero. *The Republic and The Laws*. Translated by Niall Rudd. New York: Oxford University Press, 2009.

Clarke, Desmond M. *Descartes: A Biography*. New York: Cambridge University Press, 2006.

Clarke, W. Norris. *Explorations in Metaphysics*. Notre Dame, Ind.: University of Notre Dame Press, 1994.

Conot, Robert E. *Justice at Nuremberg*. New York: Harper and Row, 1983.

Conway, David. *The Rediscovery of Wisdom*. New York: St. Martin's Press, 2000.

Copleston, Frederick. *A History of Philosophy*. 8 vols. New York: Image Books, 1993.

Corwin, Edward S. "The 'Higher Law' Background of American Constitutional Law". *Harvard Law Review* 42, no. 2 (1928): 149–85.

Crimmins, James E. "Bentham on Religion: Atheism and the Secular State". *Journal of the History of Ideas* 47, no. 1 (January–March 1986): 95–110.

Darrow, Clarence. *The Story of My Life*. New York: Grosset and Dunlap, 1950.

Davidson, Donald. "Actions, Reason and Causes". In *Essays on Actions and Events*, 3–20. New York: Oxford University Press, 1980.

Deleuze, Gilles, and Félix Guattari. *Anti-Oedipus: Capitalism and Schizophrenia*. New York: Penguin Classics, 2009.

Dershowitz, Alan. *The Abuse Excuse: And Other Cop-Outs, Sob Stories, and Evasions of Responsibility*. New York: Little, Brown, 2001.

Descartes, René. *Discourse on Method and Meditations*. Translated by Laurence J. LaFleur. Upper Saddle River, N.J.: Prentice Hall, 1952.

———. *The Philosophical Works of Descartes*. Translated by Elizabeth S. Haldane. Cambridge: Cambridge University Press, 1912.

Diogenes. *Lives of Eminent Philosophers*. Translated by R.D. Hicks. 2 vols. Cambridge, Mass.: Harvard University Press, 1972.

Dworkin, Ronald. *A Matter of Principle*. Cambridge, Mass.: Harvard University Press, 1985.

———. *Taking Rights Seriously*. Cambridge, Mass.: Harvard University Press, 1978.

Edwards, Paul. "Hard and Soft Determinism". In *Determinism and Freedom in the Age of Modern Science*, edited by Sidney Hook, 117–25. New York: Collier-Macmillan, 1961.

Emerson, Ralph Waldo. *Selected Essays, Lectures and Poems*. New York: Bantam Books, 1990.

Epictetus. *Enchiridion*. Translated by T.W. Higginson. Indianapolis: Bobbs-Merrill, 1955.

Epicurus. *The Essential Epicurus: Letters, Principal Doctrines, Vatican Sayings, and Fragments*. Translated by Eugene O'Connor. Amherst, N.Y.: Prometheus Books, 1993.

Ericcson, Lars O. "Charges Against Prostitution: An Attempt at a Philosophical Assessment". *Ethics* 90, no. 3 (1980): 335–66.

Feinberg, Joel. *Harmless Wrongdoing*. Vol. 4 of *The Moral Limits of Criminal Law*. New York: Oxford University Press, 1988.

Feser, Edward. *The Last Superstition: A Refutation of the New Atheism*. South Bend, Ind.: St. Augustine's Press, 2008.

———. *Locke*. Oxford: Oneworld, 2007.

———. *Philosophy of Mind*. Oxford: Oneworld, 2006.

Fichte, Johann. *Foundations of Transcendental Philosophy*. Translated by Daniel Breazeale. Ithaca, N.Y.: Cornell University Press, 1992.

Finnis, John. *Aquinas: Moral, Political and Legal Theory*. New York: Oxford University Press, 1996.

———. *Natural Law and Natural Rights*. Oxford: Oxford University Press, 1980.

———. "Retribution: Punishment's Formative Aim". In *Human Rights and the Common Good: Collected Essays*, 167–79. Oxford: Oxford University Press, 2011.

Flew, Antony. *There Is a God*. New York: HarperOne, 2008.

Foucault, Michel. *Discipline and Punish: The Birth of the Prison*. New York: Vintage Books, 1995.

———. "The Subject and Power". In *Michel Foucault: Beyond Structuralism and Hermeneutics*, edited by Hubert Dreyfus and Paul Rabinow, 208–26. Chicago: University of Chicago Press, 1982.

Frank, Jerome. *Courts on Trial: Myth and Reality in American Justice.* Princeton, N.J.: Princeton University Press, 1973.

Frankfurt, Harry G. "Alternate Possibilities and Moral Responsibility". *Journal of Philosophy* 66 (1969): 829–39.

———. "Freedom of the Will and the Concept of a Person". *Journal of Philosophy* 68 (1971): 5–20.

Franklin, Julian H. *John Locke and the Theory of Sovereignty: Mixed Monarchy and the Right of Resistance in the Political Thought of the English Revolution.* New York: Cambridge University Press, 1978.

Freud, Sigmund, *Beyond the Pleasure Principle.* Translated by James Strachey. New York: W.W. Norton, 1961.

———. *Civilization and Its Discontents.* Translated by Joan Rivierre. New York: Vintage Books, 1963.

———. *The Ego and the Id.* Translated by Joan Rivierre. New York: W.W. Norton, 1961.

———. *The Future of an Illusion.* Translated by James Strachey. New York: W.W. Norton, 1961.

———. *Moses and Monotheism.* Translated by Katherine Jones. New York: W.W. Norton, 1960.

Friedman, Milton. *Capitalism and Freedom.* Chicago: University of Chicago Press, 2002.

Fuller, Lon. *The Morality of Law.* New Haven, Conn.: Yale University Press, 1964.

Geach, P.T. *The Virtues.* Cambridge: Cambridge University Press, 1977.

George, Robert P. *Making Men Moral: Civil Liberties and Public Morality.* New York: Oxford University Press, 1995.

Gilson, Étienne. *From Aristotle to Darwin and Back Again.* Translated by John Lyon. San Francisco: Ignatius Press, 2009.

———. *God and Philosophy.* 2nd ed. New Haven, Conn.: Yale University Press, 2002.

Gosling, J.C.B. *Plato.* Boston: Routledge and Kegan Paul, 1973.

Gray, John, and G.W. Smith, eds. *J. S. Mill* On Liberty *in Focus.* London: Routledge, 1991.

Grisez, Germain. "The First Principle of Practical Reason: A Commentary on the *Summa Theologiae*, I-II, Question 94, Article 2". *Natural Law Forum* 10 (1965): 168–201.

Grotius, Hugo. *On the Law of War and Peace.* New York: Cambridge University Press, 2012.

Guthrie, W. K. C. *A History of Greek Philosophy*. Cambridge: Cambridge University Press, 1965.

――――. *The Greek Philosophers from Thales to Aristotle*. New York: Harper and Row, 1950.

Halevy, Elie. *The Growth of Philosophical Radicalism*. Translated by Mary Morris. Boston: Beacon Press, 1955.

Hare, R. M. *Plato*. New York: Oxford University Press, 1982.

Harris, Sam. *Free Will*. New York: Free Press, 2012.

Hart, H. L. A. *Punishment and Responsibility: Essays in the Philosophy of Law*. Oxford: Oxford University Press, 1968.

――――. *The Concept of Law*. 2nd ed. Oxford: Clarendon Press, 1994.

Hasker, William. *The Emergent Self*. Ithaca, N.Y.: Cornell University Press, 2001.

Hayek, Friedrich A. *The Constitution of Liberty*. Edited by Ronald Hamowy. Chicago: University of Chicago Press, 1978.

――――. *The Road to Serfdom*. Edited by Bruce Caldwell. Chicago: University of Chicago Press, 2007.

Herskovits, Melville J. "Cultural Relativism and Cultural Values". In *Ethical Relativism*, edited by J. Ladd, 58–77. Lanham, Md.: University Press of America, 1985.

Hitchens, Christopher. *God Is Not Great: How Religion Poisons Everything*. New York: Twelve, 2007.

Hittinger, Russell. *A Critique of the New Natural Law Theory*. Notre Dame, Ind.: University of Notre Dame Press, 1987.

――――. *The First Grace: Rediscovering the Natural Law in a Post-Christian World*. Wilmington, Del.: ISI Books, 2003.

Hobbes, Thomas. *Leviathan*. Edited by C. B. Macpherson. New York: Penguin Books, 1968.

――――. *The English Works of Thomas Hobbes of Malmesbury*. Edited by Sir William Molesworth. London: J. Bohn, 1839.

Holmes, David L. *The Faiths of the Founding Fathers*. New York: Oxford University Press, 2006.

Holmes, Oliver Wendell. "Natural Law". *Harvard Law Review* 32 (1918): 40–44.

――――. "The Path of the Law". *Harvard Law Review* 10 (1897): 457–78.

Holmes, Oliver Wendell, and Harold Laski. *The Holmes-Laski Letters*. Edited by David Howe. Cambridge, Mass.: Harvard University Press, 1953.

Hospers, John. "What Means This Freedom?" In *Determinism and Freedom in the Age of Modern Science*, edited by Sidney Hook, 26–42. New York: Collier-Macmillan, 1961.

Hume, David. *A Treatise of Human Nature*. New York: Barnes and Noble, 2005.

———. *An Enquiry Concerning the Principles of Morals*. In *David Hume, Essays Moral, Political, and Literary*, edited by T. H. Green and T. H. Grose, 1:1–8. London: Longmans, Green, 1907.

Husak, Douglas N. *Drugs and Rights*. Cambridge: Cambridge University Press, 1992.

Irwin, Dale T., and Scott W. Sunquist. *History of the World Christian Movement*. Maryknoll, N.Y.: Orbis Books, 2001.

Jackson, Robert H. "Closing Arguments for Conviction of Nazi War Criminals". Robert H. Jackson Center Website. Accessed April 24, 2015. http://www.roberthjackson.org/speech-and-writing/bibliography/closing-argument-for-conviction-of-nazi-war-criminals.

James, William. "The Dilemma of Determinism". In *The Writings of William James*, edited by John J. McDermott, 587–610. Chicago: University of Chicago Press, 1977.

———. *The Principles of Psychology*. 2 vols. Cambridge, Mass.: Harvard University Press, 1918.

Kant, Immanuel. *Critique of Pure Reason*. Translated by J. M. D. Meiklejohn. New York: Barnes and Noble, 2004.

———. *Critique of Practical Reason*. Translated by Werner S. Pluhar. Indianapolis: Hackett, 2002.

———. *Groundwork of the Metaphysics of Morals*. Translated by Mary Gregor and Jens Timmermann. Cambridge: Cambridge University Press, 2012.

———. *The Metaphysical Principles of Virtue*. Pt. 2 of *The Metaphysics of Morals*. In *Ethical Philosophy*, translated by James W. Ellington. Indianapolis: Hackett, 1983.

Kateb, George. *Human Dignity*. Cambridge, Mass.: Harvard University Press, 2011.

———. "The Value of Association". In *Freedom of Association*, edited by Amy Gutmann, 35–63. Princeton, N.J.: Princeton University Press, 1998.

Kierkegaard, Søren. *The Sickness unto Death*. Translated by Alastair Hannay. New York: Penguin Classics, 2004.

Kim, Jaegwon. *Supervenience and Mind: Selected Philosophical Essays.* New York: Cambridge University Press, 1993.

Koppelman, Andrew. "Forced Labor: A Thirteenth Amendment Defense of Abortion". *Northwestern Law Review* 84 (1990): 480–535.

Kuhse, Helga, and Peter Singer. *Should the Baby Live?: The Problem of Handicapped Infants.* New York: Oxford University Press, 1988.

Lange, Friedrich Albert. *The History of Materialism and Criticism of Its Present Importance.* London: Routledge and Kegan Paul, 1925.

Laplace, Pierre-Simon. *A Philosophical Essay on Probabilities.* New York: J. Wiley, 1902.

Lear, Jonathan. *Aristotle: The Desire to Understand.* New York: Cambridge University Press, 1988.

Lee, Patrick, and Robert P. George. *Body-Self Dualism in Contemporary Ethics and Politics.* New York: Cambridge University Press, 2009.

Leo XIII. Encyclical *Rerum Novarum* (On Capital and Labor). May 1891. http://w2.vatican.va/content/leo-xiii/en/encyclicals/documents/hf_l-xiii_enc_15051891_rerum-novarum.html.

Levine, Joseph. *Purple Haze: The Puzzle of Consciousness.* New York: Oxford University Press, 2001.

Lewis, C. S. *The Abolition of Man.* New York: HarperOne, 2008.

———. "The Humanitarian Theory of Punishment". *Res Judicatae* (1953): 224–30.

Lilla, Mark. *The Stillborn God.* New York: Vintage Books, 2008.

Lisska, Anthony J. *Aquinas's Theory of Natural Law: An Analytic Reconstruction.* New York: Clarendon Press, 1993.

Locke, John. *An Essay concerning Human Understanding.* Edited by Kenneth Winkler. Indianapolis: Hackett, 1996.

———. *A Letter Concerning Toleration.* Amherst, N.Y.: Prometheus Books, 1990.

———. *The Reasonableness of Christianity.* Edited by John C. Higgins-Biddle. New York: Oxford University Press, 1999.

———. *Two Treatises of Government.* Edited by Peter Laslett. New York: Cambridge University Press, 2009.

Long, Steven A. *The Teleological Grammar of the Moral Act.* Naples, Fla.: Sapientia Press, 2007.

Lucretius. *On the Nature of Things.* Translated by Alicia Stallings. New York: Penguin Books, 1977.

————. *On the Nature of the Universe*. Translated by R. E. Latham. New York: Penguin Books, 1977.

MacIntyre, Alasdair C. *After Virtue: A Study in Moral Theology*. Notre Dame, Ind.: University of Notre Dame Press, 1981.

Maeder, Thomas. *Crime and Madness: The Origins and Evolution of the Insanity Defense*. New York: Harper and Row, 1985.

Marquis, Don. "Singer on Abortion and Infanticide". In *Peter Singer Under Fire: The Moral Iconoclast Faces His Critics*, edited by Jeffrey A. Schaler, 133–62. Peru, Ill.: Carus, 2009.

Martin, Raymond, and John Barresi. *The Rise and Fall of Soul and Self*. New York: Columbia University Press, 2006.

Maslow, Abraham. *Toward a Psychology of Being*. New York: Van Nostrand Reinhold, 1968.

Mason, A. T. *Harlan Fiske Stone: Pillar of the Law*. New York: Viking Press, 1956.

May, Rollo. *Love and Will*. New York: Norton, 1968.

May, William E. "Contemporary Perspectives on Natural Law". In *St. Thomas Aquinas and the Natural Law Tradition: Contemporary Perspectives*, 113–56. Washington D.C.: Catholic University of America Press, 2014.

McInerny, D. Q. *Metaphysics*. Elmhurst, Pa.: Priestly Fraternity of St. Peter, 2004.

Mead, George Herbert. *Mind, Self, and Society from the Standpoint of a Social Behaviorist*. Edited by Charles W. Morris. Chicago: University of Chicago Press, 1934.

Medlin, Brian. "Ultimate Principles and Ethical Egoism". *Australian Journal of Philosophy* 35 (1957): 111–18.

Meilaender, Gilbert, "Terre es animate: On Having a Life". In *Defining the Beginning and End of Life: Readings on Personal Identity and Bioethics*, edited by John P. Lizza, 61–78. Baltimore: Johns Hopkins University Press, 2009.

Menninger, Karl A. *The Crime of Punishment*. New York: Viking Press, 1968.

Mill, John Stuart. *Autobiography*. Edited by Jack Stillinger. Boston: Houghton Mifflin, 1969.

————. *The Collected Works of John Stuart Mill*. 10 vols. Edited by J. M. Robson. London: Routledge, 1974.

————. *On Liberty*. Edited by Gertrude Himmelfarb. New York: Penguin Classics, 1985.

————. *Utilitarianism*. Edited by George Sher. Indianapolis: Hackett, 1979.

Mirandola, Giovanni Pico della. "Oration on the Dignity of Man". In *The Renaissance Philosophy of Man*, edited by Ernst Cassirer, translated by Elizabeth L. Forbes. Chicago: University of Chicago Press, 1948.

Mises, Ludwig von. *Human Action: A Treatise on Economics*. Chicago: Contemporary Books, 1966.

Moore, G. E. *Principia Ethica*. Cambridge: Cambridge University Press, 1903. Reprint, Mineola, N.Y.: Dover, 2004.

————. *Ethics*. New York: Oxford University Press, 1912.

Moore, Michael. "Moral Reality." *Wisconsin Law Review* (1982): 1061–1156.

Moreland, J. P., and Scott B. Rae. *Body and Soul: Human Nature and the Crisis in Ethics*. Downers Grove, Ill.: InterVarsity Press, 2000.

Murdoch, Iris. *Existentialists and Mystics: Writings on Philosophy and Literature*. New York: Penguin Books, 1999.

Murphy, Jeffrie G., and Jean Hampton. *Forgiveness and Mercy*. New York: Cambridge University Press, 1998.

Nagel, Thomas. *The Last Word*. New York: Oxford University Press, 2001.

Nietzsche, Friedrich. *Human, All Too Human: A Book for Free Spirits*. Translated by R. J. Hollingdale. Cambridge: Cambridge University Press, 1996.

————. *The Gay Science*. New York: Vintage Books, 1974.

————. *On the Genealogy of Morals*. New York: Vintage Books, 1989.

Nozick, Robert. *Anarchy, State, and Utopia*. New York: Basic Books, 1974.

Oates, Whitney J., ed. *The Stoic and Epicurean Philosophers*. New York: Random House, 1940.

Oderberg, David. *Real Essentialism*. New York: Routledge, 2007.

Parfit, Derek. *Reasons and Persons*. Oxford: Oxford University Press, 1984.

Pascal, Blaise. *Pensées*. Translated by A. J. Krailsheimer. New York: Penguin, 1995.

Pasnau, Robert, and Christopher Shields. *The Philosophy of Aquinas*. Boulder: Westview Press, 2004.

Plato. *The Collected Dialogues of Plato*. Edited by Edith Hamilton and Huntington Cairns. Princeton, N.J.: Princeton University Press, 1961.

Priest, Stephen. *The British Empiricists*. London: Penguin Books, 1990.

Priestly, Joseph. *Essay on First Principles of Government*. New York: Gale ECCO, 2010.

Ratzinger, Joseph Cardinal. *Introduction to Christianity*. San Francisco: Ignatius Press, 1990.

Rawls, John. *A Theory of Justice*. Cambridge, Mass.: Harvard University Press, 1971.

Raz, Joseph. *The Morality of Freedom*. New York: Oxford University Press, 1986.

Reid, John Phillip. *The Concept of Liberty in the Age of the American Revolution*. Chicago: Chicago University Press, 1988.

Richards, David A.J. *Sex, Drugs, Death and the Law*. Lanham, Md.: Rowman and Littlefield, 1986.

Rommen, Heinrich. *The Natural Law: A Study in Legal and Social History and Philosophy*. Indianapolis: Liberty Fund, 1998.

Rorty, Richard. *Philosophy and Social Hope*. New York: Penguin Books, 2000.

Ross, W.D. *The Right and the Good*. Oxford: Oxford University Press, 1930.

Rousseau, Jean-Jacques. *Discourse on the Origin of Inequality: The Social Contract and the Discourses*. Translated by G.D.H. Cole. London: J.M. Dent and Sons, 1973.

———. *The Social Contract*. Edited by Maurice Cranston. New York: Penguin Classics, 1972.

Rowan, J.P. "Platonic and Christian Theism". In *God in Contemporary Thought: A Philosophical Perspective*, edited by Sebastian Matczak. New York: Learned Publications, 1977.

Russell, Bertrand. *On God and Religion*. Buffalo: Prometheus Books, 1986.

———. *The Problems of Philosophy*. New York: Barnes and Noble, 2004.

Ryle, Gilbert. *The Concept of Mind*. Chicago: University of Chicago Press, 1949.

Sandel, Michael J. *Liberalism and the Limits of Justice*. Cambridge: Cambridge University Press, 1982.

Searle, John R. *Freedom and Neurobiology*. New York: Columbia University Press, 2007.

————. *Mind, Language, and Society: Philosophy in the Real World*. New York: Basic Books, 1998.

————. *The Rediscovery of the Mind*. Cambridge, Mass.: MIT Press, 1992.

Seneca. *Moral Letters to Lucilius*. Translated by Richard Mott Gummere. WikiSource. http://en.wikisource.org/wiki/Moral_letters_to_Lucilius.

Shiner, Roger A. "Aristotle's Theory of Equity". *Loyola Law Review* 27 (1994): 1245–64.

Skinner, B. F. *About Behaviorism*. New York: Alfred Knopf, 1974.

————. *Beyond Freedom and Dignity*. Indianapolis: Hackett, 2002.

————. *Science and Human Behavior*. New York: Free Press, 1953.

Singer, Peter. *Animal Liberation: A New Ethic for Our Treatment of Animals*. New York: Random House, 1978.

————. *Practical Ethics*. 3rd ed. New York: Cambridge University Press, 2011.

————. *Rethinking Life and Death*. New York: Macmillan, 1996.

Smilansky, Paul. "Hard Determinism and Punishment: A Practical Reductio". *Law and Philosophy* 30 (2011): 353–67.

Snell, Bruno. *The Discovery of the Mind: The Greek Origins of European Thought*. Oxford: Blackwell, 1953.

Spade, Paul Vincent, ed. *The Cambridge Companion to Ockham*. New York: Cambridge University Press, 1999.

Spinoza, Baruch. *The Ethics and Selected Letters*. Translated by Samuel Shirley. Indianapolis: Hackett, 1982.

Stace, W. T. "Man against Darkness". *Atlantic Monthly* 182 (September 1948).

Stevenson, Charles L. *Ethics and Language*. New Haven, Conn.: Yale University Press, 1944.

Stevenson, C. L. "Ethical Judgments and Avoidability". In *Facts and Values: Studies in Ethical Analysis*, 138–52. New York: Praeger, 1975.

Strauss, Leo. *Natural Right and History*. Chicago: Chicago University Press, 1953.

Stump, Eleonore. *Aquinas*. New York: Routledge, 2003.

Sulmasy, Daniel P. "Human Dignity and Human Worth". In *Perspectives on Human Dignity: A Conversation*, edited by Jeff Malpas and Norelle Lickiss, 9–18. New York: Springer, 2007.

Sunstein, Cass. "Legal Interference with Private Preferences". *University of Chicago Law Review* 53 (1985): 1129–74.

Taliaferro, Charles. *Consciousness and the Mind of God*. New York: Cambridge University Press, 1994.

Taylor, Charles. *Sources of the Self: The Making of the Modern Identity*. Cambridge, Mass.: Harvard University Press, 1989.

Tooley, Michael. *Abortion and Infanticide*. Oxford: Claredon Press, 1983.

Tully, James. *A Discourse on Property: John Locke and His Adversaries*. New York: Cambridge University Press, 1980.

Urmson, J. O. *The Emotive Theory of Ethics*. Oxford: Oxford University Press, 1969.

Veatch, Henry B. *Rational Man: A Modern Interpretation of Aristotelian Ethics*. Bloomington, Ind.: Indiana University Press, 1962.

———. "Telos and Teleology in Aristotelian Ethics". In *Studies in Aristotle*, edited by Dominic J. O'Meara. Washington, D.C.: Catholic University of America Press, 1981.

Waldron, Jeremy. "A Right to Do Wrong". *Ethics* 92, no. 1 (1981): 21–39.

INDEX